DIRECTING PLAYS

DIRECTING PLAYS

A WORKING PROFESSIONAL'S ■ METHOD ■

STUART VAUGHAN

Longman
New York & London

Directing Plays: A Working Professional's Method

Longman, 10 Bank Street, White Plains, N. Y. 10606

Associated companies:
Longman Group Ltd., London
Longman Cheshire Pty., Melbourne
Longman Paul Pty., Auckland
Copp Clark Pitman, Toronto

Acquisitions editor: Kathleen Schurawich
Development editor: Virginia Blanford
Production editor: Dee Amir Josephson
Text design: Irmegard Lochner
Cover design: Irmegard Lochner
Cover illustration/photo: Mark Sadan
Production supervisor: Anne Armeny

Library of Congress Cataloging-in-Publication Data

Vaughan, Stuart.

    Directing plays : a working professional's method / by Stuart
Vaughan.

      p. cm.
    Includes bibliographical references and index.
    ISBN 0-8013-0623-X

    1. Theater—Production and direction. I. Title.
PN2053.V34 1992
792'.0233—dc20   92-16875
                                    CIP

1 2 3 4 5 6 7 8 9 10-HA-95 94 93 92

CONTENTS

PREFACE:
A LIFE IN THE THEATRE

In Terre Haute, Indiana, before World War II, directing plays was a profession I'd never heard of. I played in the band. I sang in the glee club. I took parts in school plays.

I confess that studying agreed with me, though I avoided all courses involving mathematical matters and all games played with balls. We found out in due course that I couldn't see the balls coming, and thenceforth I was confined to a life behind spectacles. No cure was ever found for my aversion to numbers. In addition to my musical and dramatic activities, I was high school class president, and in the Boy Scouts I was patrol leader, then senior patrol leader, then junior assistant scoutmaster, and then camp counselor. These activities came my way not because of my popularity but because I seemed to have an ability to get things done. My career aspirations focused on anthropology, the result of an unusual exposure to Native American culture.

Enter the Children's Theatre of Terre Haute, director Lillian Decker Masters, and their production of *Robin Hood*. They found me somehow, and I found myself playing an Errol Flynn-influenced Robin Hood, complete with steel broadsword. I have never recovered.

College became a succession of parts in plays. I no longer had time to play in the dance band to earn my pocket money, so I took on a paid job as technical director for the Children's Theatre, using my drawing, painting, and carpentry skills. I even did a little directing in college. Graduate school followed. I chose theatre, and anthropology faded away.

At about the time I was finishing my M.A. I auditioned at Terre Haute's Community Theatre for a visiting director. He was Walter Young, a true professional of long standing—70 years old, with Broadway, London, films, and stock behind him. There was no part for me, but he took an interest.

"What do you want to do with your life?" said he.

"Oh, I'll get a Ph.D. and head my own university theatre department," said I.

"Is that what you want, really?"

Gulping, I confessed. "I'd really like to go to New York and be an actor."

"Why don't you?"

I was taken aback. No one had ever suggested that as a possibility. "I'm not good-looking enough. My voice isn't good enough. I'm not all that tall . . ."

"What's that got to do with it?" he answered. "Each human being is unique. The actor must find his own unique human essence and learn to expose and project it for the stage. Voice and beauty and all that—secondary."

"But—I don't even know how to make people laugh!"

"That's easy. Haven't you even heard of the five parts of a joke?" Of course I hadn't, so he generously shared a piece of the theatre's oral tradition, which I shall pass on later in this book.

Upshot: I scraped up some money and went to New York that September. I was cast in my first Equity role in a touring company the very week I arrived. Luck does come into it.

In the air, at this time, was a fresh current—the yearning for professional theatres all over the country, not just in New York or the few outposts like Pasadena or Cleveland that *Theatre Arts Magazine* condescendingly called "the tributary theatre." Shortly after my attack on New York, I fell into a Fulbright Grant for a year in England—1949–1950, the first year of the theatre Fulbrights. My grant let me visit and work with more than twenty British repertory theatres, including Stratford, the Bristol Old Vic, the Glasgow Citizens' Theatre, and several smaller companies. I wanted to find out why Britain had regional repertory theatres and we had none. I worked, watched, and learned.

Coming back from England, I went on acting, in stock and later in New York. I was studying in New York with Harold Clurman, co-founder of the Group Theatre, when someone learned enough about my patrol-leader proclivities to ask me to direct an Off-Broadway event—a staged reading of Sean O'Casey's I *Knock at the Door*, adapted by Paul Shyre. It opened on a Sunday afternoon, in a blizzard, to thirty people and Brooks Atkinson, critic of the *New York Times*, who next day wrote wonderful things about the show and about my direction. So my directing career began in earnest, and in New York, at a crucial time in the American Theatre.

The O'Casey excitement developed into two limited Broadway engagements. Next, Joseph Papp, still a stage manager at CBS, asked me to direct the new outdoor Shakespeare project he was starting on the Lower East Side. None of us realized we were beginning what was to turn into the crowning glory of America's new not-for-profit regional theatre movement. For the next four years I was artistic director of what we decided to call the New York Shakespeare Festival. Four years after that I headed a resident acting company at New York's Phoenix Theatre, formed by Norris Houghton and T. Edward Hambleton. The Ford Foundation created a grant for directors that gave me a season's leave of absence from New York to visit the Berliner Ensemble, Piccolo Teatro di Milano, Sweden's Royal Dramat, and several major theatres in Germany, and to make a return visit to my earlier British haunts. Coming home refreshed, I became founding artisitic director of the Seattle Repertory Theatre, where for three years we did genuine "rotating rep," after which I founded Repertory Theatre, New Orleans under the auspices of the new National Endowment for the Arts. After three seasons of this I came back to New York, directed some more for Papp in Central Park, wrote and directed some plays that played in regional theatres around the country, and with my wife, founded and ran The New Globe Theatre, a classic touring repertory theatre. We were actor-managers in the old style, acting, producing, directing, designing. Our private "down-with-institutional-bigness" campaign was instructive, invigorating, exhausting, and ultimately impossible to maintain.

Along the way, I had short stints in educational theatre as a visiting professor, but now came an oportunity to accept tenure as a full professor in a permanent academic situation. I did! We bought a house! It was strange.

Three years later an invitation came from Joseph Papp to direct a summer production in Central Park. Why not? After it opened, he said,

"There's a big office back there, and I'd like you in it full time, as our resident director." So, with plays scheduled to direct, back to New York we came. By the time you read this book, who knows what life will have turned up? Well, that's how things are in the theatre.

Shaw said, "Be careful what you ask for; you may get it." I've often had what I've asked for, for better or worse. I've been up, down, and sideways. Along the way I've learned how to do my job. I am happy to pass on whatever it is I know to others, to use as they can. And one thing I am quite sure of: never in over four decades in the professional theatre have I had a moment when I seriously wished I had taken up another line of work.

ACKNOWLEDGMENTS

The theatre does not happen in a vacuum, and those who trusted me to create theatre under their auspices have contributed greatly to my career and to this book. Among them I must single out with respect and gratitude the late Joseph Papp of the New York Shakespeare Festival, T. Edward Hambleton and Norris Houghton of the Phoenix Theatre, Lucille Lortel, Vincent Curcio, Ewen Dingwall (whose efforts brought me to Seattle), Roger L. Stevens, and the late Paul Shyre. I was introduced to theatre by those excellent teachers Robert and Lillian Masters, and F. Cowles Strickland of Stanford University influenced me greatly.

This book was enhanced by the encouragement of Michelle Macau and Alexander Brietzke, associates of mine at the New York Shakespeare Festival, and I am particularly grateful to Alexander Brietzke for his contribution of the exercises that appear throughout this book. Still, this book would never have come about without the support of the late Gordon ("Tren") Anderson, of the Longman Publishing Group, who, though he did not live to see its publication, was mainly responsible for my setting forth on it. Longman editors Kathleen Schurawich and Virginia L. Blanford have admirably carried on in helping me to bring the project to fruition. My friend and colleague Dr. Yvonne Shafer read the manuscript and has offered many useful observations. I am grateful, too, for the thoughtful and constructive comments of Ronald A. Willis, University of Kansas; Judy E. Yordon, Ball State University; Femi Euba, Louisiana State University; Kathleen Elizabeth George, University of

Pittsburgh; Rex McGraw, The Ohio State University; and Bruce Halverson, Ithaca College.

My wife Anne Thompson Vaughan has accompanied me, not only through many of the theatrical adventures cited in this book, but also in every phase of its writing.

To all these, and to the many actors and other collaborators who also shared these theatre experiences with me, my thanks.

Stuart Vaughan
High Bridge, New Jersey

KING LEAR
Seattle Repertory Theatre, 1963
The opening production of the Seattle Repertory Theatre.
Edgar (Stephen Joyce) speaks to the dying Edmund (Harvey Solin).
Director: Stuart Vaughan.
Photo: Paul V. Thomas

# INTRODUCTION

The director is the one person in the theatre who can have a successful career without knowing his job.

Every actor who reaches opening night must finally pass the test of meeting the audience and surviving the evening. The designers' sets and costumes have to be built; the designs must be turned into something with physical form and substance. The lights actually have to light the stage on cue, the properties must be on hand, and, to get the show on, actual money must be raised, press releases must be written and placed, and the play must be advertised if an actual audience is to come. Only the director can be confident that if he cannot do his job, someone else will.

A particular off-Broadway director of the fifties and sixties comes to mind. He had a series of successes spanning nearly a decade. Every one of his productions finally reached the point, late in rehearsals, at which the actors banded together and said, "Listen, you," which was not his name, "sit down, shut up, and *we'll* get this thing on!" Why wasn't he fired by the producer? He *was* the producer. The actors, in desperation, saved themselves, and in so doing saved his theatre and made his reputation.

When we watch a production we can perceive things about the acting; it's in front of us. We know what has moved us to tears or laughter. The composer's work, the work of the designers, the playwright's work—all are visible as distinct entities. We can tell who has done what.

The director's work takes place during the preparation and rehearsal process, and no one can discern from viewing the finished product, except in the case of an especially incoherent production, what the director's contribution really was.

Then, if a production turns out all right—if the audience likes it and the reviews are good—has the director succeeded? Not necessarily. The *production* has succeeded, perhaps because of an accidentally felicitous combination of elements, or perhaps because of the particular strength of some elements—a strong script, or performances powerful enough to carry the evening. It may be, too, that the sure hand of a sensitive director has brought all the elements together creatively to produce an harmonious whole.

The director is, or should be, the person responsible for everything that reaches the stage in the finished production. The shape of the play itself, its length, the number of intermissions, what the play is about—all these elements are in the director's sphere, with the playwright, living or dead, receiving the benefit of the director's nurturing and guiding hand. The casting of the play and the creation of the acting ensemble are the director's responsibility, including the reality, depth, humor, pace, and all other aspects of the playing. The visual concept should be the director's, realized in a collaboration with the scene designer, and so also with the design of lighting and costumes. The director's taste and choice must be involved everywhere—music, properties, makeup. Every aspect of the production must owe its presence and validity to directorial oversight.

The person who maneuvers the course of the unwieldy juggernaut of ideas, visual effects, volatile personalities and public relations called a theatre production will succeed most effectively if he is conversant with a wide spectrum of skills. In the early periods of the theatre, certainly among the Greeks and the Elizabethans, the person who drilled the actors and coordinated the production was the playwright. Later, those responsibilities fell to the actor-managers—stars who formed their own production companies, selected (or, as in the case of Molière, wrote) plays that exhibited their talents to advantage, and led their employees (actors, scenic artists, and others) as they performed their various support functions.

The director began to emerge as a figure separate from the actor or playwright in the latter part of the nineteenth century. In Germany, the wealthy Duke of Saxe-Meiningen, whose hobby was theatre, developed a company of actors. He himself took on the task of unifying the play, settings, lighting, costumes, and acting style into a carefully selected and orchestrated whole. In Russia, Constantin Stanislavski, another wealthy amateur, was a seminal figure in establishing the director's artistic function and primacy. The Moscow Art Theatre, of which he was co-founder, survived the transition from Czarist to Communist Russia to become one of the world's great theatres.

The role of the director as controlling artistic force has been reinforced by time, and now the need for someone exercising that function is universally recognized. Other directors who have put their imprint on the position have been David Belasco of the United States, Max Reinhardt of Germany, Margaret Webster and Tyrone Guthrie of England, Bertolt Brecht of Germany, Elia Kazan and Antoinette Perry of New York's Broadway—all these people have contributed their own genius to enhancing the status of the director as artistic leader.

The people mentioned above, and all their colleagues up to, say, 1945, evolved as directors from beginnings in other theatre jobs. Many were actors. The actor gets exposure to many directing methods, and he learns about directing from being directed. Elia Kazan, Margaret Webster, and Laurence Olivier are examples of actors who became directors. Olivier, of course, never stopped acting. Writing has often led to directing. David Belasco moved from stage managing to adapting to writing plays of his own to producing. Bertolt Brecht is best known as a playwright, but his directing and his theories about it have influenced a generation of modern directors. The designer's gift for visual concept and spatial relations has sent some of them into directing. Until the emergence of director training in universities shortly before World War II, the only way to become a director was to take a side-step into directing from some other theatre job.

Whatever the starting point, a combination of talents, skills, and knowledge is needed to shape the complete director. Being of the male gender is *not* one of the requirements. One of the joys of directing is that it enables the director to leap past the physical limits of sex and type that always constrict the actor. The director can work with every kind of material his taste leads him to, and women have been wonderfully successful in the profession, though they are only now coming into their own in terms of numbers. Having said this, I must immediately acknowledge a difficulty presented by the English language, which offers no graceful way of avoiding the "he or she" construction when referring to individuals who, in the context in question, might be of either sex. Although the plural is available to me, directors do in fact work alone, so the plural is not a blanket solution to this writing problem. I will try several things: I will use second person and direct address where it seems appropriate in talking about you, the readers of this book, as potential directors. I will use the plural where I can. And I will occasionally alternate between "he" and "she" where neither of the previous solutions seems to work. When called upon to deal with "actor/actress," I find the problem particularly perplexing. If you find an annoying preponderance of male pronouns, I beg your indulgence; the task is a difficult one.

Though gender is not at issue in the nature of the kit-bag you bring to your task, breadth of your background is of great significance. Directors need a sense of history. A wide-ranging knowledge and love of literature—not only of plays but of novels, poetry, and criticism—will enlarge your scope. A grounding in the classics of philosophy will add to your intellectual armament. A commonsense background in human psychology and the basics of psychotherapy will help the director through many a tight spot. Art history, color theory, design theory, the basics of music (a sense of the piano, an ability to read music, basic harmony and arranging)—all these will be useful if the director's experience includes them. Of skills peculiarly theatrical, it has been well said that the director should be qualified to work professionally at any of the positions that will come under his supervision—as actor, playwright, designer, electrician, carpenter, and so on. You will be better able to imagine the potential in a given area if you have had direct experience of it. You will be able to deflect the automatic "No" to your question "Can you . . ." with "Yes, you can. I have." Of course, one cannot ask the potential director to be gifted in all these areas or expect everyone to acquire this amount of broad experience. Remember, though, that every time you have to depend on a specialist because you don't know enough, you lose some degree of control over the artistic product. As a director you must work constantly to extend the horizons of your knowledge of both practice and theory.

Director training in universities, when it began in the late thirties and early forties, consisted of one or two courses, called something like "Directing" and "Advanced Directing." Full-fledged directing programs are a relatively recent development. Books on directing available for use in such programs are still few in number and vary considerably in their nature.

There seem to be three kinds of books about directing to which one can refer. One category is the book by the "name" director. Part memoir, part manifesto, these books instruct, inform, infuriate, and are an essential part of one's professional reading list. Another category is the textbook, written by teachers to help other teachers teach. Some among these books are very sound indeed. Then there are "manuals," written to guide the beginner (the English teacher stuck with the class play) through the maze of steering a production to completion.

This book belongs in part to each of these three categories. Its origin is in my own experience, and the anecdotes in it are included as examples of actual events from which I have extracted principles. The book means to pass on an approach to directing, one rooted in both English and American theatre practice, with the American professional theatre of my own experience as its primary source. It is also a "manual," or "cookbook," in that it contains a great deal one needs to know, set down so one can follow it step by step and attain an efficient result, when dealing with plays from the kind of theatre I am focusing on.

I hope that instructors and students will find the text enhanced by the exercises, created by my colleague Alexander Brietzke from the New York Shakespeare Festival, which appear throughout. These exercises follow a single play, Samuel Beckett's *Waiting for Godot*; they are designed to allow students of directing to apply the concepts and guidance provided in the text itself to the direction of their own production of *Godot*—whether actual or theoretical. Where page references are cited, the edition referred to is the one published by Grove Press (1984). The choice of *Godot* was a considered one. As you will find as you read on, I took some time to come to an appreciation of *Godot* myself. But the cast is small and the set can be spare, allowing for a certain ease in workshop productions, and the text offers a wide range of opportunities for interpretation, critical thinking, and experimentation.

The theatre I emphasize in this book is the theatre of the spoken word, the plays that have come down to us from the distant and immediate past as literature. My approach to directing has practical application to producing plays from Greek drama, through Shakespeare, Molière, the Restoration, and the eighteenth and nineteenth centuries. The plays of Ibsen, Shaw, Wilde, Coward, and the American realistic drama all respond to this method of preparation and rehearsal. The "theatre of the absurd" is open to approach in the fashion that I advocate here, and indeed, if the play can be written down and is based on human behavior, the principles of sound professional practice, careful preparation, and an orderly and commonsense conduct of rehearsals that I am trying to communicate will serve the director well in dealing with the plays of today, yesterday, and tomorrow.

I am particularly concerned to pass down some of the living, oral traditions of the working theatre. Professional theatre people have not been given to writing books that give away "the tricks of the trade." Indeed, until well into this century, professional theatre people were not usually college-educated. Today, there is a great deal of interchange between the professional theatre and the campus. I hope to add to the store of practical knowledge available to the student of directing.

In addition to the broad spectrum of interests and the variety of theatre skills and practical common sense that you must bring to the task, to be a good director you must have three essential abilities:

1. You must be able to read a play, sift it for its core, and find exciting theatrical means to make it speak to audiences.

2. You must be able to get a group of creative people to collaborate successfully with you to realize your vision.

3. You must be able to get all this done efficiently, on time, within budget, with everything coming together at the opening.

A director who is to bring each production to a sound creative destination needs a method of work, a path for setting out from the beginning and reaching the destination intact and triumphant.

This book sets forth an approach to the sequence of tasks that the director will meet in every production. Each production provides a challenge to discover creative solutions to its problems. This book is not about solutions. It attempts to define the problems you will encounter as a director and to suggest a path by means of which you can find specific solutions, such solutions arising from the special combination of tastes, talents, and skills assembled to create each specific production.

There is no one correct way to do any particular play. Nor is there any one correct method of work. Technique exists to create channels for the release of creativity, and this is equally true in the case of piano playing, acting, furniture making, and directing. This book outlines one tested method of going about the job of directing plays. As a reader you may choose to direct plays by this method forever after. Well and good, assuming you enrich your personal kit of tools through your own experiences along the way, and provided you remember that each play is itself alone—in other words, that method is not formula.

Norris Houghton, in his important book on the Russian theatre of the thirties, *Moscow Rehearsals*, speaks of the Stanislavski Method as a "codification" of what good actors had been doing instinctively down through the ages. I have always been grateful for that comforting and demystifying description.

"Codifying" means setting down the obvious, capturing oral tradition by means of writing, spelling out as a system what many people have taken for granted. That is what I am trying to do in this book: marking out a path through the director's tasks that can lead to a successful production. I will be pleased if my practical guide through the directing maze helps others get through the underbrush that can clog the way.

True creativity emerges from our unconscious, and genius proceeds through flashes of insight. Flexibility and responsiveness to the moment are surely important aspects of talent. Still, talent can only flow through channels that are open. The directing skills I attempt to codify here are simply tools, to help those who have some talent for this most complex of crafts to achieve more immediate access to their own gifts and to employ them to even better effect.

PART ONE

THE DIRECTOR'S PREPARATION

PROLOGUE

An actress I know spent a summer in a "new-play-every-week" stock company some years ago, in which the same man directed every play. "A play a week for twelve weeks—that's tough," I said. "He must have spent all spring studying the plays." "Not at all," she answered. "He didn't even read them before the first rehearsal. They used the ground plan in the acting edition and just followed the stage directions." I saw two of the plays that summer. They weren't bad. The actors were competent, and the stage directions that had been borrowed from the Broadway production made for adequate staging. This fellow who hadn't read the play got his cast together, took them through the printed moves, and had a show a week later. That's not directing, but that's what they called him—"director."

At the Actors' Studio, Lee Strasberg had a wonderful way of working with scenes he didn't know. The actors would perform the scene. At the end, Strasberg would ask, "What did you try to do?" The actors would then explain what acting problems they wanted to work on for which they had selected the scene, what additional problems the scene had presented, and what they had emphasized as they worked. Having heard them out, he would then turn to the audience (other Studio members) and ask, "What do you have to say?" The members, among them usually some celebrated "names," would then offer constructive thoughts about what had gone on.

After all this, Strasberg would finally offer his own comments, sometimes developing something that had been said but often taking a new and revealing tack.

When teaching myself, I find this technique most useful when the scene has baffled me, either because I am ignorant of the play or because the scene has been done so badly the mind boggles. After hearing from both actors and audience, I usually surprise myself, and perhaps others, by finding something worthwhile to say.

I have no reason to doubt that my friend's summer stock director could, in a similar way, contribute order to chaos and supply some useful guidance. Being a sensible and theatre-wise fellow, he could, without reading the play, after a few hours of watching see where the laughs and climaxes were supposed to be and which actors should be standing next to each other to make the scenes work. So could I; so could you. That's still not directing.

Indeed, almost any normally intelligent member of any playgoing audience can spot what's wrong with a production. The audience sees the gaps. The audience tends to be well aware of inadequacy.

This is not to say that the audience, or even experienced theatre people, can accurately *express* their negative feelings. In this connection an anecdote comes back to me. A Broadway director, seeing one of his major financial backers at an intermission of a preview, unwisely inquired, "How do you like the show?" "Well," said the angel, "the first act is great, but the second act is just awful." "What's wrong with the second act?" asked the director, his heart quailing at the thought of hours of rewrites or cast changes that might be required to keep this bozo happy. "My wife says the way that girl irons that shirt at the top of Act II simply ruins the play!" "I see," said the director. "I'll fix it." Next night, same intermission, same backer and director. Director: "How's the second act?" Backer: "Really marvelous. Kitty loved it!"

Anybody can *see* what's wrong. Understanding the relative importance of what's wrong takes a specialist. Understanding how to *fix* what's wrong—that's part of directing. Understanding how to *achieve what's right*—that's *really* directing!

A piece of timeworn theatre wisdom goes, "Once the ground plan of the setting is worked out and the casting is finished, 85 percent of the director's work is done." I would accept the truth of that adage, if only to keep directors humble. I would add, however, that "a production's chances of succeeding are in direct proportion to the thoroughness of the director's preparation."

The director's preparation begins with a detailed study of the play to be produced.

A play is a work of art. What is this particular kind of art work meant to do?

Shakespeare, in *Hamlet*, Act III, Scene 2, says, in discussing the purpose of playing,

". . . whose end, both at the first and now, was and is, to

hold, as 'twere, the mirror up to nature; to show virtue

her own feature, scorn her own image, and the very age

and body of the time his form and pressure."

A "mirror up to nature." What kind of mirror—a simple reflector, or "a glass where you may see the inmost part of you"? Both comments are Hamlet's—the first, to the players before the play within the play; the second, to the Queen in her closet, just after the play within the play. Aristotle, in his *Poetics*, called tragedy "the imitation of an action." Here, too, we have the sense of art drawn from nature, reflections of nature, reflections *on* nature—that aspect of nature the artist wants us to see through his eyes. In a play, as in a painting, the artist sets up boundaries, inside of which he works. In a painting, on the two-dimensional picture plane, the boundaries are spatial, within a frame. On the stage, the boundaries are in time. Shakespeare again: "The two hours' traffic of our stage."

The playwright's time is of several sorts. There is the length of the performance, as in Shakespeare's apparently simple reference. But the playing time of the uncut *Hamlet* is *four* hours. Its internal time seems to cover a few days, but in those few days Voltimand and Cornelius go to Norway and come back, and Hamlet goes almost to England and returns. *Macbeth* does play in two hours' time but seems to cover twenty years. "Pleasure and action make the hours seem short," observes Shakespeare's Iago.

Within his frame of flexible time, the playwright shapes a world—not the *whole* world in two hours, or four, however expansively the writer uses time. He has to leave some things out. Indeed, that is how all art works—by leaving things out. Life itself is cluttered, filled with clogging and irrelevant detail. What if you heard all the noise in the world, going on simultaneously, at the same volume? Or what if your TV set received all signals, all channels, without your being able to select from the jumble of images the program you wanted to watch? The artist—playwright, painter, filmmaker—chooses a limited scope. He leaves out what he isn't interested in, in order to make us see what he has depicted, and see it "strangely," as playwright Bertolt Brecht says, with new eyes. We can see the familiar as new and "strange" because the artist has distilled only an essence of reality for us to focus on—an essence we miss in life because of its obscuring details.

The playwright's world centers around "an action," as Aristotle puts it. The author sets in motion a human conflict—"man against man, man against himself, man against God." Within the limits of the chosen world of the play the author pits the invented antagonists against one another to work out the moral solution to the struggle the play poses. Yes, *moral*. A play makes a judgment, demonstrates the playwright's judgment, about right and wrong, good and bad, as shown in the world of the play. Comedy, tragedy—either angle of vision can provide a judgmental view.

The playwright says, "If I set this human being, with these attributes, against this group, with these attributes, this will be the result, in a world that operates by these rules." From the playwright's choice of characters, from the nature of the conflict, and from its outcome, we can determine why he wrote the play and what he wanted it to do to his audience. Discovering the playwright's intention is that part of the director's work upon which all his other choices depend.

To state the obvious: first the director must decide *what* he is trying to do to his audience before he can decide *how* he will go about it.

But today, someone is sure to ask, can we really know what the author meant to say? No, not with certainty. We can only try, with every tool of scholarship and literary detective work at our disposal, to ferret out the playwright's meaning in spite of almost insurmountable obstacles. Religious, political, sexual, economic and other attitudes will certainly have changed since the play of the past was written. No matter what sort of production we eventually envision, we must first strive to understand the period play in terms of the assumptions of the author's day.

Even with a modern play, delving into the author's biography and psychology may be necessary for finding the key to that which would otherwise be obscure. And even with plays of the very recent past, the social and ethical values underlying the piece require assessment.

When all has been studied that can be studied, we still filter the play through our own individual consciousness. Try as we may to penetrate to the author's meaning, we can finally discover only what *we* think he meant.

Then why bother to study at all? Why not turn the eye in upon the self and use the play to reflect—that self? Some will answer with a hearty "Amen," and fall to, creating a "concept" production, a shocking "new" reading, a director's subversion of the play to his own purposes.

It strikes me, however, that the self's ability to contemplate itself is, without outside stimulus, limited to only a few narcissistic postures. Directors who fail to study each play carefully for its own particular meaning—granted, to *them*—end up doing the same production over and over, like star actors who always play the same part, only in plays with different names. One must read, study, examine each play from as many points of view as possible in order to arrive at a distinct and creative interpretation—one that is subjective, to be sure, but that is thoroughly informed about the *play*. To achieve the interpretative depth we should be seeking, we need all the outside stimuli we can come by.

To my question, "What makes you paint?" a painter friend of mine came back with, "To color in all the white places between the lines." Many directors cannot make themselves work on a production before rehearsals begin because they fail to give themselves an outline to fill in. Part One of this book, "The Director's Preparation," is about how to create outlines and fill them in. To get the right answers, you first need to ask the right questions.

CHAPTER 1

SELECTING AND READING THE PLAY

Selecting a play for production sets in motion a complicated machinery, involving subjective and introspective activity, scholarship and research, and eventually the bringing together of people and the building of objects and the spending of money. Even the student director of a classroom project or a workshop at the graduate level will quickly discover how institutional considerations affect the choice of material. The decisions about which play to do and who is to do it are thus rarely matters of individual whim.

PLAY SELECTION IN INSTITUTIONAL THEATRES

In institutional settings, such as resident theatres or university theatre departments, the play-selecting process is usually a part of creating a season. This season is aimed at satisfying the theatrical expectations of a particular public. Resident theatres and university theatres tend to depend on a body of season-ticket holders—a group of supporters who have come to rely on this particular theatre to provide them with a level and type of production that they find acceptable, and who endorse the mission of the theatre in question.

What is the function of a particular theatre? In the case of a university theatre, must its productions provide a training ground for theatre majors as well as a cultural experience for its audience? In the case of a community theatre, must it provide theatrical opportunities of a recreational nature for its performing members? How much does the local audience rely on the resident, university, or community theatre to provide its entire theatre diet? Must the theatre institution in question take on the responsibility for being all things theatrical to all people? Must it find a balance between musicals and classics, comedy and drama, the experimental and the conventional? Is it the task of the theatre in question to be sure its audience gets to see the latest thing from Broadway or Off-Broadway? Or is the echoing of New York fashion anathema to this particular audience?

In large population centers, with a range of theatrical institutions, the individual theatre may have carved out a special mission—new plays, ethnic plays, plays written only by women, experimental musicals. Play selection in such theatres is hedged about by precise limitations and definitions, as opposed to the almost unlimited range of choice available to some university theatres.

Too, in the construction of a season, the matter of rhythm and variety must be dealt with. "Start with a comedy, end with a comedy," was an old rule of thumb. "Do your big classic at Christmas when the kids are out of school, so their parents will bring them," can as easily be reversed to, "Don't do your big classic at Christmas, because then the teachers can't bring busloads of kids." "Do a big musical once a season to get the people in; then you can slip in a classic once in a while and gradually build audience taste." Maybe, but maybe "Do a musical once a year that sells out and pretty soon nothing will sell out *but* musicals—which you'll have to do in increasing number." Have stars once in a while and pretty soon the audience will expect you to have stars all the time. Can one indeed develop audience taste, or is audience-building a matter of finding different audiences for different material?

One piece of wisdom (and now we enter the realm of economics and actors' salaries) holds: "Start your year with a small-cast comedy, to make money; build to your largest and most expensive show two-thirds of the way through the season; and then gradually reduce cast size, ending with a small-cast comedy, so you'll have some money in the till to start next season with." Traditional wisdom gives us another choice: starting and ending with large-cast shows. Indeed, traditional wisdom gives us an axiom for almost any course of action we choose to justify.

One thing is clear: the more productions a theatre offers in the course of a season, the more chance it has of pleasing all the people some of the time. The five-play or four-play season will always be under attack from almost all quarters: "More new plays!" "More classics!" "More recent New York hits!" "More experimental theatre!" Those institutions with more than one stage can present simultaneous productions in theatres of different configurations to suit the demands of diverse kinds of plays. Rotating repertory (more than one play playing in a given space in a given week) also helps satisfy the audience's need for variety.

The institutional theatre's artistic leadership usually works out some formula for organizing its season: so many slots for new plays, so many for classics, so many for contemporary revivals, and so on. The plays themselves may be chosen by the artistic head or by a committee; in some university theatres, a given slot (''the Shakespeare'') is designated for a particular director, who makes the actual choice of play himself. In a few university situations, each faculty director directs one play a year, and has almost total freedom to choose whatever play to which he feels drawn.

PLAY SELECTION IN THE COMMERCIAL THEATRE

The Broadway and Off-Broadway theatres offer other paths toward play selection. The usual commercial procedure (either off- or on-) is for a producer to choose a play on the basis of reading plays submitted or from seeing productions in regional theatres, in London, or in one of the marginal workshop situations that abound. Once the producer has found a play and optioned it (by paying a fee that reserves exclusive right to produce the play for a stated period of time) the producer then selects a director and assembles a creative team, at the same time reserving a theatre space. The director in question, having been contacted by the producer, then reads the play, and if he likes it and is available to do it, enters into contract and the work begins.

The Broadway or Off-Broadway director has an alternative to waiting for the phone to ring, and indeed in today's theatre many productions begin in this alternative way. The director can go on a search for plays, by joining one of the many Off-Broadway groups devoted to developing new plays, or, in an informal way, meeting writers and reading their plays. Having found a play to do, the director can then contact a workshop group or someone who controls a space, and make arrangements for a reading, a staged reading, a showcase production, or all the above, in sequence. At any stage in this process, a producer looking for a play to do may well take an interest—and the project is launched. This path can lead directly to Off-Broadway, or to the play's passage through various regional theatre productions, and the eventual destination may well turn out to be Broadway.

Through this circuitous passage, the likelihood of the director's maintaining a connection with the new play is good—so long as the relationship with the author remains intact. Producers are unlikely to replace a director who has the author's confidence. The author is apt to remain grateful to the director whose faith and energy gets the work on. Still, contractual arrangements often carry rocky personal relationships through crises, and if there is some way in which author and director can devise and hold to a written agreement, the director will have a better chance of staying with the play for the duration of its voyage.

THE DIRECTOR'S CRITERIA FOR CHOOSING A PLAY

No matter what complexity of institutional or commercial convolutions may affect the play selection process, the director does finally have to confront the question, "Do I like this play enough to do it?" Sometimes this question appears first in the form of an imperative: "I need a job"; "I need recognition"; "I need a project to keep from going batty." Even then, the real question remains, "Do I like this play enough to do it?" Because if you don't, you may lose the job, fail to get recognition, or go batty anyway because you discover you actually hate the damned play.

How can you fail to know whether you like the play? Believe me, it happens. As an actor, I came across a play about the French resistance in World War II, *The River Line* by Charles Morgan. I was asked to read the central character, Heron, in a public reading. Paul Shyre was directing. A year later, the play was done Off-Broadway, and I was asked to direct. The play had struck me as strongly pacifist in theme—Heron, the role I'd read, seemed to articulate that—and, in the rush that always seems to accompany these decisions ("We go into rehearsal next week!"), I accepted the job. I was sure I knew what the play was about. We cast one impossible actress and one inadequate actor, although the splendid Beatrice Straight almost saved the day. The impossible actress was replaced by Sada Thompson, who won an Obie award for her work. My work was damned with faint praise, but a real lesson was learned. Midway through the not-very-fluent rehearsals, I discovered that the play was not what I thought it was. It actually embodied a rigid "eye-for-an-eye" conservatism, and I lost confidence in it.

About *Waiting for Godot* I was at first very clear. I didn't like it, because I though it shapeless, negative nonsense. In spring, 1968, I was asked to direct it at the Cleveland Playhouse. I was available because at my own theatre in New Orleans the last play had already opened. "I'd never choose it myself," I thought, "but here's a chance to tinker with something like this at somebody else's expense." On close study, I learned to love the play, and the production was extremely successful, both artistically and commercially—we had a sold-out run.

I turned down the chance to direct the New York premiere of Pinter's *Birthday Party* because I completely missed the sense of menace we all now know hangs over the play. I didn't know how to read the play when it was brought to me. Time has passed, and I have seen *Birthday Party* done well. I could enjoy doing it now. Then, it simply didn't speak to me.

LISTING YOUR PERSONAL REQUIREMENTS

All directors should, I think, draw up lists, very personal lists, of things they are looking for in a play—sets of characteristics to which they respond. I give you my set of personal requirements, as an example of what such requirements might be.

1. *Story.* I look for a play with a clear beginning, middle, and end—a shape, a progression that adds up to something.

2. *Language.* I like strong, eloquent, articulate language—verse, if possible. I want music and intensity of thought on my stage.

3. *Theme.* I want a theme that is socially or politically or psychologically constructive. My theatre teaches a lesson, and it teaches it through conflict.

4. *Characters.* I want somebody as a protagonist with whom the audience can identify—somebody the audience can be *for.*

Now, you will note that this covers a lot of ground—I can include tragedy, comedy, social drama, farce. It leaves in Shakespeare, the Greeks, Shaw, Wilde, Molière, Ibsen—in fact, most of the "hits of all times," from today back to the drama's beginnings, offer most of the qualities I look for in a play. If I *don't* find these qualities—if, for example, the play is basically nonverbal or themeless—then I will probably choose not to direct it. You, on the other hand, might find it very appealing.

ASKING THE RIGHT QUESTIONS

Every director's list of needs will be different. Certainly, each list will be highly personal. Let me, then, propose the beginnings of an all-purpose screening tool—a list of questions we could all ask ourselves about plays, even though each of us may come up with different answers; questions that fit any play, new or old.

1. Does the play excite you—does it give you what someone has called a strong "gut reaction"?

2. *Why* does it excite you? Do you react to the elements of

Language	Atmosphere
Inventiveness	Timeliness
Story	Novelty
Theme	Psychological insight
Humor	Emotional impact
Characters	Humanity
Opportunities for actors	Compassion
Opportunities for spectacle	Harsh truths
Opportunities for music	Etc., *ad infinitum*

3. Is it a good play by your standards? That is, is it good in the sense of

Structure	Conflict
Characters	Relevance
Development	Etc.
Theme	

These criteria, and your answers to these questions, must then be balanced in an equation with the practical considerations of season, casting, money, space, and audience interest in order to determine your final choice intelligently.

READING THE PLAY

Financial and logistical questions aside, as a director your positive response to a play depends on your ability to read it *as a director.*

The only difference between getting acquainted with a new play and getting to know an old play is that one may already know too much about the old play. In fact, one very often decides to do a classic without rereading, whereas, with a new play, there is always a real "first time." New play or old play, one should clear one's mind of all that one has heard or read about its author, period, productions, reputation, critical response, and whatever other impedimenta may clog one's consciousness disguised as knowledge.

Read for the story, freshly. Read like a child.

Ignore, for this reading, the parade of theatrical problems—scene changes, lighting needs, casting requirements—the play undoubtedly poses. There will be time enough for that. The first reading is the time of perspective, the last time the director can easily sit in the audience's seat, expectant, waiting, unknowing, curious.

A recent discussion of David Henry Hwang's play M. *Butterfly* revealed how easily the theatre community, and even the audience, can forget the importance of what an author intends as a surprise. The play's story deals with a French diplomat's sexual involvement with a Chinese performer whom he discovers, only late in the relationship, to be a man. The author carefully lets the audience meet the Chinese performer without revealing his masculinity, saving that for a later *coup de théâtre*. The moment the play was reviewed, and indeed, after the first audience, the secret was out. From that point on it was impossible to view the first scenes uncorrupted by that knowledge. This play sustains itself handily anyway—but something is lost. The colleague with whom I discussed the play had entirely forgotten that no exposition provided by the author reveals the sexual disguise at the beginning of the evening.

As you read the play this first time, don't make any notes. Read straight through without interruption. A play is not a novel, to be taken in small bites. Don't reread any passages this first time. The audience can't play it back. Plough on. Visualize, yes—but like a movie or a novel, not as one directs. Don't read aloud. You'll have time for that later. Just experience the play.

You may simply not get it. If nothing happens, if it isn't any fun, than perhaps it's not the play for you. But perhaps you aren't doing your part; perhaps your receptors aren't working. Try again. Things may come into focus. If the play still fails to come to life for you, maybe you should choose another play.

Perhaps, however, you *do* need the job. Perhaps you have been *assigned* the play—as a graduate student project, or as the play that has your name on it, since you are on the staff. Perhaps the play is *Hamlet*, and it's a great play and this is the time to do it and you yourself are the artistic director who says this is the time to bite this particular bullet.

In that case, the techniques we will be discussing for analyzing the play, for enriching your understanding of it, for helping you to bring life to it for the actors, will bring your own imagination and instinct to the fore, producing excitement and affection by technical means, to replace your earlier apathy.

Remember that good piece of advice about the Stanislavski Method. When the actor's instincts are alive, when everything is going well—forget the analyzing. Just be grateful the work is going well. When nothing happens, when the work is going badly, when you can't find the character—that's when the techniques of "The Method" are most valuable. We in the theatre are very lucky to have these techniques for awakening inspiration and feeling. We don't have to wait around for the muse to strike or to recover from writer's block. Creativity is within our grasp, through the techniques of our craft.

FINDING THE PLAY'S STORY

After this first and freshest reading, try to tell yourself the story of the play, the sequence of its events, in your own words. If you need to, write out a summary of the plot. It is probable that, while you'll be able to describe the plot in general terms, you will not be able to remember the exact sequence in which certain things occur or are revealed.

Consider this plot summary of *Charley's Aunt*, by Brandon Thomas, taken from Theodore Shank's *500 Plays*:

> This still delightful play concerns two college boys who dress a friend in woman's clothes to impersonate a rich aunt from Brazil. The aunt was to chaperone a tea for the boys and their lady loves, but was delayed. Then, unexpectedly, the real aunt arrives, accompanied by her beautiful ward. The father of one of the boys,

CHARLEY'S AUNT
Repertory Theatre, New Orleans, 1966
This looks like a publicity still, but it is really a production photo, capturing how Fancourt (Steve Perry), in unwilling disguise, takes advantage of his position with the girls (Kitty—Anne Thompson, and Amy—Gretchen Corbett) to the discomfiture of Jack (R. Scott Thomas) and Charley (Rex Thompson).
Director: Stuart Vaughan.
Photo: Frank Methe

Sir Francis Chesney, and Spettigue, the girls' guardian, both attempt to improve their fortunes by proposing to the false aunt while the real aunt looks on. The unmasking finally occurs; the widowed aunt turns out to be an old love of Sir Francis; her ward is the missing love of the suffering masquerader; and the two young ladies admit they are anxious to wed the hosts.*

An intelligent reader will surely remember the story of any play he reads in at least that much detail. This, however, is not the kind of summary the director needs.

Act One of *Charley's Aunt* introduces Brassett, the servant; the boys; their girls; their guardian, Spettigue; Sir Francis, the father of Jack; and establishes the problem of the absent chaperone and the disguise solution—and then immediately begins the round of comic complications which this "solution" creates.

After reading the play for the first time, in preparation for directing it in 1966 in New Orleans, I found I had real trouble remembering how the author constructs his story. So I invented my "list of events," a technique I have used ever since to trace through the structure of a play I am learning to know.

Here is the list of events for the first ten pages of Act One of *Charley's Aunt*. The scene is Jack Chesney's suite of rooms at Oxford, 1895.

1. Jack, writing a love letter to Kitty, shares and works out his problem with the audience.

2. Brassett interrupts him, wanting to appropriate some cast-off items of Jack's clothing. Jack agrees, dismissing him.

3. Charley interrupts and Jack is impatient.

4. Jack apologizes and explains his letter-writing problem.

5. Charley shares his own similar dilemma, regarding *his* girl, Amy.

6. Charley asks Jack's help.

7. Jack diagnoses Charley's difficulty.

8. Jack begins to dictate a letter to Charley, at the same time creating his own letter.

9. Charley interrupts to explain he must especially tell Amy about his aunt, whom he's never met, who is coming to visit—giving Jack a newspaper clipping describing her as a Brazilian millionairess.

10. Charley explains that he wants to write to Amy, but he has to meet his aunt's train.

---

*Theodore J. Shank, ed., *500 Plays: Plot Outlines and Production Notes* (New York: Drama Book Publishers, 1988), p. 98.

11. Jack gets idea of luncheon party, with aunt chaperoning, so that he and Charley can tell the girls about their love.

12. Charley raises objections; Jack convinces him.

13. Jack calls Brassett to get a messenger for taking a note to the girls.

14. Jack dictates girls' invitation to Charley, who writes.

15. Brassett takes note to messenger.

16. Jack calls Brassett back and orders lunch for five. There is a discussion about charging the bill at Bunter's.

17. There is a discussion about the wine.

18. Jack and Charley discuss how to get the girls alone and what to do with the aunt.

19. They reject alternative "extra men"—and decide to invite Lord Fancourt Babberly.

20. They send Brassett to invite Fancourt to join them.

I proceeded through the entire play in this fashion, telling the story of each event in a succinct way. Gradually, I found myself able to grasp the sequence of incidents comprising the action of the play.

EXERCISES

1. Page 20—Design a well-balanced season of five plays that includes Samuel Beckett's *Waiting For Godot*. Choose as if you were: (1) an artistic director of a professional regional theatre; (2) an artistic director of a community theatre; (3) a director of a college theatre program. How do the producing circumstances alter your selections? What are the assumptions behind the term "well-balanced"? Prepare to defend your season as well-balanced based upon your definition of the term.

2. Page 20—The author claims that he hated *Godot* when he first encountered it, but later loved the play when he had a chance to direct a production. Speculate about how this change of feeling occurred. Have you ever had a similar experience?

3. Page 22—Prepare a list of ten plays that you most want to direct. Use this list to articulate your values and beliefs concerning drama and the theatre. Based upon your tastes, would you be a good director for *Godot*? As a producer, would you hire yourself for the job? As a director, would you accept the assignment?

4. Page 24—After an initial reading of *Waiting for Godot*, write a fable of the play from memory. Do not consult the text again. The fable should describe the action of the play as you remember it and should emphasize the sequence of events. What do you remember most vividly? What elements have you forgotten? Limit the fable to two pages. Does this exercise reveal your prejudices about the play? Can you begin to form your interpretation of the play?

CHAPTER 2

TYPES OF DRAMA

Y ou have read the play, freshly. You have read it again, and outlined it. You have noted the play's special excitements and riches.

Now, you must define what kind of play it is, before deciding how to do it.

There are several ways to categorize plays.

There is the nature of the play's content to consider. Here we can talk about tragedy, comedy, farce, melodrama, historical drama, social drama, comedy of manners, folk drama, and so on.

The style in which a play is written can be a means of classifying it. Here we find ourselves talking about representational and presentational approaches, about naturalism, realism, selective realism, expressionism, constructivism, theatricalism, theatre of the absurd, theatre of cruelty, and so forth.

Also, we can consider the play from the historical perspective—the period in which it was written. The generally recognized historical periods of drama are Greek, Roman, Medieval, Renaissance, Elizabethan, French Neoclassic, Restoration, Eighteenth Century, Nineteenth Century, Twentieth Century.

I shall look at plays from these various points of view in the course of this discussion, but, let me reiterate, always from the director's position. One must try to assess what is theatrically distinctive about each type of play. "So it's a melodrama—what does that mean I *do*?" This book is not going to tell you everything there is to know about every type of drama, but I will try to indicate what to emphasize in the principal types of drama in order to make them work effectively.

IDENTIFYING STRUCTURAL ELEMENTS

All types of plays have certain structural aspects in common that can be identified at the outset.

EXPOSITION

Exposition is the portion of the play that lays out information the audience needs. It sets the scene. It identifies the characters and gives their history. It supplies background information about what happened before the play begins, and it sets up the situation the characters find themselves in as the play starts.

A bad play, a primitive or early play, or an immature play by a talented but inexperienced playwright may have very bald exposition. One character, new to the court (or town, or country), asks another character to tell him what's going on. Or the playwright, to get on with it, may do as Plautus does in *The Braggart Soldier*, and have a character say to the audience:

> "Now, folks, if you'll be kind enough to hear me out,
> Then I'll be kind and tell you what our play's about."*

A more sophisticated, or at any rate a more realistic playwright, will help the audience attend to his exposition by wedding it as much as possible to his play's conflict. The adroit handling of exposition incorporates it so that one or more of the characters clearly and strongly *need* the information and the other characters on stage *need* to impart it, in a situation requiring that the information be given, not to the audience, but to people onstage.

In dealing with exposition, the director will be well advised to seek out and emphasize whatever aspects of conflict and/or dramatic action demand that one character tell another character what the audience needs to know. As long as the characters *need* to speak and hear, audience faith in the dramatic illusion is enhanced. Insofar as the audience is given the information baldly, the artificiality of the play and its conventions is emphasized. Sometimes, of course, emphasizing artificiality will serve the director's purposes.

CONFLICT

Conflict, the opposition of people or forces, is the essence of drama. The director must identify the nature of that conflict and describe how the characters relate to it. A play is a world created by the playwright, populated by charac-

---

*Erich Segal, trans., *Plautus: Three Comedies*, Harper Torchbooks (New York: Harper and Row, 1963), p. 18.

ters invented by him and placed in precise juxtaposition to one another. A question is posed in this invented world to which there are divergent answers. The conflict within the world of the play has to do with which answer will prevail. The *protagonist* is the character with whom the audience identifies, the *antagonist* is his opponent, and the other characters are usually connected in some way with one or the other of these functions, either acting or acted upon. Sometimes, too, there may be characters who are observers or commentators upon the action—almost an onstage audience, assisting the real audience by serving as a reflection of the *norms* of the world in which the conflict takes place.

The exposition sets up the world in which the conflict occurs, defines its characters and the potential array of forces involved. The conflict begins with the *inciting incident*—an event that, after the play starts, makes the conflict unavoidable and sets things on a collision course. The Ghost asking Hamlet to revenge his murder at the hands of Claudius marks the start of the real action of *Hamlet*, although the preceding exposition scenes reveal clearly enough Hamlet's antipathy toward his mother's marriage, his desire to escape to Wittenberg, and the fact that something is rotten in Denmark. *Othello* seems to get off to a slower start, if we think the play is about sexual jealousy, for not until Act III, scene 1, with Iago's "Ha! I like not that," does the jealousy theme of Othello versus Cassio begin. If, however, we view the main action of *Othello* as Iago's revenge on Othello for not promoting him, then the inciting incident is Iago and Roderigo goading Brabantio to interfere with Othello's marriage to Desdemona, with the jealousy plot figuring simply as the successful means Iago uses to effect his goal. My point here is that while in some plays the structural elements of the plot may be easy to distinguish, in others the director's view of the structural function of certain scenes may depend on an overall sense of the play. How the director defines the elements of exposition, inciting incident, and the nature of the conflict has an important effect on the production's meaning and impact.

RISING ACTION

After the main action has begun, *complication* and *development* contribute to the *rising action*. In other words, the plot thickens. There may even be *subplots*—actions among secondary characters that echo or contrast with the main action. In *The Taming of the Shrew*, as Petrucchio tames Katherine, Bianca is won by the wealthy Lucentio, disguised as a poor Latin teacher. The director must decide how such a subplot relates to the main plot—perhaps, as in *Shrew*, as a mirror, or perhaps as a contrast. If you shake the play does the subplot fall out, unattached by essential connections—merely an ornament on a Christmas tree—or can the director make the contribution of the subplot even more revealing?

What have Medvedenko and Masha in *The Seagull* to do with Nina and Constantine? The director must discover and enhance.

CLIMAX

The *climax* is the point at which the conflict begins to head inevitably toward its final solution. The suspense of the rising action and the tightening of the complications finally reach such a pitch that a final tension is released—and the action of the play gradually unwinds from there. The word *climax* in Greek means "ladder," and the mounting tension in a play is indeed like climbing a ladder, culminating, in our sense of the word *climax*, with the arrival at the top. The director must identify and properly build toward the play's climax.

DENOUEMENT

After that, the *falling action* begins, pointing toward the *denouement*, or "the untying of the knot," when the conflicts are at last resolved. The *resolution* has been reached when the world of the play settles into a hard-won calm, as in *Hamlet*, when Fortinbras begins his "Let four captains . . ."

Once again, as director you *must* identify these structural landmarks in the play you are preparing. If you are doing a classic, you will find an abundance of critics who have expressed opinions in books and articles as to the play's structure. Reading critics may help you think. But in the final analysis, you must make up your own mind as to how the play works and about the nature of the tensions in your own production. We can all use "a little help from others," as Algernon says in *The Importance of Being Earnest*, when asked if his hair curls naturally. Remember, though, that the best use you can make of scholars and critics is for the stimulation of your own imagination.

TRAGEDY, COMEDY, MELODRAMA, AND THEIR NEAR RELATIONS

Aristotle, whose *Poetics* has set the standard for critical writing for more than two thousand years, said enough about the "laws" governing tragedy to stoke the critical fires ever since. Had his material on comedy survived, who knows what an enormous quantity of verbiage might have been inspired? For those who want theory, quite enough material exists. Now, however, I want to consider how to make tragedy, comedy, melodrama and their near relations effective in the practical, workaday world of the theatre.

TRAGEDY

Who wants to see plays with unhappy endings? Apparently, lots of people have, down the centuries. There must be more to it, then, than just the chance to cry.

THE ORESTIA: PART I: AGAMEMNON
This photograph from the German director
Peter Stein's Berlin production conveys what
"purging with pity and terror" can be
in the theatre.
Photo: Courtesy German Information Center

Aristotle wrote of tragedy "purging us with pity and terror." Most people have taken that to mean that going to a tragedy gives our pent-up emotions an outlet, after which "purging" we feel better. F. L. Lucas, writing on *The Poetics* in 1928, ingeniously suggests that most people lack the capacity for large feelings, and that tragedy, rather than channeling feelings, awakens them.* Whichever description is accurate, both fall short of helping the director move audiences with tragedy in the theatre.

It seems to me that two kinds of tragedies have made the list of "dramatic hits of all time." In one kind, the hero is a (relatively speaking) "good guy," like Hamlet, Oedipus, or Saint Joan. In the other kind, the protagonist is a "bad guy," like Macbeth, Richard III, or Medea.

"Good Guy" Tragedy.   Let's take the "good guy" kind first. What is the appeal?

Remember, in real life, the death rate is 100 percent. "None of you guys

---

*F. L. Lucas, *Tragedy* (London: Chatto and Windus, Ltd., 1928, rev. ed. 1957), pp. 35–78.

are gonna git outa this alive." The vulgar bumper-sticker motto "Shit happens, and then you die," could be said to describe the human condition. If that's all, why bother? To live is to participate in a futile exercise, and thus, why not end the nonsense as soon as possible?

Tragedy—the "good guy" kind—helps us to experience, vicariously, that life, though finite, can be lived gloriously, for a worthy purpose, and, like Hamlet's, can be expended nobly. Look at Lear—the strongest man in his world, still vital at eighty, not senile—so confident in his strength that he delivers himself into unworthy hands. Even the strongest man in the world has a lot to learn, and in the journey of the play, we see him learn humility and forgiveness. Far from being a study in futility and senility, *King Lear* seems to me to be a study in insight and redemption. The "good guy" tragedy leaves us uplifted, with the life-confirming forces in us roused, with our courage and faith renewed.

"Bad Guy" Tragedy. The "bad guy" tragedy (and I nominate *Macbeth*, *Richard III*, and *Medea* as examples) gives us a protagonist vastly gifted, a man or woman of great power, a "Lucifer"—and then shows these gifted ones in the service of evil purposes. For a time, in such plays, we may follow the hero with admiration, as in *Richard* III, where Richard's wit, intelligence, and sheer energy make him far outshine those characters who surround him. Macbeth is a man of action in the prime of life, with everything going his way. He is tempted to evil and chooses it. Richard and Medea have in common that each has been wronged, to some extent. So has Iago, to cite another example—at least in his own eyes. Richard's deformity, Jason's perfidy toward Medea, Iago's having been passed over for promotion—these are not depicted as justifications for evil, but they do constitute initial injustices from which evil retaliation springs. We as spectators enjoy seeing the wronged one "get her own back," as Eliza Doolittle puts it in Shaw's *Pygmalion*. When, however, real damage is done, and then repeated, as in *Macbeth* and *Richard* III, our gorge rises and we demand punishment for the wrongdoer. The author usually provides this (though Medea gets away in her magic chariot), and we leave the theatre with a renewed sense of justice. In the "bad guy" tragedy, *waste* is the element that operates on our feelings. Macbeth, Richard III, Medea—each in his separate way has genius. As with Lucifer, the gift of special power is used for evil, not for good. What a waste! What a tragedy.

Modern Tragedy. The tragedies I have mentioned involve events "of a certain magnitude," to use Aristotle's phrase from his *Poetics*, in the lives of kings, queens, princes, and legendary figures from ancient literature. What about today's tragic figures—like Willy Loman of *Death of a Salesman*? Some critics hold that real tragedy is impossible today. The argument goes that modern life lacks that shared belief in moral and spiritual values received from God which gives rise to heroes who can defy that God. Willy Loman is not a king or a man of heroic stature; he's just a common man like us, so there can be no tragedy. This particular bit of intellectual jockeying may offer a valid area for academic discussion, but it is of little practical use in the theatre. For the play to work, Willy Loman must be played as a hero among men, a God to his sons, a person of special size and power. His problem, which Miller states so clearly, is that he has bought the wrong values—the values of a salesman, of being "well liked"—when he should have been a man of his hands, of the soil. Play him like a petty, little, ordinary man, and the play goes out the window. In the theatre, it works as a tragedy should work. So does A *Streetcar Named Desire*, devised as it is of a more delicate fabric. Blanche is a modern heroine of stature, and the struggle between her sensitive and spiritual nature and the brutish and philistine Stanley gives us modern tragedy of a high order.

Casting the Tragic Hero.   For successful impact in the theatre, both "good guy" and "bad guy" tragedies require a magnetic and heroic casting of the protagonist. The audience puts its identity in the hands of the leading character. They invest him with power over their vicarious experiences. He stands for them. He must be worthy of sympathy and identification. I have seen a Richard of Gloucester so repulsive of countenance and so misshapen of body that he required an external skeleton of aluminum to stand upright. Ghastly, horrible, repulsive. You bet. And why does Lady Anne succumb to these charms in Act I, scene 3 of Shakespeare's *Richard* III? I don't think she would. Watch Olivier, in his film, play that scene with Claire Bloom as Anne. Sexual attraction is what brings Lady Anne around. That takes the magnetism of the best and sexiest actor you can find, for Richard. As for Macbeth: the moment he becomes a temporizing, guilt-ridden procrastinator the play is lost. He is the man who "unseamed" the merciless Macdonwald "from the nave to the chops." True, he waffles more about killing Duncan than Lady Macbeth finds manly, but he soon gets on with it. The headlong pace of Shakespeare's music for this play should be sufficient to convince anyone sensitive to it that its hero is no hesitator. Medea must excite our admiration, with her beauty as well as with her animal vitality. Even if we understand that Jason's weakness leads him to seek out a weaker partner, we still comprehend and identify with Medea's sense of betrayal and her desire for revenge.

"The world is out of joint," as Hamlet says of the world of *his* play. The protagonist may try to "set it right," or be himself the cause of the lack of balance. In either case, sympathy with the protagonist is what holds our interest, and, in both cases, the end of the tragedy restores the balance, and thus the audience receives its sought-for redemption and fulfillment.

RICHARD III
New York Shakespeare Festival, 1957
George C. Scott, in his first New York appearance, succeeded in being both heroic and
grotesque in the role that brought him to prominence. Director: Stuart Vaughan.
Photo: George E. Joseph

COMEDY

In tragedy, the protagonist usually loses his struggle, and with it his life, whether the struggle has been of man against man, man against himself, or man against God. In comedy, he usually wins his battle. If tragedy teaches, by example, that life's battle can be worth the fight, even if we inevitably succumb, comedy puts life's everyday problems into proportion and reduces them to manageable size, often through ridicule. Laughter gives us power over events.

Much has been said by Freud and others about humor as sublimated aggression, a socially acceptable way of expressing hostility. I certainly accept the premise of humor as sublimated aggression, but it hasn't done much for my directing. I mean, if it is aggression, the author has sublimated it, right? So it is his sublimation that concerns me. It is clear enough that Joe Orton, in *Loot*, is thumbing his nose at society. To make the play entertaining, I have to find out what's *funny* in it.

THE IMPORTANCE OF BEING EARNEST
Seattle Repertory Theatre, 1965
Kay Doubleday (Gwendolyn) and Anne Thompson (Cecily) demonstrate that
"comedy is a very serious business." Director: Stuart Vaughan.
Photo: Dudley, Hardin and Yang

Humor: The Four Types.   I offer here a rough-hewn but theatrically service-
able classification of the sources, or types, of humor. Look at your play and
see what's funny in it, using these simple guidelines. I hasten to say, these are
not my formulations. They are part of the oral tradition of the theatre which,
like all professionally experienced people, I have absorbed along the way. If I
could remember where I learned them, I would cheerfully give credit. I don't
remember. But even if I did, I expect credit would not be due, for whoever
passed this on to me got it from someone else—and so on, perhaps back to
Thespis, the first actor—the first one who earned star billing, anyway.

1. *Exaggeration.* Sometimes things are funny simply because they are shown
on the stage larger than life. The clown's baggy pants—baggier than you'll ever
see; his red nose, redder than any drunk's; his orange, stick-up wig, more orange and wild than any real hair. A hugely fat man, an extraordinarily tall and
skinny person, big feet, ears that stick out—these are often seen as funny, along

with things that are exceptionally fast, slow, high, low, and so on. Exaggeration is a fairly primitive kind of humor, and it consists largely of visual elements, or "sight gags."

2. *Incongruity.* This is the humor of putting things together that don't belong together. The tiny Volkswagen "beetle" that is driven into the circus ring is not inherently funny. The man who gets out of it isn't, either. But when, one after another, thirteen men get out, it will be funny—because it is so incongruous that so many people could get into such a little car. Another example of incongruity, still in the realm of the visual: the fat man in the top hat and fur-collared coat isn't funny; the banana peel lying on the sidewalk isn't funny. But when the fat man steps on the banana peel and falls on his behind, it *is* funny—funny incongruous (so much dignity deflated)—as long as he doesn't break his hip. A joke *on* somebody, visual or verbal, won't work if it trespasses into the area of the *painful*, for then sympathy and not laughter is aroused for the object of the joke. The pie-in-the-face is funny as long as the person hit is surprised or deflated. If, however, he rubs his eyes in pain, laughter ceases. The aggression has peered out from behind its acceptable mask of humor, and resistance, not release, is aroused. In the verbal realm, incongruity often has to do with *what* is said *when*. The great French writer of farce, Feydeau, when asked his recipe for a comedy scene, said, "I decide which characters must not, under any circumstances, meet each other, and then I bring them together." It is under such incongruous circumstances that the most banal of lines, like, "Well, here I am!" can bring down the house.

3. *Wit.* By wit I mean the humor created by words alone. The author may get a joke from the character's conscious creation of an epigram or from the quite ordinary remark made in a particularly loaded situation. In any case, most wit comes from the sharp juxtaposition of incongruous *ideas*. For example, in Act I of Wilde's *The Importance of Being Earnest*, Lady Bracknell inquires of her nephew Algernon about an acquaintance who has recently lost her husband:

Lady Bracknell: I had some crumpets with Lady Harbury, who seems to me to be living entirely for pleasure now.
Algernon: I hear her hair has turned quite gold from grief.

4. *Recognition.* The fourth humor yardstick is recognition, or that feeling in the audience, "Isn't life just like that!" One can almost say, "*fond* recognition," for very often there is the surprise of a sudden affectionate emotional recall that the play produces. We laugh in recognition. Whole plays work from this kind of humor: family plays, like *The Glass Menagerie* (Williams calls it "a memory play"); and folk or ethnic plays like *Playboy of the Western World* and *Steel Magnolias*.

In *The Glass Menagerie*, two jokes occur close together. Tom has come in late and drunk. He goes to sleep on the living room couch, and the lights go down. We hear the alarm go off in the dark, and Amanda calls out, "Rise and shine, rise and shine!" The audience laughs, from recognition of our mothers doing just that, and also the sense of how it is to wake up too early. Tom answers, "I'll rise—but I won't shine." The audience recognizes this too, remembering what a hangover Tom must have—and there is, too, the incongruity of "shining" in his condition.

This example illustrates how the four categories of humor may be combined. Exaggeration may be blended with incongruity, wit with recognition, recognition with exaggeration. Still, the four divisions themselves have proved a durable starting place, over the years, for answering the question, "Why is this funny—what's the joke?"

Classic Comedy.   Comedy descended from the Greeks and Romans, as did tragedy, and that ancestry has left its imprint on the comedies still on our stage today.

David Scanlan, in his *Reading Drama*, sets forth what the classic comedies are about:

> In Bella and Samuel Spewack's 1935 comedy *Boy Meets Girl*, Hollywood screen-writer J. Carlyle Benson sums up the traditional comic plot in a simple formula: "Boy meets girl. Boy loses girl. Boy gets girl." This formula has surprisingly wide application. It describes a fundamental aspect of most comedy written since the time of the Greek playwright Menander (342–292 B.C.), including the comedies of Shakespeare, Molière, Bernard Shaw, Oscar Wilde, Noel Coward, and Neil Simon.
>
> "Benson's law," however, does not give an adequate idea of the richness of the comic resolution, when boy finally gets girl. Whatever happens along the way, we know the comedy will end with one or more pairs of lovers, and perhaps their elders, their servants, and their neighbors (whatever combination is appropriate to the historical period and social level of the play), assembled in the dramatic space in anticipation of a wedding and a happy life ever after. This resolution celebrates love, prosperity, sanity, and renewal. Like a real-life wedding, it is not meant to remind one of everyday reality, but of our highest hope for the future.*

The classic comedy relies on one or more pairs of lovers, stern parents or guardians who may constitute an obstacle to the union, servants or friends who act as confidants to the lovers, and devices like smuggled letters and disguises (often girl as boy, for protection or freedom in a man's world).

Money versus love is very often the nature of the conflict, with aristocratic parents holding out for marriage as an economic contract, pitted against the desire of the couple to marry for love. A resolution usually occurs that reconciles love with financial security. Sometimes the same conflict is enacted with

---

*David Scanlan, *Reading Drama* (Mountain View, CA: Mayfield Publishing Company, 1988), p. 45.

THE TWO GENTLEMEN OF VERONA
New York Shakespeare Festival, 1987
The pairs of lovers, reunited, at the end of this classic comedy.
From left to right: Deborah Rush, James Goodwin, Thomas Gibson,
and Elizabeth McGovern. Director: Stuart Vaughan.
Photo: © 1991 *Martha Swope*

gentle versus common birth. As theatre audiences became more democratic
and society's strictures separating the classes were gradually relaxed, the formula "Boy meets girl, loses girl, gets girl" became less entangled with economics.

Modern Comedy.   Modern comedies still deal with the vicissitudes of lovers,
but instead of money and stern parents, the major obstacles seem to concern
the battle of the sexes, involving questions of dominance, dependence, inde-
pendence, and social mores. Who lives with whom, the nature of commitment,
the consequences of divorce, sexual identity, the status of women, the inner
dynamics of marriage—these are the questions that have dominated comedy
in the late twentieth century. The family constellation still gives rise to domestic comedies, such as the autobiographical plays of Neil Simon, but rarely is
the conflict simply over money and social position; more often it is in the area
of human relationships. Social issues—race relations and the stock market—

were the subject matter of two of the most successful American comedies of the late eighties: *Driving Miss Daisy* and *Other People's Money*. The British writers David Hare and Caryl Churchill are writing biting comedies about politics today.

Types of Comedy.   Within the area of comedy, there are certain special categories that deserve identification.

Farce is that type of comedy (*Charley's Aunt*, *The Girl from Maxim's*, *Room Service*) that depends on a rapidly spiraling series of physical events. The author chooses a situation that lands his hero in a very awkward kettle of fish. *Charley's Aunt*, to which we have referred earlier, builds on the difficulties Lord Fancourt Babberly's disguise as an old lady gets him into. In *The Girl from Maxim's*, by Feydeau, Petypon, respectably married to a very pious wife, awakens with a terrible hangover, to discover that, after a night of unaccustomed drinking with a medical colleague, he has brought home with him a can-can dancer, nicknamed "The Shrimp." He tries to conceal her presence from his wife, leading to hilarious complications, further heightened when General Petypon, his rich uncle, calls unexpectedly, mistakes The Shrimp for Madame Petypon, whom he's never met, and invites his nephew and "wife" to a party at his country estate. The real Madame Petypon turns up there, looking for her husband, and further madness occurs as Petypon tries to keep the two women from meeting. All turns out well in the end, with The Shrimp and the General embarking on a love affair.

These two plays, and others like them, make use of quite improbable situations, which these authors adroitly succeed in establishing as both possible and probable. Of course, in farce as in all drama, the impossible but probable is preferable to the possible but improbable. All that matters on the stage is that the audience, for the duration of the performance, believe in (find probable) the events depicted in the play. In farce, once the audience has accepted the author's premise, he is able to add layer upon layer of complicating problems. As the tension mounts, the speed with which the unexpected and disconcerting twists of the plot occur serves to keep the audience from questioning the increasingly absurd heights of humor that the play scales.

The protagonist, in farce, is always a victim. He may, as in *Charley's Aunt*, be an innocent victim, so that, after his initial embroilment in troubles, the audience will enjoy seeing "the worm turn." Often, though, the victim has, through qualities inherent in his character, been responsible for the plight in which he finds himself. Petypon, in *The Girl from Maxim's*, did bring the girl home. We understand his dismay on finding her, half-dressed, in his consulting room, but The Shrimp reveals herself to be a cheerful and accommodating creature. As Petypon gradually shows himself to be a hypocrite, ashamed of her presence and her profession, the audience becomes increasingly willing to see him

CHARLEY'S AUNT
Repertory Theatre, New Orleans, 1966
There are nice chuckles, but no real laughs, in *Charley's Aunt* until Fancourt enters in disguise, but after that the laughs never stop. The "aunt" pulls up her skirts to get at her pockets, smokes cigars, flirts with the two older men—all highly physical humor.
Steve Perry as "the aunt," Dillon Evans as Mr. Spettigue. Director: Stuart Vaughan.
Photo: Frank Methe

get his comeuppance. His wife, too, is a good sort, and the audience begins to side with the women. *Charley's Aunt* is sunny and without the slightest hint of the naughty. *The Girl from Maxim's*, constantly near the edge of impropriety, titillates without ever exceeding the bounds of good taste.

Chases, disguises, mistaken identities, notes, concealment behind doors or under beds or *in* beds, compromising meetings—all are characteristic of farce. There is little "wit," in the sense of epigrams or jokes that can be quoted out of context, aside from the comic "character tag" like "I'm Charley's aunt from Brazil, where the nuts come from." This kind of identifying tag, used throughout the show (in *The Girl from Maxim's*, the General is always saying "Keep to the right!") is usually a sure-fire laugh. (I am reminded here of Teddy's "Charge the blockhouse!" as he runs up the stairs in *Arsenic and Old Lace*.) The verbal laughs in farce are almost all situational, in that the remark is only humorous because this person says it in this particular situation. Otherwise, laughs in farce are largely sight laughs.

Charley's Aunt reminds me of another characteristic of farce. When I was about to embark on directing it for the first time, my very gifted designer said, with relish, "Let's do it in black and white, like an old-time movie." "Wrong," said I. Let me clarify. Farce shares with melodrama the mounting tension of a series of physical incidents stemming from a situation that skates on the edge of the improbable. As the tension increases, the audience's credulity must be maintained, though it may be sorely tried. Thus, farce, along with melodrama, requires a special attention to realism—walls that enclose and conceal, doors that really work, props that have solidity and reality, clothing that could have been worn in life. The more theatrically stylized (distant from naturalism) the physical production and the acting are, the less the audience will connect empathically with the threatening precariousness of the dramatic situation.

Comedy of manners is a term that usually refers to the comedies of Restoration England, of Molière, and of the eighteenth century. They poke fun at the fashionable foibles of their age and satirize the very audience that comes to see them. The plays of Oscar Wilde, George Bernard Shaw, Somerset Maugham, and Noel Coward are comedies of manners. All these plays are inhabited by characters recognizably typical of their time, and they deal with social situations and issues that were of immediate and topical interest to their audiences. They depend for their humor in great measure upon wit. Their upper-class characters are deliberately witty, and their lower-class characters bring their own brand of wit to bear, in contrast. In these plays of elegant language, the production must encourage the audience to listen. The play may contain farcical elements (disguises, concealments, coincidences) but the physicality must never be so boisterous as to lead the audience into *watching* for the next joke, instead of *listening* for it. Too, although institutions and characters may be depicted so we can laugh at them, the delicacy and wit of the best comedies of manners avoid the harshness and vulgarity of burlesque or parody. The observations of society must remain accurate enough that truth is not violated. Amusement, not mockery, is the aim. Ridicule hurts—the fat man has broken his hip.

Satire, however, has more latitude. *The Beggar's Opera* and its modern adaptation, *Threepenny Opera*, compare the relationships and commerce of the criminal world with those of the everyday world, and that comparison is tart and stinging. The savageness of the comparison makes the lesson of the piece work. *Parody* involves criticism by imitation. A parody ridicules the original it "takes off." Parody is intended to rebuke, and if we, as audience, enjoy the parody, we accept its intent to sting. *Burlesque* achieves its effect by exaggerating the qualities it selects to imitate. To recapitulate: I see comedy of manners offering amused observation, satire as tartly ridiculing social institutions, parody as ridicule by harsh imitation, and burlesque as poking fun by exaggerated imitation. In parody and burlesque, the characterizations partake of caricature.

In comedy of manners and satire, the one-dimensional quality of the char-

THE RIVALS
Repertory Theatre, New Orleans, 1967
Herbert Nelson as Sir Anthony and R. Scott Thomas as Jack manage hats, staff, sword,
wigs, high heels, ruffles—all that, and acting, too. Director: Stuart Vaughan.
Photo: Frank Methe

acterizations is part of the style. It has been said, comparing Molière with
Shakespeare, that where Shakespeare gives us a broad, many-faceted portrait
of his characters, Molière is interested in intensely examining his people in only
one aspect. He sets out to tell you everything he can about miserliness, or
hypocrisy, or affectation, or hypochondria. Ben Jonson, too, examines his characters in this intense and deliberately one-dimensional way for their "humors,"
rather than for their full humanity. This is not a fault of Jonson's or Molière's;
it is their method. To try to flesh out a Molière character with a full range of

human quirks would be a mistake; to miss Shakespeare's broader and more detailed palette would be to fail to take advantage of one of this author's greatest strengths.

This seems to be the place, too, to suggest that characters develop in tragedy, but not in comedy or melodrama—develop in the sense of grow or change. Macbeth develops, from a man with criminal inclinations but a conscience, into a determined and implacable villain. Hamlet grows, in the course of the play, into a person who can finally act on his charge to exact revenge. In comedy or melodrama, the character is placed in a situation of conflict. As the plot unfolds, his situation changes, and by the end of the play, his conflict is resolved. He may even have learned things about himself he didn't know before. Tracy Lord in *Philadelphia Story* finds out that she, too, is only human, with feet of clay. Still, she hasn't developed or changed. The protagonist in comedy or melodrama may know more, feel better, and be better off than he was at the beginning of the play, but he remains intrinsically that same person. Oedipus, Richard III, Hamlet, Lear—all have developed. To seek directorially for character development in a comedy or melodrama is to distort an essential element of the form. Not to ask how the character develops or changes in a tragedy is to ignore part of the author's purpose.

High comedy is a rather imprecise term that refers to a genre of a gentler and more lifelike nature than comedy of manners. T. S. Eliot's *The Cocktail Party*, his *Confidential Clerk*, Enid Bagnold's *The Chalk Garden*, the plays of S. N. Behrman and Philip Barry—these are examples of high comedy. These plays usually deal with people in the higher social strata, they have fairly complex and realistic stories, and they may well have significant social or psychological themes. The plays are rich in language and ideas, and their humor is verbal—wit. There is little physical humor and often little physical (in the sense of muscular) action. Let me quote some remarks of Ina Claire, one of America's greatest actresses of comedy, who starred on the Broadway stage almost continuously from the twenties to the fifties. She talked about high comedy when we worked together on *The Confidential Clerk*, she as star and I in a more lowly capacity, one of the happiest chores of which was cueing her through her part. Like many other actresses, she preferred talking to working. Her excursions, though, were particularly fascinating, since they were filled with theatrical lore. "Don't expect many laughs in high comedy," she said. "Chuckles, yes, and many smiles, but not many big laughs. Remember, too," she said, "there is pain—but it's always remembered pain. Pain in the past. With a memory speech in a high comedy, don't work to make it immediate—don't try to relive it all over again, as you would in a drama. Look back on it, let it be distant, seen through a veil." She never let a chance for humor slip, but, like all able comedians, she would always sacrifice several little laughs in order to get one big one.

Folk comedies are usually family plays. *The Glass Menagerie, Playboy of the Western*

World, *Crimes of the Heart*—plays like this depend on recognition for their humor. O'Neill's *Ah, Wilderness!*, one of the finest folk plays and his only comedy, evokes the simpler, gentler New England of the turn of the century. We recognize this past as part of the American legend, and there is a fondness and affection for it that spreads over the play as we watch the young protagonist, Richard (an idealized picture of the author as young man), live through the pangs of growing up in the bosom of a kindly family very unlike the Tyrones of *Long Day's Journey into Night*.

The best folk plays walk a wonderful tightrope of memory. Tip toward one side—it's funny. Tip the other way—there are tears.

MELODRAMA

Melodrama got a bad name because the nineteenth-century stage was occupied by many effective theatre pieces of little literary merit, most of which could be classified as melodramas. Literary merit as a qualification for success in the theatre has become important only recently. Remember, prior to the invention of cinema, theatre was the *only* dramatic form. It served all levels of people with material suited to their taste and education. Of what literary merit is the television sitcom? In the past, as now, "all the drama fit to print" was a very small portion of the drama consumed by the public.

The Characteristics of Melodrama. Melodrama is a very accessible form. There is always a hero or heroine with whom to identify, and there is always a villain. Good and evil are clearly established and personified. The story line, or plot, is apt to be heavily complicated and "crowded with incident," as Wilde puts it, and these incidents are characterized by vigorous physical action. Exotic or elaborate settings are characteristic of the form, since spectacle was important to melodrama's earlier audiences. The characterizations, at the worst, are at a very thin level, but well-rounded characters are not uncongenial to the form. The cheaper plays of this type abound in sentimental clichés and sensational but not fully justified shocks and surprises, but good writing can avoid the obvious, as in any other form of drama. Shocks and surprises can be motivated, coincidences do occur, even in great plays, and truth of emotion is not excluded from melodrama. Disguises, intercepted letters, eavesdropping, and similar devices figure in melodrama as they do in classic comedy and the older tragedies. But in melodrama, almost invariably "the good ends happily and the bad unhappily," to paraphrase Oscar Wilde.

Dion Boucicault was an actor-manager-author of the mid-nineteenth century with an international career in London, Paris, and America. His *Octoroon*, *London Assurance*, and *The Poor of London* (in New York called *The Poor of New York*) all represent well-crafted and commercially successful examples of the older melodrama. Walter Kerr, reviewing my 1959 Phoenix Theatre revival of Boucicault's *The Octoroon* in the *New York Herald-Tribune*, said, ''If we can't have good new plays, thank God for bad old ones.'' No, Boucicault is not Ibsen, but even today, his plays *work*.

Melodrama is far from dead. Both well-crafted and preposterous examples crowd our film and television screens today. Almost any cop show, murder mystery, or Western drama is a melodrama. The social drama is usually in the melodramatic form, with its hero doctor, social worker, or newspaperman struggling against the business interests, the environmental polluter, the profiteer, the corrupt politician.

Differences Between Melodrama and Tragedy. Melodrama, like tragedy, can deal with very serious material. Usually in melodrama the bad people are defeated and the good emerge triumphant, but not every time. That can sometimes raise the question, for the director, ''Which is it, tragedy or melodrama?'' Shakespeare calls it ''The Tragedy'' of *Romeo and Juliet*. Is it? I hasten to say there is no one right answer to this question, only the creation of productions different in tone. Two families are involved in a blood feud. A boy and a girl of opposing families meet and secretly fall in love. They are secretly married. A quarrel is forced on the boy by her cousin, who is killed, and the boy is banished. Under the threat of what would be a bigamous marriage proposed by her parents, the girl fakes death with a potion concocted by her priest, planning to slip out of her tomb and flee with her husband. The letter telling him of this plan is never delivered, and instead, the boy receives word of her death. He comes back and kills himself over her body—just before she wakes up. She awakens to find him dead and kills herself. When both deaths are discovered, the parents realize that the blood feud is at fault, and the families, in mutual sorrow, finally make peace.

Now, the kids are very sweet, it is a great love story, and what happens to them is a damned shame. It is also a great play. But let's look at it carefully.

The kids are not ''of a certain magnitude.'' They are just bright kids, not repositories of the fate of nations. They are undone, not by special qualities inherent in their characters (although sexy and young they certainly are) but by the outworn social convention of the feud, bringing with it the accidental death of Mercutio when Romeo tries to stop the fight, leading to Tybalt's death, and by the failure of a message to arrive—undone by accident.

This is not a play in which everything points inevitably toward a result grounded in the inherent nature of its complex protagonist. This play, in my view, is a social drama, a melodrama, which superficially resembles a tragedy. The director, deciding that, can enjoy his street fights, make Tybalt as nasty as he likes, find humor where he will, relish the scheming of the friar, go with the romanticism and sexiness of the love stuff, and emphasize the theatrical quality of the coincidences. And at the end, the play teaches that outworn social

ROMEO AND JULIET
New York Shakespeare Festival, 1957
This was the first of the Shakespeare productions in Central Park. The permanent set was clad in arches, with various curtains and gates, and was *terra cotta* in color.
The touching but courageous Juliet was Bryarly Lee. The manly but tender Romeo was Stephen Joyce. Director: Stuart Vaughan.
Photo: George E. Joseph

conventions can kill (think of Ibsen's *Ghosts*) within the same dramatic form that lets the film *On the Waterfront* effectively show the consequences of corruption.

Melodrama and the Comedic.   Melodrama, as well as verging on the tragic, can also partake of the comic. The classic social drama is Ibsen's *An Enemy of the People*. Though it lacks some of the violent physical incident typical of melodrama, it has a clear hero and villain and shares other aspects of the form. Dr. Stockman discovers that the waters of the health spa he has created are fouled by waste from the tannery, so that the town's greatest tourist attraction, the baths, should be closed. For this discovery, he is denounced as "an enemy of the people." Heaven knows, in Arthur Miller's adaptation, all this is earnest

AN ENEMY OF THE PEOPLE
Repertory Theatre, New Orleans, 1969
The long speech in Act IV was staged with the onstage audience downstage,
so the theatre audience could get the full effect of the doctor's argument.
Stuart Vaughan was Dr. Stockman, Donald Perkins was the newspaper editor behind him,
and David Scanlan directed.
Photo: Frank Methe

enough, with villainy triumphant and our upright hero, in the midst of his family, holding the fort alone.

Ibsen's play, in spite of being susceptible to such a reading, is actually a comedy. Dr. Stockman is, of course, right, but he is also foolishly impractical and lacking in political sense. In the face of opposition, he is optimistic, stubborn, and finally implacable. The original play has many laughs. Stockman has a boyish, impulsive, bull-in-a-china-shop quality that makes him a sympathetic comic hero. The play is actually the most Shavian of Ibsen's plays—a comedy-melodrama of ideas, that works on many levels.

LAUGHTER AND THE "WORTHWHILE"

Laughter as a way of dealing with serious subjects is not for everyone. I directed *Waiting for Godot* at The Cleveland Playhouse some years ago in a very popular production. One night there was a seminar after the performance. The panel assembled onstage was made up of a prominent Cleveland psychiatrist, a member of the English faculty of a local university, and myself, as director of the play. The discussion quickly revealed that the English professor was appalled that the production got so many laughs—in such a serious play. The psychiatrist and I were easily able to accept that the absurdity of the play's situation (humanity, stranded) leads to helpless laughter, that the characters are whistling in the dark, and that Beckett recognizes that humor is a potent way to deal with the abyss around us. Shaw's French translator fled the Paris theatre, the first time one of his translations was played, crying out, "But— they *laughed!*" We must remind ourselves that serious subjects may be dealt with in a humorous manner, that there can be laughs in tragedy, that farce and melodrama are worthwhile forms, and, too, that earnestness of purpose does not necessarily a great play make.

EXERCISES

1. Page 32 —*Godot* has been described as a play in which "nothing happens twice." Is this an accurate assessment of the play? Does the play have any action at all in a traditional sense? Develop an answer that responds to your interpretation of "tradition."

2. Page 32—Who is Godot and why are Didi and Gogo waiting for him? In what ways do your answers reveal more about your biases as a director than about either character motivations or Beckett's view of the world? Can you base your interpretation on evidence in the text?

3. Page 45—Beckett's subtitle reads: "A tragicomedy in two acts." Does this definition

travesty the notion of genre or does it sincerely attempt to alert the reader to a particular kind of experience? List the tragic and comic elements in the play and demonstrate how they interact. Is the result of this collision a critique of dramatic form or the creation of a viable new genre? Relate your answer to your own experience of the world at the end of the twentieth century.

4. Page 50—The American premiere of *Godot* at the Coconut Grove Playhouse in Florida was billed as "the laugh hit of two continents." How would you promote your production? To what extent does generic classification enhance or reduce an appreciation of the play?

CHAPTER 3

STYLES OF PRODUCTION

Before casting and before dealing with designers, the director must determine in what *style* the production will be presented.

DEFINITIONS OF "STYLE"

"Style" is a word everybody uses that seems to have a variety of definitions. "He has great style" refers to manner, having a distinguished "air." "Lifestyle" has become a way of referring to the totality of a person's choices as to clothes, food, housing, recreation, human relationships, politics—all those areas in which we exercise our personal taste. "Stylish" can mean fashionable. "In style" means "up to the minute." "Out of style" means *passé*.

For your purposes as a director, the term *style* is a useful way to describe your choices in answering three important questions:

1. What relationship will there be between the conventions of the historical period from which the play comes and this particular production?

2. Is the play to be produced "representationally" or "presentationally"?

3. In what style relative to day-to-day reality will this production be mounted?

HISTORICAL STYLES

The first task of the director in selecting a production style is to assess how the author related to the theatrical conventions of his own period. Each period evolves a set of established practices, "ground rules," accepted by both audiences and practitioners of theatre as "the way things are done." The acceptance of masks, of men playing women's roles, a "realistic" box set with its "fourth wall" removed, the aside, the soliloquy, the entire "illusion of the first time"—all these are examples of theatrical conventions which both artists and audiences have agreed to believe in at particular times in the theatre's history. As director you must ask yourself, then, how did the author expect the play to be acted? In what sort of theatre was the play produced and what effect did

PEER GYNT
Schaubühne am Halleschen Ufer, Berlin, 1971
This photograph is included to show to what vigorous lengths "stylization" can go in the hands of an imaginative and creative director—in this case, Peter Stein.
Photo courtesy German Information Center

the theatre's design have on the play's construction? What kind of setting did the author envisage? Only when you have addressed these questions will you have enough data on which to base your own stylistic decisions.

This is where your knowledge of dramatic literature and theatre history will serve you well. Without trying to provide that background here, let me suggest for each historical style the principal production elements its authors would have expected and those that are especially important and useful for the modern director to reckon with.

CLASSICAL GREEK AND ROMAN DRAMA

Outdoor theatres in Classical times consisted of a semicircular forestage, backed by a permanent, raised structure pierced with doors. The plays were verse dramas, with masked actors, sometimes wearing built-up shoes. There

OEDIPUS REX
Darmstadt Theater
Here is a modern interpretation of the conventions of the Greek stage,
including an inventive solution for the actors' masks.
Photo courtesy German Information Center

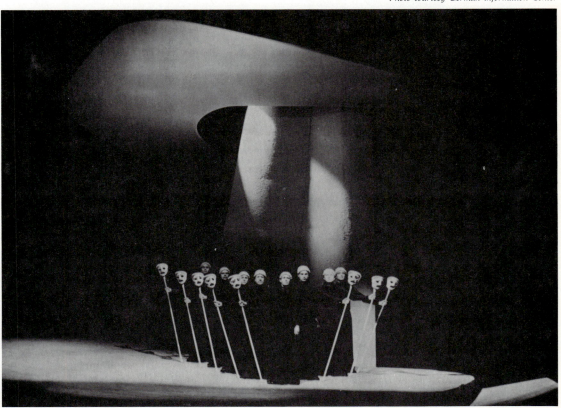

THE BIRDS
Bad Hersfeld Festival, 1974
This outdoor production of Aristophanes' comedy made a greater effort at authenticity of costume and mask, with what appears to be less theatrical success.
Photo courtesy German Information Center

was evidently a rhetorical and formalized acting style. A chorus was used, variable in size, that supported and commented on the main action in song and dance. The Roman theatre, resembling the Greek in physical production, degenerated into increasing emphasis on spectacle, violence, and sexual display.

MEDIEVAL DRAMA

Heaven and Hell were indicated on opposite sides of the acting area. Wagon stages were drawn through the streets, or various stations were set out simultaneously in the town square to which the audience moved in sequence. Semiprofessional performers were used. Plays were based on the lives of saints or the life of Christ and performed on feast days. Performances sometimes took place on church steps. Outdoor playing probably led to broad and "explanatory" acting.

RENAISSANCE DRAMA

Latin verse plays based on classical models began to be performed in university dining halls on temporary platforms. Curtains might indicate doorways right, left, and center leading to a neutral "forestage." Probably the acting was modeled on someone's ideas of Quintilian's instructions for orators.

ELIZABETHAN AND SPANISH SEVENTEENTH-CENTURY DRAMA

This period saw the evolution of professional writers and acting companies, performing at first in inn-yards with balconies on three or four sides, used by the audience, with a platform stage thrust out into the yard, surrounded by standing members of the audience (the pit). This stage usually had an upper level, permitting scenes to be played "above." These inn-yard stages were copied, with improvements, when permanent structures like the Globe were built. The subject matter, comedy or tragedy or history, was presented episodically, with many changes of locale, scene changes indicated in the words but played within the same physical areas. Soliloquies and asides preserved the actors' option to speak directly to the audience. Evidently, movement was circular and frequent, so that audience members on all sides could see.

COMMEDIA DELL'ARTE

This was an entirely continental (non-English) development. The rough platform stage was inhabited by conventional masked characters (Harlequin, Columbine, Pantalone, etc.) in comedy plots with improvised dialogue, studded with memorized set speeches and elaborate comic business, all performed with much audience contact and broad physicalizations.

MASQUE AND EARLY OPERA

Supported by the princely courts, these productions combined music and spectacle. An emphasis on scenery led to the development of indoor proscenium theatres. Actors sang, danced, or stood in formal tableaux. Often, courtiers performed.

MOLIÈRE, RESTORATION, AND NEOCLASSIC DRAMA

The proscenium theatre evolved further. Side boxes for the audience were still on the stage, with doors right and left under or near them opening onto the forestage (the proscenium doors, with us for more than 100 years). Scenery, mostly painted screens and drops, was behind the actors, who played on the forestage. Sets (drops, flats, and cut-outs) were changed simultaneously by an arrangement of ropes and pulleys. Tragedies were in verse and adhered to the "classic unities" of place, time, and action. The subjects of tragedy were drawn from mythology or history. Comedy was based on the court life of the time and was witty and satiric. The audience was fashionable and elite. Asides, soliloquies, and audience eye contact were much in evidence. Remember that, until the invention of gaslight and the ability to control light intensity, the auditorium was as well-lit as the stage. This continued the custom of artificially "playing front," even though the actors were presumed to be realistically portraying people very much like their audience members.

EIGHTEENTH-CENTURY DRAMA

The style of playing and setting was basically unchanged, though plays became more sentimental, more domestic, and less satiric. Asides and soliloquies still abounded.

NINETEENTH-CENTURY DRAMA

With the Industrial Revolution and the growth of the middle class, theatres became larger, stage boxes retreated into the auditorium, scenery became more elaborate, and scene changes took place behind a curtain. Gaslight and, later, electric light allowed increasing subtlety in the acting, and the advent of realism can be connected with these inventions. Soliloquy and aside were gradually dropped. Plays became less declamatory. "Naturalism," at the end of the century, introduced "slice of life" reality.

TWENTIETH-CENTURY DRAMA

Realism dominated the early part of the period, though stylistic experiments were made by Strindberg, O'Neill, Pirandello, and others. As film began to take over the realistic function, particularly after "talkies" came in, theatre increasingly produced styles distant from reality, leading to "theatre of cruelty," "theatre of the absurd," various kinds of agit-prop drama, and "Brechtian" theatre. Scenery evolved from the box set toward "open" staging, "space" staging, much reliance on the flexibility of electric light, and an increasingly imaginative use of space and materials. The theories of Stanislavski dominated realistic acting for a time, but later many nonrealistic approaches to acting

Minna von Barnhelm
Hamburg, 1978
Lessing's eighteenth-century play, which some regard as Germany's greatest comedy, is here being given a truthful and realistic production in fully authentic costumes. Plays of the 1700s need not be played as exercises in affectation.
Photo courtesy German Information Center

LONG DAY'S JOURNEY INTO NIGHT
Düsseldorf
This German production, directed by Karl Heinz Stroux, is also scrupulously within the style for which it was written. The actors, clothes, set, and props could all be American. Such a production lets the *play* speak.
Photo courtesy German Informaiton Center

emerged. The form of the theatre itself evolved to include "theatre in the round," the thrust stage, flexible seating, and so on.

My point about historical style is this: as director you must understand what conventions the *author* took for granted—real doors, walls that enclose, a forestage, formalized acting, and so on—and if you decide to work within *other* conventions, you must assess the artistic functions of the conventions you are *rejecting*, and the comparable value of the conventions you are *invoking*.

REPRESENTATIONAL VERSUS PRESENTATIONAL

Every production must take a position on one side or the other of this question: Should the audience members be encouraged to remember that they are watching a play in a theatre, or should they be influenced to lose themselves empathically in the production's illusion of reality?

Representational means a manner of playing and a means of setting designed to support the author's effort to persuade the audience it is looking through a big keyhole or a removed "fourth wall" at "real life." The play/production does not acknowledge the presence of the audience. The audience, carried into and identifying with the world of the play, looks on as the production creates the illusion of an actual human event as it transpires. The front curtain, the proscenium stage, the box set—these are some of the devices of the representational play. The setting, however, may be unrealistic or nonexistent and the structure of the play itself unconventional. What is important is that the characters speak only to one another, as people speak in real life. There are no soliloquies, asides, narrations—there is no direct contact between stage and audience to disrupt the illusion of reality and to remind the audience of its separate existence.

Presentational refers to that kind of writing and those devices of production that remind the audience it is in a theatre, watching actors on a stage—actors who are aware of the presence of the audience and who, in their performing, acknowledge that they are part of a dramatic presentation. The writing devices that indicate a presentational attitude on the part of an author are soliloquies, asides, narrations in direct address to the audience, songs sung to the audience. Some presentational production devices involve entrances through the audience, a "Brechtian" curtain over which the audience can see, nonrealistic scenery, a thrust or nonproscenium stage, house lights up during the performance, signs, projected titles, visible scene changes, masked actors, and so on.

Having discovered that the author's attitude is clearly, let us say, presentational, does that mean that the director is bound to be guided by the author's position?

What we know of the Elizabethan stage tells us that Shakespeare's theatre was presentational: the architectural stage with its lack of scenery, the soliloquies and asides, the use of verse, the audience on at least three sides, etc. Elizabethan plays work in the theatre when these devices are accepted and fulfilled. Even as subjective a speech as "To be or not to be . . ." can be played in direct address, including the audience as "imaginary playmates" or partners, and bouncing the arguments off them.

However, the director could well choose to give this presentationally written play a representational production. Each scene could be performed in its own realistic setting on a proscenium stage. Asides and soliloquies could be played, and often have been, as if the character were talking to himself. Indeed, the whole piece could be played as if behind an imaginary fourth wall, removed to show us real people.

As director, your taste will dictate which way of doing *Hamlet* you choose. Following the Elizabethan conventions may seem more faithful to the author's intentions, but the representational approach can be entirely faithful to itself and persuasive to an audience—as Olivier's film version of *Hamlet* demonstrates.

Once again, you should be fully aware of the author's attitude and of the effect he intended. Then you should choose your own approach, well aware of what will be gained and what will be given up.

Keep in mind that one must go fully with the choice one makes. One cannot be just a little bit presentational or just a little bit representational. The audience gets its signals at the beginning of the play—even, in the case of an open stage with no curtain, before the play begins. As director you set up the conventions—the ground rules—for the performance. Having chosen them and established them, you must stay within them. They become the rules of the theatre game you invite the audience to share with you.

The table on page 62 suggests some of the signals regarding representational/presentational style that the director may send.

STYLE RELATIVE TO DAY-TO-DAY REALITY

In the theatre, naturalism is the style closest to a "slice of life"—a "bloody slice of life," it has been called. The author (and director) attempt, in a naturalistic piece, to show life as it really is in all its details, the indecent along with the decent, the mundane along with the unusual. The movement had its beginnings in the late nineteenth century. Hauptmann's *The Weavers* is usually cited as an early example. Gorky's *The Lower Depths* is usually mentioned in the same breath. The dramatization of Erskine Caldwell's *Tobacco Road* is a 1930s example. Now, if the purpose of theatre is, as Brecht said, "to shock, to surprise, and to make us see familiar things strangely," then theatrical naturalism runs into some trouble on the last count. It may well surprise us to see real life on the stage, that temple of artifice. It may well shock us to see people on the stage doing things in public that they close the doors and turn out the lights to do in private. But, insofar as art's mission is to reveal the strangeness in things we look at every day, naturalism falls short—it simply shows us real life in the midst of real life, and meanings remain as diffuse as always.

Theatre artists, and other artists, *take things away*—they subtract details—in order to reveal those things we miss in life because of its familiarity and its proliferation of detail: sights, sounds, family rituals, all the distracting impedimenta of living.

Realism selects what it wants to show of "real life" and leaves out the rest. The illusion is still sufficiently intact that a play like *Long Day's Journey into Night* seems just like real life passing by—what artifice! What art! We simply don't notice that nobody goes to the bathroom. The author has *left out* the stories he chooses not to tell and *left in* only the story he wants to tell.

Look at a style from the art of painting—cubism. One could think, I suppose, of a cubist painting as something added—built up out of cubes. More

DIRECTORIAL SIGNALS ON STYLE: PRESENTATIONAL VERSUS REPRESENTATIONAL

Devices	Presentational	Representational
Front curtain used		X
No front curtain—stage open as audience comes in	X	
Raked stage	X	
Flat floor		X (perhaps)
Box set		X
No walls	X (perhaps)	
Direct eye contact with audience	X	
Fourth wall		X
Actors enter through audience	X	
Acting within frame		X
Proscenium theatre	X (depends on how you use it)	X
Theatre in round	X (depends on how you use it)	X
Thrust stage	X	
Brechtian front curtain	X	
Proscenium door	X	
Use of narration, asides, monologues	X	
Pantomimed hand props	X	
Visible lighting instruments	X	
Doors that open and close		X
Visible scene changes	X	
Set changed behind curtain or in dark		X

accurately, however, cubism is "seeing the cubes in things"—reducing familiar structures to their underlying "cubishness."

The various stylistic movements of the nineteenth and twentieth centuries away from the depiction of "real" life in art are too numerous to examine here. Look for the "ism's"—surrealism, structuralism, expressionism, theatricalism, and so forth. Look too for the "theatres of": theatre of cruelty, theatre of the absurd, theatre of ritual; poor theatre, rough theatre, etc.

DER UNTERGANG DES EGOISTEN FATZER
Schaubühne am Halleschen Ufer, 1976
This unfinished fragment by Brecht, mentioned in 1929 by Piscator as under consideration
by his company, was given a documentarily naturalistic production by the same company
that did the stylized *Bacchae* of Plate 19. Director: Frank-Patrick Steckel.
Photo courtesy German Information Center

The director must, then, assess what elements of reality are *left out* in the writing or production style in question, not what ornamentation is *stuck on*. Remember that, in the person of the actor, we in the theatre are always left with his humanity at the core of whatever we do. We can, say, strip away everything but the mechanics of his movement and speech, to get the robotlike figures in Rice's *The Adding Machine*, but remaining at the center of what is left on view is the humanity of the actor's physical presence. The surrealist painter Dali, stylizing his slippery watches and clocks, did not have to contend with the pervasive humanity of his subject.

Part of the permanent collection at the Zurich Art Museum, on view when I was last there, is a collection of theatre costumes from the twenties, designed

THE BACCHAE
Schaubühne am Halleschen Ufer, 1974
Euripedes' play is here given an extremely modern production by what had, by 1974,
been acknowledged as the most important current German-language theatre.
Director: Klaus Michael Grüber.
Photo courtesy German Information Center

by Klee and Arp and others of the Bauhaus school. The costumes were created
as an experiment in destroying the line of the human figure and animating
nonhuman shapes by putting actors' bodies inside them. Armatures of whale-
bone, wire, or buckram were covered with fabric to create odd forms. Pads,
cushions, stuffings, and layers of cloth were employed. Height and body structure were concealed by means of an amazing variety of constructions. The
fascinating thing, though, was that the experiment struck me as totally unsuc-
cessful. Interesting "sculptures" were achieved, to be sure. But the human figure was simply *there*—and whatever was stuck on, built up, or made to protrude
from it, just looked artificial and attached. Of course, these constructions were
exhibited on mannequins, but seeing them in motion on actual people would
surely have contributed even more fully to the failure of the attempt.

In other words, at the heart of any enterprise using live actors, an unextinguishable core of reality—human truth—resides and must be reckoned with. Use the scalpel of stylization to pare away everything possible, and yet something essentially truthful (realistic) remains for the actor to do or be. Keep this always in mind as you take up the tool of stylization.

EXERCISES

1. Page 59—There is a huge fund of critical material devoted to Beckett and his plays. Find five articles or books that would be useful to your production. Explain why the materials you chose support your ideas about the production.

2. Page 59—Criticism is only one source of information. There might be other books that influence you greatly—books that have nothing directly to do with Beckett. Also, consider music, pictures, paintings, prints, cartoons, poetry, as excellent sources of information and inspiration to help you to establish a style for the production.

3. Page 59—What kind of library do you want to build for yourself: words or pictures? What does your answer tell you about yourself as a director?

4. Page 61—Imagine that you are cast in a production of *Godot* directed by Constantin Stanislavsky, whom you've heard a great deal about and with whom you've always wanted to work. He delivers a very inspirational speech to the cast in which he outlines his view of the play, and then rehearsal begins. After three weeks, however, the producer visits the first run-through and elects to fire Stanislavsky. The next day a new director, Bertolt Brecht, arrives. He, too, gives an impassioned speech about what the play is about, his intentions, and his plans for the production. Describe the two very different productions in which you have played a part. Which version did you like better and why? If you were the director, what would you have done differently?

5. Page 62—What questions are appropriate to ask of the characters in the play? Why can't the characters remember anything? Where are they? Explain the contents of Vladimir's pockets. Why do Didi and Gogo continually check the insides of their hats? Can you account for the vast number of references to Christianity? Develop a set of questions to fire your imagination: To what kind of world do the characters belong? How will you proceed to create this world?

CHAPTER 4

PLAY ANALYSIS AND THE DIRECTOR'S PROMPTBOOK

PLAY ANALYSIS

Only what it sees and hears conveys to the audience the story that the director and actors are trying to tell. No telepathy, no mystical communion exists. If they can't hear it or see it, it's not part of the show! The playwright has written the words and described the skeleton of the physical action he envisaged accompanying the words. Using the written guidebook for performance that is the author's script, the director and actors must search for, select, and rehearse the score—the articulated coordination of sound and movement—that the audience will receive in the theatre.

The director is the author/conductor of this score.

Theatre is a combination of visual and aural elements, and to ensure that all elements stem from an organically derived conception of the play, the director must analyze as many of the internal aspects of the play as he can, prior to making design, casting, and other decisions about externals. The director's talent will prompt him toward instinctive and impulsive notions about how the play should look and sound. These thoughts may well be valid, but he should use a battery of analytic tools to slow down and check up on his decision-making zeal, to be certain that each of his choices throws light on the heart of the play.

By this time in his creative process, the director has:

1. Selected the play

2. Read the play, as director

3. Examined the play's structure, as to:
   a. How the story is told
   b. What kind of play it is

4. Determined a basic style for the production

Now the director is ready for a detailed examination of the play, unit by unit, finding its *spine*, the *super-objective* of each character, dividing the play into units, or *beats*, and within each beat finding each character's *intention* and the *adjustments* by means of which the character carries out that intention.

This scheme of study is a product of the Stanislavski Method, as it developed in this country. "The Method" was introduced here by members of the Moscow Art Theatre company who elected not to return to Russia. Lee Strasberg, Harold Clurman, and Stella Adler, founding members of the Group Theatre, were among their students, and they, as teachers and directors, have passed their learning on. I met this way of looking at plays early in my career, but taking acting classes with Harold Clurman helped me to understand it more fully. In his book *On Directing* he has written what he said in class. Since 1956, when I first heard him on the subject of directing, I have prepared every play I have directed in the fashion I am about to describe. I have developed my own application of Clurman's principles, and this is what I am going to outline in the next several pages. The purpose remains: to accomplish a thorough examination of the play's meaning as it emerges through dramatic conflict.

THE SPINE

The first and most encompassing element the director must define and enunciate is the play's *spine*. The *spine* is a brief statement—one sentence, if possible—of the play's message: what it teaches, what it was written to convey, its "theme," if you will, but stated as a proposition. Every complication of the play's plot or plots, every action of every character, and each and every scene of the play must contribute to the accomplishment of the spine. If any aspect of the script cannot be viewed as contributing to the spine, the director has chosen the wrong spine.

Here are examples of two spines I used in production:

Romeo and Juliet: The outworn social convention of the family blood feud is finally abandoned only after the innocent children of the opposing families are sacrificed to its destructive momentum.

Hamlet: Something is rotten in Denmark, and the rightful king finally restores order by killing the usurper, revenging his father's death, and sacrificing himself.

Choosing a spine is an informed interpretative act. Any spine is "correct," which is not contradicted by anything in the text and to which every portion of the text contributes. A different spine could offer a *Romeo and Juliet* as a tragedy of star-crossed lovers, not a social drama. That production would have an entirely different tone, but it could be equally correct, and faithful to the play as written. *Hamlet*, with the spine given previously, becomes a play about politics and power. Its hero, after he determines that the ghost is an ''honest'' ghost and not a creature from hell, acts as decisively as he can. Another spine might give us a psychological study of inaction, or, as Olivier put it for his film, ''a man who cannot make up his mind.'' Certainly equally correct, this choice would give us a very different protagonist and a very different set of theatrical decisions.

The spine is the beacon by which the director sets the course. Every choice is checked against it. Does the color of the set support it? Does the nature of the music support it? Does the casting support it? The spine focuses and unifies the decisions made. A strong spine, well carried through, helps to shape a forceful and coherent production.

THE SUPER-OBJECTIVE

After choosing a spine for the play that expresses the production, the director must define and state clearly each character's *super-objective*.

The super-objective is the overall activating purpose that carries that character through the play, in his contribution to the play's driving force, or spine. The director's statement of a character's super-objective must encompass absolutely every task the character takes on in the course of the play. Let us look at some possible super-objectives in familiar plays, remembering that just as the choice of the spine represents a major interpretative decision about the play, so do the choices of super-objectives represent basic interpretative paths for the characters.

Using the spine given earlier as an example for *Romeo and Juliet*, Romeo's super-objective might be: ''To win possession of his lady love in spite of all obstacles.'' ''Possession'' includes consummated marriage and living together. He realizes she is the daughter of Capulet, but he scales the wall, marries her secretly, climbs to her bedchamber for the wedding night, and expects to work out a way to be with her. Finally, even death is no obstacle to that. Juliet's super-objective in this production might be: ''To stand by her commitment to Romeo, in spite of all obstacles.'' Juliet's concern in the balcony scene is to be thought not a ''light'' love. She arranges contact through the Nurse and goes through with the secret marriage. When Paris is suggested as a match for her, she fights back. Even after Tybalt is killed and Romeo banished, when the Nurse suggests simply marrying Paris and concealing the earlier marriage, she stands by her commitment. This force carries her through the taking of the potion and to her final joining of Romeo in death.

Romeo and Juliet are the central figures in the play, and they are ''sacrificed to the outworn social convention of the family blood feud,'' as the spine states. Tybalt personifies the blood feud, the ''obstacle'' in the play. His super-objective, too, contributes to the accomplishment of the play's spine. Tybalt's super-objective might be: "To prove the honor of his family in the blood of the enemy." If the play has a villain, he is it, but his every action supports the code of honor to which he is devoted, and he sees himself as an upright person. The Nurse's super-objective might be: "To do anything she can to help Juliet to fulfillment." The Nurse clearly dotes on Juliet, the apple of her eye. She wants Juliet to be well-bedded and happy, on those physical and material levels that define the Nurse's idea of happiness. Thus, she can support the secret marriage and the secret consummation, but in the end, by advising the bigamous marriage to Paris, she reveals her incapacity for understanding Juliet's true nature.

Let us look briefly at *Macbeth* in regard to the relationship between spine and super-objective. A view of *Macbeth* based on the Witches as emissaries of Fate and on Banquo's Ghost as further evidence of the "reality" of the supernatural in the play would perhaps not be compatible with the spine and super-objectives I am about to suggest. I opt for Macbeth making his choice from free will, in order to provide a theatre piece with as much suspense as possible, and

ROMEO AND JULIET
New York Shakespeare Festival, 1957
Left to right: Stephen Joyce—Romeo; J. D. Cannon—Mercutio; Patricia Falkenhain—Nurse; Jerry Stiller—Peter. Director: Stuart Vaughan.
Photo: George E. Joseph

for the same reason I view the Witches, Banquo's Ghost, and the Apparitions as personifications of Macbeth's own evil desires and his consequent guilt for acting on them. Another view, equally correct and perhaps more to another director's taste, would produce a different spine and different production decisions.

A spine for *Macbeth* might be: "A strong and charismatic man of action, yielding to his own evil impulses, usurps the reins of power, only to find that his method of attaining his prize renders it empty of satisfaction, finally perpetuating evil and leading to his own destruction."

Examples of related super-objectives for some characters in the play:

Macbeth: "To seize and hold what the 'right of might' places in his grasp."

Lady Macbeth: "To do everything to help her husband realize his ambitions."

Duncan: "To rule justly, and justly to pass on the succession."

Malcolm: "To serve worthily as rightful guardian of his heritage."

A diagram of the relationship between the spine and the super-objectives would look something like Figure 4.1.

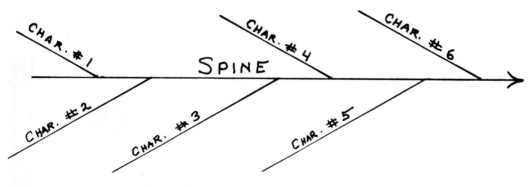

FIGURE 4.1

Notice that the super-objective is a statement of what the character wants, and is always stated in the form of an infinitive: "To . . . something." Further discussion of this verbal way of stating the actor's objectives will come in the next section—on "beats."

BEATS—UNITS OF CONFLICT

A play is an action, and the director's chosen spine defines that action. The play's action (chief conflict) is divided into units of conflict like a set of Chinese boxes, one within the other, each with a beginning, a middle, and an end. Thus, each unit of action, however small, recapitulates a play's shape. Lots of smaller plays are contained within the bigger play. Plays are divided into acts, acts into scenes, scenes into "beats," each with its beginning, middle, and end.

Figure 4.2 diagrams the relationships between the play's units of conflict.

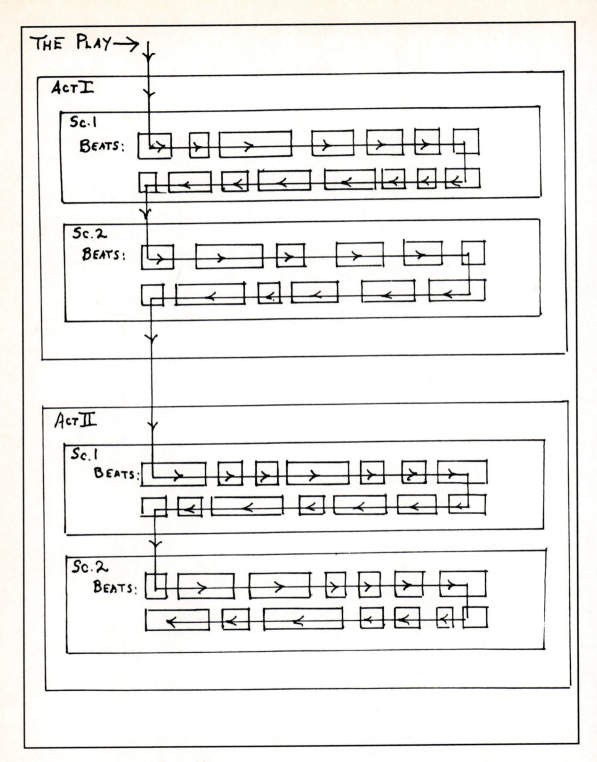

FIGURE 4.2

Each *beat*, or unit of a scene, is a play in miniature. In each beat, a single unit of conflict is played out. There is a struggle about something. Somebody wins while others lose, or else the struggle is interrupted. In either case, a new unit of struggle (a beat) begins, and so on till the end of the play.

The origin of the word "beat" deserves to be mentioned here. As part of the oral history of the American theatre, this story comes in several versions. I will repeat it as it was told to me.

It seems that one of the early Russian defectors from the Moscow Art Theatre, rehearsing with his American acolytes, kept saying, "Let's do that beat again, starting from . . ." Back in the corners of the rehearsal room, his listeners, hanging on every word in order to absorb new truths, would say to themselves, "Beat. He means a unit of rhythm, as in music—or heartbeat! That's it—the pulse of the scene! Or a phrase, like a phrase in music!" And so the word "beat" for a unit of conflict came into permanent use in the American theatre—when all the dear old Russian director with his dear old Russian accent was trying to say was, "Let's do that *bit* again . . ." Such is legend.

Now follows a portion of Shakespeare's *Twelfth Night*, from Act I, scene 5, broken down into its *beats*, as I see them. A horizontal line across the page separates one beat from the next.

Olivia: . . . *(exit Maria)* Now, sir, what is your text?

Viola: Most sweet lady—

Olivia: A comfortable doctrine, and much may be said of it. Where lies your text?

Viola: In Orsino's bosom.

Olivia: In his bosom? In what chapter of his bosom?

Viola: To answer by the method, in the first of his heart.

Olivia: O, I have read it! It is heresy. Have you no more to say?

Viola: Good madam, let me see your face.

Olivia: Have you any commission from your lord to negotiate with my face? You are now out of your text. But we will draw the curtain and show you the picture. *(Unveils)* Look you, sir, such a one I was this present. Is't not well done?

Viola: Excellently done, if God did all.

Olivia: 'Tis in grain, sir; 'twill endure wind and weather.

Viola: 'Tis beauty truly blent; whose red and white

Nature's own sweet and cunning hand laid on.
Lady, you are the cruel'st she alive
If you will lead these graces to the grave,
And leave the world no copy.

OLIVIA: O, sir, I will not be so hard-hearted. I will give out
divers schedules of my beauty. It shall be inventoried,
and every particle and utensil labeled to my will:—as,
item, two lips, indifferent red; item, two grey eyes, with
lids to them; item, one neck, one chin, and so forth. Were
you sent hither to praise me?

Viola: I see you what you are—you are too proud;
But if you were the Devil, you are fair.

My lord and master loves you. O, such love
Could be but recompens'd though you were crown'd
The nonpareil of beauty!

Olivia: How does he love me?

Viola: With adorations, fertile tears,
With groans that thunder love, with sighs of fire.

Olivia: Your lord does know my mind; I cannot love him.
Yet I suppose him virtuous, know him noble,
Of great estate, of fresh and stainless youth;
In voices well divulged, learned, and valiant,
And in dimension and the shape of nature
A gracious person. But yet I cannot love him.
He might have took his answer long ago.

Viola: If I did love you with my master's flame,
With such a suff'ring, such a deadly life,
In your denial I would find no sense;
I would not understand it.

Olivia: Why, what would you?

Viola: Make me a willow cabin at your gate
And call upon my soul within the house;
Write loyal cantons of contemned love
And sing them loud even in the dead of night;
Halloo your name to the reverberate hills
And make the babbling gossip of the air
Cry out "Olivia." O, you should not rest

> Between the elements of air and earth
> But you should pity me!

Olivia: You might do much.

>   What is your parentage?

Viola: Above my fortunes, yet my state is well.
> I am a gentleman.

Olivia: Get you to your lord.
> I cannot love him. Let him send no more,
> Unless, perchance, you come to me again
> To tell me how he takes it. Fare you well.
> I thank you for your pains. Spend this for me.

Viola: I am no fee'd post, lady: keep your purse;
> My master, not myself, lacks recompense.
> Love make his heart of flint that you shall love;
> And let your fervor, like my master's, be
> Placed in contempt! Farewell, fair cruelty. (*Exit*.)

Finding the Beats.   Just as the choice of spine and super-objective are inter-pretative as well as analytic tasks, so too is the division of the play into beats.

Playwrights do not consciously write beats. At any rate, pre-Stanislavski playwrights didn't. Playwrights *are* conscious of theme, conflict, and transitions. By and large, they just write, follow their scenario, letting the characters fight it out among themselves in the most effective and truthful fashion available. This business of finding the beats is the director's and the actor's business. Speaking for a moment as a playwright who has directed his own work, I was surprised to find that I didn't think about beats at all during the writing process. As *director*, preparing to direct my own work, I found them to exist in my play, and finding them helped me to define the theatrical structure of my own play in a specifically directorial way.

The nature and duration of the beats you, as director, perceive, and your definition of the conflict they each contain, depend on the spine you have selected and the stated super-objectives of the characters involved. Two equally gifted directors with different points of view may see the scene's beats quite differently.

Still, there are ways to recognize, in reading, likely places where beats may begin and end.

1. Look for a change of subject. Note that, in the scene above, Viola and Olivia are first talking about "text, doctrine, bosom, chapter, method, heresy." Then they begin talking about Olivia's face. Why? The answer to the "why" is

GHOST DANCE
Ohio State's Thurber Theatre, 1974
Written and directed by Stuart Vaughan. William Cody demands that James Laughlin,
Indian Agent, release Sitting Bull from house arrest.

a clue to what's happening, but the change of subject is a clue that there is probably a change of beat.

2. Look for a change in *who is leading the scene*. The character leading the scene is the one making things happen, initiating the subject, taking the offensive. As the scene begins, Olivia is leading: "Now, sir, what is your text?" But at "Good madam, let me see your face," not only does the subject change, but Viola starts calling the tune.

3. Look for where somebody enters, thus interrupting or bringing a new

note to the scene, or where somebody leaves, thus putting an end to what had been going on before.

    4. Look at where someone, in her own speech, finishes with one problem and takes up another. Viola finishes sizing Olivia up at "But if you were the Devil, you are fair," and at "My lord and master loves you," begins to talk about, not Olivia's beauty, but Orsino's passion for her. In other words, the beat can change, not only between speeches, or at entrances and exits, but *within* speeches.

INTENTIONS

In each beat, each character has something he *wants to do*—either to another character, or to an outside object, or to himself—a result he wants to accomplish. It is the success, or failure, or interruption of that effort that brings about the beginning of the next beat. These "wants" of the character are called his *intentions*.

    Having broken the play down into its beats, the director must then go back and, always remembering each character's super-objective and remaining consistent with it, now decide, in each beat, what each character's intention is.

    The theatre is not an exact science with a precise vocabulary. Some of its tenets, like those of the Stanislavski Method, cross international borders, but linked as it is to each country's language and literature, the theatre is, by its nature, parochial. Even within our American theatre, teachers use different vocabularies. So—in some circles, what I have learned to call an "intention" will be called an "action," as in "What's your *action*?" and others use the term "objective" for the same thing.

    In any case, all the Stanislavski-derived subsystems concur that the "intention," "action," "objective" is expressed in the infinitive form: "to (verb)." The character "wants to (verb)."

    The words chosen to express the intention must be *actable*. They must express something *physical*, something done with the body, or with the voice, or through the eye, or simultaneously with all the above. An intention might be:

To batter him down with the words

To cut through to her meaning

To soothe her nerves

To tread water

To give her enough rope

To hear the distant melody behind his words

To smell out the lie

To walk a tightrope

These are actable, human tactics, applicable to the simplest of realistic plays or to the most complex verse dramas. Such phrases are the vocabulary of acting. They involve what human beings do to one another in trying to achieve their goals.

All the practitioners of "The Method" agree, too, that nobody can act a "state"—a state of being, a state of feeling. "He feels happy"; "He is filled with love"; "Rage consumed him"—these are *descriptions*, possibly accurate. An audience might so describe a character as acted in a performance. The playwright might so describe his character's feelings in the script. But the actor cannot achieve a truthful result by trying to show feelings; that will merely produce *indicating*, like someone playing charades. The director and actors must analyze the beats to find the human tasks of the characters. Find the intention; if that is played, the feelings that prompt it will be clear. The actor cannot literally "show love for her," except by intention: "to drink in her beauty through his eyes"; "to memorize every tiny portion of her face"; "to dissolve her into his embrace"—these are actable; "Show your love for her" is not, though it may describe what the director wants the audience to see the actor do. "Show your love for her" must be translated by the director and actor into the language of the theatre—into verbs of *doing*.

Objects, How's, and Obstacles.   Three other elements are part of this "doing" transaction.

1. The character wants to (verb) him, or her, or it. Each intention has an *object*—someone or something it is directed at—and director and actor must know what or who that object is.

2. The character wants to (verb) the object *by means of*. One must ask *how* the character means to accomplish his purpose—by what means.

3. What is the character's *obstacle* for this intention? What is keeping him from attaining his goal? Usually, one character's obstacle is another character's intention, unless the obstacle is within himself, or is an inanimate object—a door he wants to break down.

Playable intentions constitute the universal language of the theatre. Choosing and being able to carry out and fulfill recognizable human intentions are what distinguish the fine actor from the mere speaker of lines. But, after all, the playwright wrote the words, so isn't it enough to say them? No—spoken language is only one of the means human beings use to express their needs. How does your dog know what you want? He grasps your *intentions*. The actor in a foreign language armed with only a beautiful voice and a beautiful face and the acting clichés of an operatic tenor conveys nothing to those who do not know his native tongue. The great actor, playing human intentions, can reach us all with an astonishing amount of the play's meaning, even when we can't comprehend the words of his spoken language.

As a director you should make your own *Thesaurus of Human Intentions*. You should list hundreds of infinitives for verbs of "doing." These will become your vocabulary of interpretation, for use in every type of play and any kind of human situation, no matter what language or cultural barriers you need to overcome.

ADJUSTMENTS

Within each beat, the actor's entire effort is to *fulfill* the character's intention— that is, to carry out the stated intention by every possible means, until it is accomplished, defeated, or interrupted, bringing the beat to an end. These moment-to-moment efforts of the character to fulfill the intentions are called *adjustments*. These involve reactions, looks, moves, line readings, and all the elements of speech and behavior required of the actor on stage. The director can perceive a clear but general outline of these adjustments from his script work. By finding a "stage direction" for each section and phrase of the lines each character must speak in a given beat, the director can carve out the shape of each actor's moment-to-moment conduct of the role. The adjustments are the *how's* by means of which the character carries out his tasks, and it is the director's prerehearsal investigation of these how's that puts him in touch with directing the actor's progress.

Later, in rehearsal, the actor will, through trial and error and improvisation, find connections between the segments of text—looks, moves, activities— all of which will, defined by his super-objective and his intentions, comprise a score for his part. The table on page 80 shows the relationship between intentions and other aspects of the actor's investigations.

Actors do not *play* intentions, not "on the night." Finding the spine, finding the beats, selecting the intentions—these are part of the director's, and later the actor's, *analytic* process. Adjustments, too, insofar as they have to do with speaking the text, can be analyzed, as can the movement. In the collaboration of rehearsal, the intentions are "played" as a way of testing how everything fits together. Adjustments are evaluated in terms of how they help fulfill the intentions. However, when it comes to *playing through* (whether playing a whole beat, or whole scene or whole act or whole play), the actor plays only from moment to moment, knowing that the underlying intentions, which guided the selection of the adjustments and the contents of the moments, are there, having been thoroughly rehearsed. The connection of one adjustment to the next carries the actor along, and he exists only in the moment he is playing.

FOR EACH AND EVERY BEAT AND MOMENT OF ANY PLAY, THE ACTOR MUST BE ABLE TO MAKE THE FOLLOWING STATEMENT: "IN THE GIVEN CIRCUMSTANCES (WHATEVER THEY ARE) I WANT TO DO (WHATEVER IT IS—INTENTION) TO (WHOEVER OR WHATEVER IT MAY BE—OBJECT) FOR (WHATEVER REASON—MOTIVATION) IN SPITE OF (WHOEVER OR WHATEVER—OBSTACLE) IN THE FOLLOWING MANNER (BODY, VOICE, MOVEMENT, BUSINESS—PHYSICALIZATION)."

Technical Term	Definition	How to State
Given circumstances	All that has gone before: the story, your character's bio, the place, the time, the weather, the historical period, political atmosphere, etc.	Review all that has bearing on the scene (beat, moment) while making choices
Intention or Action	What you are doing	"To _____" as in "to needle," "to quiz," "to slash," "to tease"
Object	The person or thing you are doing it to	"him," "her," "them," "it"
Motivation or Objective	For what purpose: . . . Why?	"In order to . . ." or "because . . ."
Obstacle	What's stopping you: usually another character's intention	"In spite of . . ."
Adjustments	In what manner; how you are carrying out your intention: vocally bodily choreographically	Adverbially, as: "swiftly," "as if walking on eggs," "gasping," etc.; or describing and defining the tool, as: "grabbing his dagger, he jabs repeatedly at the air, gasping for breath."

THE DIRECTOR'S PROMPTBOOK

The director's tool for recording the results of his play analysis and preproduction preparation is his *promptbook*, as we in this country tend to call it—not with any precision, since the director these days rarely prompts from it. Brecht called it his *Arbeitbuch* (workbook), a more exact description.

Let me reassert some basic principles behind my work as director, and behind this book, before developing my recipe for the director's promptbook.

1. Everything to be accomplished in the theatre must be accomplished by technical means—things we understand how to do. Even happy accidents ("Keep it in!") must be assessed and repeated by technical means.

2. The "technical" is not the opposite of the "organic" or the "internal." There is the technique of the "internal" as well as the technique of the "external," and the word "organic" in the theatre only means "drawn from the script and not imposed upon it from outside."

3. Flexibility and emotional release are achieved only by learning everything one can possibly know about the work in question, leaving no question unraised and nothing to chance. Only in this way can a performance be achieved that captures the illusion of truth and emotional spontaneity and that penetrates to the depth of the work in question.

4. Only actors thus rigorously rehearsed can become so genuinely liberated from the toils of accident that they *can* stir an audience.

The promptbook, as described here, offers you a device for attaining control over your play—if you have the self-discipline to use it fully.

I use the promptbook the way my painter friend uses the white spaces on his canvas, as a graph to fill in. The empty space makes me think. It tells me how much work I have to do.

I am happy once again to credit Harold Clurman with having put me on to this way of preparing and using the promptbook. I have, however, adapted his ideas to my own needs. For what he has written about this subject, see his book *On Directing*, pp. 74–86 and pp. 280–289.* Here is my version of this well-known but underused tool.

MAKING YOUR "GRAPH"

First, you must prepare your empty graph—the space that will demand that you fill it.

If you will be working from a copy of the typed manuscript, open the play out flat on your desk. The back of the page preceding the page you will be working on will be on your left. This blank back page is the "white" you are going to "color in." If you are using a printed text, use two copies, pasting script pages on typing paper so that the pages appear in proper sequence on the right, with a blank page-back on your left. You could also interleaf the printed page with white paper in order to provide yourself with writing space opposite each script page.

Mind you, you have already worked out and stated for yourself the spine of the play and the super-objective for each character.

Now, block out the beats. Go through the whole play and draw ruled horizontal lines marking the change of beats across the script page, carrying them on across each blank facing page.

For the rest of the graph: On each blank facing page, draw two vertical

---

*Harold Clurman, *On Directing* (New York: Collier Books, Macmillan Publishing Co., Inc., 1974).

lines, making three vertical columns, spaced as in the table on pages 84–85, with the column farthest from the script page narrowest, because less will be written there. The widest column should be the center one, because you will need most space there. Label the column farthest from the script, which should also be the narrowest, "Intentions"; the center column "Adjustments"; and the third column, nearest the script, "Activities."

So—the empty graph is complete, saying, "There's a whole play ahead of you. Fill me! I dare you!"

FILLING IN YOUR GRAPH

The first two columns in your promptbook, *intentions* and *adjustments*, must be attacked first, and I shall discuss them first. What the play means and what the characters do dictate what the scenery will be. The nature of the intentions and the adjustments, beat by beat, determines the physical action on the set. I never fill in the third column, *activities*, until I have worked through the whole play, filling in *intentions* and *adjustments*. Then and only then do I work on the movement, writing down the *blocking* in my third column. Chapter 7, *Staging*, deals entirely with the filling of this third column. At this point in your analysis of your production, you too should leave the question of the stage movement until later.

Begin on page 1 of the play. Read the first beat, as already determined by the reading when you drew the horizontal lines. Do you still agree with your own decision about where the beat changes? If not, change your mind. This process is not about rigidity but about thinking. Accepting the beat's shape, then ask yourself, "What's going on—who's doing what to whom?" Find the intentions for the first beat and write them in the narrow column on the left. Now, look at the lines, and ask yourself, "*How* are they trying to do it?" Then, phrase by phrase, moment by moment, direct the adjustments in your head and write your decisions in the middle column, using small numbers next to phrases in the text which key to numbers in the adjustment column—and so on through the play. (Note that at this time, the "Activities" column is left blank.) In making these notes, I use the first letter of the character's name to designate him, and if two characters' names begin with the same letter, I'll add another letter to one of them: "O" for Orsino, "Ol" for Olivia.

The table on pages 84–85 is taken from my director's promptbook for Shakespeare's *Henry VI, Part Two*, part of the 1970 *Wars of the Roses* for the New York Shakespeare Festival in Central Park. It provides an example of beats and adjustments, as actually employed.

I prefer, schedule permitting, to work out the intentions and adjustments in this fashion straight through the play, *before designing the set*. What *happens* in the play should determine what the production *looks* like. If one could, like

HENRY VI, PART TWO (WARS OF THE ROSES)
New York Shakespeare Festival, 1970
Henry VI—Nicholas Kepros; Queen Margaret—Barbara Caruso. Three plays were played in
rotation: *Henry* VI in two parts and *Richard* III making up the series. Ming Cho Lee
designed the scenery, Theoni Aldredge designed the costumes, and Stuart Vaughan
directed. All three plays were given in one marathon night at the midpoint of the run.
Photo: George E. Joseph

Stanislavski at the Moscow Art Theatre in the thirties with all the money and
time in the world, rehearse with the actors for a month with the designer on
hand, so the set could be designed from rehearsal discoveries, that would be
even better. Failing that, the director can at least, in his study, find the *play*

Intentions	Adjustments	Text from *Henry* VI, *Part Two* by William Shakespeare
		(*Sound a sennet.* Enter the KING, YORK, SOMERSET, DUKE HUMPHREY, CARDINAL BEAUFORT, BUCKINGHAM, SALISBURY, WARWICK, *and the* QUEEN.)
K. to push it off	K. (1) repeating what he said before (2) ending it	KING [1]For my part, noble lords, I care not which: [2]Or Somerset or York, all's one to me.
Y. to stand on the record	Y. stiffly and proud	YORK If York have ill demeaned himself in France, Then let him be denayed the regentship.
S. to match him	S. tit for tat, equally snotty, perhaps an invitation	SOMERSET If Somerset be unworthy of the place, Let York be regent; I will yield to him.
W. to set him straight	W. (1) smoothly (2) the snapper	WARWICK [1]Whether your grace be worthy, yea or no, Dispute not that. [2]York is the worthier.
C. to cut the ground out from under him	C. superciliously	CARDINAL Ambitious Warwick, let thy betters speak!
	W. bluntly	WARWICK The cardinal's not my better in the field.
B. to put him in his place	B. coldly	BUCKINGHAM All in this presence are thy betters, Warwick.
	W. darkly, to himself	WARWICK Warwick may live to be the best of all.
S. to caution W.	S. to him aside	SALISBURY Peace, son.
S. to assert voice of reason	S. stoutly, standing on his age	And show some reason, Buckingham, Why Somerset should be preferred in this.
Q. to intervene (assert K's right)	Q. indignantly	QUEEN Because the king forsooth will have it so.

continued

DIRECTOR'S PROMPTBOOK PAGE (WITHOUT COLUMN—3 ACTIVITY)

Intentions	Adjustments	Text from *Henry VI, Part Two* by William Shakespeare
G. to shut her out	G. interposing firmly but finally	**GLOUCESTER** Madam, the king is old enough himself To give his censure. These are no women's matters.
	Q. hotly persisting	**QUEEN** If he be old enough, what needs your grace To be Protector of his excellence?
	G. holding himself in	**GLOUCESTER** Madam, I am Protector of the realm, And at his pleasure will resign my place.

before firming up his physical concept. Working through the "internals" first prevents the director from seizing on "a bright idea," a "concept," which too often may reveal its superficiality after they are already building the scenery.

The choices made when writing down the intentions and adjustments may not actually prove to be the final ones. They are, however, guided by the chosen spine and super-objectives, and they are made in a reflective period of "sifting through." Start somewhere. You can always change your views. Brecht says we should examine every line in every play from the point of view of the author's (character's) choice: he says, not *that* (some opposite that he might have said) but *this*. Select, choose, be sure you have thought of many possible intentions and "how's"—so that, when you choose, you have covered all the ground your actors may have to cover. As you begin, the area of choice may seem limitless, but, as you choose carefully and well and get further and further into the play, your field of choice will gradually become narrower and more inevitable. These choices, remember, are *not final*. They are your best effort at interpretation before rehearsals. This is *preparing* to work, not building yourself a straightjacket.

The material that actually gets written down in the small space the graph allows is, of necessity, brief. I have developed a promptbook handwriting about one-third the size of my ordinary scrawl. What gets into my book looks like a code, or a kind of shorthand. I want the promptbook notes to *remind* me what I think, not to embody an essay on the subject at hand. Sometimes my reminders are highly personal—similes or metaphors from private experiences. Sometimes the imagery may be scatological, sexual, vulgar, or obscene, so it will vividly bring back what I want to remember. Sometimes it will be what I want to remember to *tell the actor*, as distinct from what I want to remind myself. In any case, the promptbook must not become an effort at "great writing" or, indeed, "writing" at all. One need not sit staring at the page waiting for the right word to come. If it does come, good—but if it doesn't, write a word that will serve, and get on with it. Nobody but you will ever see it, anyway.

Now, when you meet the actors, will having written all this stuff down in the promptbook make you rigid? Of course not. If the actor says, "Why not do it this way?" you'll be able to tell her why not, if not. Or you'll be able to say, "That's right," with conviction, if her instinct mirrors yours. But if by chance she thinks of something that has never crossed your mind, you will know enough, in the light of your thorough preparation, to be truly grateful. No one is so defensive as the person who has only one idea. You, with your promptbook, are prepared. You are ready to be flexible and open-minded, because you are too well-prepared to be defensive, too well-prepared to lose your way in a babble of actors' "Wouldn't it be funny if's?"

Of what use is the director's promptbook during rehearsal? During the actors' first reading of the play, I read what I wrote in the promptbook and compare it with what they are bringing in. I refer to it in the reading/discussion rehearsals that follow, although I remember it all pretty well. In blocking rehearsals I refer to the moves I have worked out in advance. Prior to each day of "detail" rehearsal in week two, time permitting, I review the scenes to be worked on that day, going over my promptbook notes to refresh myself as to their content. Also, when the actors go through the scene for lines for the first time, I can follow along in the promptbook to check on the nature of the directing task immediately before me. After that, for the rest of the rehearsal period, the promptbook remains in my briefcase. It may, on occasion, be used as a reference, particularly if an actor wants to recapture something said early in rehearsal. Generally, however, I rely on having ingested all its lessons and allow the momentum of rehearsals to guide the work.

EXERCISES

1. Page 68—Consider Pozzo's speech in Act Two:

"Have you not done tormenting me with your accursed time! It's abominable! When! When! One day, is that not enough for you, one day we'll go deaf, one day we were born, one day we shall die, the same day, the same second, is that not enough for you? (Calmer.) They give birth astride of a grave, the light gleams an instant, then it's night once more. (He jerks the rope.) On!"

How does this speech relate to the spine of the play as you have defined it? How does it relate to the super-objective of each character?

CHAPTER 5

DESIGNING
THE PHYSICAL
PRODUCTION

With the internals of your play thoroughly under your belt, you are now ready to create the specifics of your physical production. Usually each area—scenery, lights, and costumes—has its own designer, so after coming to some basic decisions about the nature of the physical production, you will embark upon the earliest of the collaborative relationships in which bringing your play to life will involve you.

Before meeting with designers, however, you must address certain practical and artistic considerations that relate to every production.

DESIGN CONSIDERATIONS

THE THEATRE ITSELF

What is the theatre's shape—proscenium, thrust stage, in-the-round, black box? What is its size and nature—700 to 1,500 seats, formal, demanding through its large stage and elegant appointments a very strong or elaborate physical production? Or is it intimate, with little room for scenery? Or is it a space that can accept a variety of physical treatments, from minimal to sizable? How well equipped is it—are there full flies or a ceiling grid or no grid? How deep is the stage? How much wing space is there? Are there any special sight-line problems—stage height from auditorium floor, height and pitch of any balconies,

THE TWO GENTLEMEN OF VERONA
New York Shakespeare Festival, 1987
Scenery, lighting concept, and the early scenes
of any production in Central Park must deal
with the fact that the play starts at 8:00 P.M. in
the full rays of the setting sun. No addition of
stage lighting is even visible, so that device
cannot be used to get attention. In this
instance, since Valentine is about to leave
Verona for the court at Milan, we chose to start
the play with some elaborate and amusing
lowering of baggage from the upper level.
Director: Stuart Vaughan.
Photo: George E. Joseph

any boxes, etc.? Is the house equipped with lighting instruments and board,
or must equipment be rented? Are there sufficient instruments, circuits, and
dimmers? Are there adequate lighting positions—any severe limitations? Are
dressing rooms adequate for the size of the cast and properly equipped for
Equity standards, if applicable? When is the theatre available—for rehearsal,
for technical rehearsals, and for previews?

BUDGETARY FACTORS

How much money is available for scenery, for costumes, for lighting, for props?
Does the budget figure include labor, or are staff and crew salaries accounted
for in another line? How much new scenery and costume construction does

THEATER FÜR KINDER
Berlin, 1976
Note, here, the special design problems posed by having to play in school situations in a
variety of spaces. The picture shows a small flat-floor auditorium. The company has set
up its two tents on the floor, with a playing area in between, and is utilizing the room's
small stage for audience seating, to supplement the seating areas on the floor.
Photo courtesy German Information Center

the budget permit and how much must the production rely on pulling from
stock?

TIME FACTORS

How much time does the schedule allow for design and construction? How
much time for load-in, for technical and dress rehearsals and previews? How
much time is there between striking the last production and your load-in and
set-up (changeover time)? How much leeway (in both time and money) can
you expect for making changes in the physical production after the technical
rehearsals begin?

LEVEL OF PRODUCTION SKILLS AVAILABLE

What level of design talent is available? What about shop facilities and equipment—can they handle the concept's demands? How skilled are the painters, cutters, milliners, and other workers?

The audience only sees what it is given, and it extends no congratulations for grandiose but failed concepts. Better a simple scheme completely realized than an ambitious one that is incomplete or badly executed. Better a production scheme that can be created in the time allowed (by the people available) than an ideal conception that breaks everyone's back and is still unfinished "on the night." A realistic view of what money can buy will keep the creative goals sensibly attainable. The theatre building is like a picture frame, and a production within it must fit its scale (or the theatre must be chosen to fit the production's scale, a sequence that is likely to occur only in choosing a house for a New York or a London West End production.) Too, the production's scheme must fit not only the play's needs, but the artistic and production team's ability to bring it off. If your means are small, think spare and simple.

THE PLAY'S DESIGN ESSENTIALS

What do you *have to have* in order to do the play? For *Hamlet* must you have a grave trap, or is there another solution? For *Arsenic and Old Lace* do you *have to have* enough height for the landing and stairway down which Teddy charges? Does Act II of *Man and Superman require* a practical motor car? Does *Abe Lincoln in Illinois demand* the rear end of a railroad observation car that can pull out, for Lincoln's departure? Acknowledging and meeting these demands are the first production tasks required of director and designer.

Is there a design element that conditions the design of the play? *Blithe Spirit* ends with a series of effects as the "ghosts" spitefully attack the living room. If the effects don't work, the set hasn't worked, so the design starts there. Where the bed is stored can dictate the design for *Othello*. One doesn't want four stalwarts to carry on the bed so Othello and Desdemona can play a private scene in it. So—does it pivot from behind a wall, slide out from under a platform? Do units roll aside to reveal it? Is it lowered like a Murphy bed? The solution to these problems will condition other design decisions. The need for an open stage for *Julius Caesar's* battle scenes dictates that design. Whatever suggests Rome in the first half of the play must be cleared away. Any production of Ibsen's *Ghosts* has to manage a good offstage fire effect as the orphanage burns to the ground. Hedda Gabler, in Ibsen's play of the same name, has to be able to close off the upstage room for her suicide—that same up-center area from which Judge Brack and George have watched Hedda and Eilert look at the album without being able to overhear. The set for *A Flea in Her Ear* must incorporate the secret bed.

STYLE

Is the production to be done representationally or presentationally, and what scenic devices will be employed to convey the chosen message? (See the table on p. 62.)

Is the production to be done in period style?

Where does the production stand in relation to realism versus stylization?

All those questions discussed in Chapter 3 in the light of the director's early preparation must now begin to find their expression in terms of design.

SCENE CHANGES

How many scene changes are required and how are they to be accomplished?

METHODS OF CHANGING SCENERY

Wing and drop—Painted drops flown in and out, to suggest change of locale. The "wings" are vertical flats masking the sides. For stages without flies, sliding flats in and out on tracks can accomplish the same effect.

Wagons—Low platforms carrying full or partial sets that are moved in and out from offstage or upstage, or sometimes pivoted in from the sides like two blades of a jackknife. Suitable only for stages with large wing spaces.

Unit set—A basic set altered by plugging arches or windows, or opening hinged walls, or by turning double-sided flats, or by revolving some platform elements.

Permanent set—An architectural unit, like Shakespeare's stage, that doesn't move, but that has a variety of playing areas for suggesting different locales, perhaps assisted by varied lighting emphasis.

Simultaneous setting—A version of the permanent set that shows several places at the same time, like the cutaway walls of a house showing different rooms, or various buildings along a street.

Revolving stage—A low disc, or revolving platform, or revolving segment of the floor turned behind a proscenium to reveal, one at a time, the several settings on it.

Space stage—A form of permanent set, usually just platforms and steps and no walls, in which change of locale is achieved by light.

The conventional box set—Realistic settings made of flats, struck and reset behind the curtain at intermission.

A *vista* changes—Teams of servants, dancers, or actors coming onto the stage in sight of the audience to change scenic elements or props. Any other scene change performed in full view of the audience.

Projections—Images projected on drops, walls or other scenic elements to accomplish change of locale, sometimes in combination with one of the other methods listed previously.

Tracks—Tracks embedded in the stage floor for taking props and/or set pieces on and off.

Periaktoi—Turning towers or units, usually three-sided, presenting three different faces when turned simultaneously. Usually used in a row, forming a back wall.

Traps—Elevators from the floor, motorized or hydraulic or operated by winch, for altering the height, pitch, or shape of the stage floor, or for taking set pieces or full sets in and out, as in certain opera houses.

Contour curtains—Drapes with many vertical guidelines raised in changing shapes to suggest arches, entrances, closures, etc.

Method of moving—Most of these devices can be moved by concealed manpower, by motor, by hydraulics, or by compressed air. The technology is always expanding.

SOME DESIGN PRINCIPLES TO REMEMBER

- Tall scenic units and/or wide-open spaces suggest themes of importance and grandeur.

- Low units, solid walls, and enclosed spaces suggest domestic themes, smaller problems.

- Comedy works better down front, in shallow spaces, close to the audience.

- To make the set look crowded, to make your mob or army look bigger, make your space smaller. To dwarf your cast, put a few people in a large space.

- If the audience can't see, it can't hear.

- Lighting comedy calls for brighter and paler colors. Tragedy can be dimmer, in more saturated colors.

Anecdote: Guest-directing *Waiting for Godot* in a regional theatre some years ago, I asked for the full stage, bare except for Beckett's two low mounds and his almost naked tree, and a Raoul Dufy-style pastel drop behind—a gauzy, frivolous sky with both a painted sun and a painted moon showing. The drop arrived, and it was wonderful—whimsical and wistful all at once. The technicians turned on the lights (technical rehearsal) and there were about fifteen spotlights in all, plus the strips to light the drop. A discussion ensued.

CORIOLANUS
Berliner Ensemble, 1964
This photograph of this famous production demonstrates how height in the scenic pieces adds significance and dignity to the stage picuture. Director: Manfred Wekweth.
Photo courtesy German Information Center

I: "Where's the light?"

They: "That's it."

I: "You haven't got enough light here to light any play."

They: "I suppose you're one of those New York directors who wants two hundred instruments."

I: "Yes, please."

They: "Don't tell me lighting. Did you know I invented the high hat for Jed Harris?"

I: "Invent me seventy-five more spots. The actors are saying jokes in the dark down in the corners and up center!"

They: "It's a just a little four-character comedy. I'd play it downstage in one, in black drapes, about ten feet deep, and they'd be lit."

I: "It's *not* just a little comedy, it has cosmic intimations and needs space. Now get me some more light."

And they did.

- Beware of sets lighter in color than the actors' faces.

Anecdote: Cecil Beaton, famed photographer and designer of women's clothes, who sometimes did scenery, designed the Broadway production of Enid Bagnold's *The Chalk Garden*. He gave it a light beige, almost white, set, with brown cross-hatchings on it, like a sepia engraving, to indicate shading and shadows on the walls. It was a charming set, representing a charming British country house, charmingly dotted with costly furniture, costly vases, costly gew-gaws, and acres of expensive but fake silk flowers. Out of town (New Haven, Boston, Philadelphia) they found that the audience couldn't see faces. (Can't see, can't hear.) Everyone who lit plays was called in to fix it, including the owner of Century Lighting—talk about adding instruments! Finally, someone quietly said, "It's not the light—it's the paint." In came a scenic artist, down went the white of the set to a darker beige (which still looked pretty white) and the problem was solved—you could see, you could hear, and we ran almost a year.

- Wing and drop sets create movement and groupings in straight lines. Do you want that?

- Glitz—satin, sequins, shinies—competes with actors' faces. Do you want that? What about pattern in fabrics—prints like florals or plaids? Competition. White anyplace on the stage—be careful.

- If there is any likelihood that the running order of scenes may be changed (as in the case of an original revue or musical) be careful that the scenery and production scheme can easily be adjusted to a change in the running order, even if no change is as yet contemplated.

- Will the set go through the loading door? If built for outdoors, will it stand up to wind, rain, weather? Obvious, yes. Overlooked? Alas, often.

- Be careful that the pitch of stairs and the pitch of raked stages is not such that actors have trouble moving. They can get used to a lot, but *there are limits*. Be careful that the treads of onstage stairs are wide enough for feet, otherwise actors look awkward going up and down.

- Remember that plunging offstage from bright light to pitch dark is dangerous, because the eyes can't adjust. An effect may be esthetically pleasing, but how pleasing is the effect of a plaster cast on the leading lady?

- Scene changes must be safe for actors. This often has to do with design, sometimes with construction.

Anecdote: Gretchen Corbett, an actress friend, was appearing in *Forty Carats* with Julie Harris and Evelyn Varden on Broadway. The prologue was played in a Greek taverna set, very small, which was flown out in its entirety when the first scene was finished, after which it spent the evening suspended high above the stage, down center. The other sets were on wagons on the floor and were changed in the dark. The actors, in these changes, went to prepared positions, indicated by glow tape, where they would not be hit by the moving platforms. Well on in the run, at the particular change in question, on the night in question, Gretchen's place was down center, below the moving sets. Standing there in the dark she was suddenly seized by panic and began to whimper. Miss Varden, from her upstage position in the dark, whispered to Gretchen, "What's the matter? Come here, darling!" Gretchen ran to her comforting arms, just as the entire taverna set broke loose from its moorings in the flies and crashed to the stage floor. Had Gretchen been in her appointed place she would have been killed. What made her panic—subliminally hearing the cables creak? Who knows? Moral; anything that *can* go wrong . . . !

- The more moving parts, the more light cues, the more props to reset— the longer the technical rehearsal will be, and the more worn out the actors will get, with the play drifting away with every mistimed and repeated cue. If you have doubts about the theatre's efficiency, simplify!

- Symmetry–asymmetry: Shall the setting provide a formal and symmetrical balance, with something like a door or stairs or a platform at center, and the sides equally weighted and alike—or should the balance be occult, with mass and space composed pleasingly, but not symmetrically? The formality or classicism of one play may suggest symmetry, while the quirkiness, or informality, the folksiness or grotesque qualities of another play may suggest imbalance and lack of symmetry. Remember, though: the symmetrical setting can, by a shift of emphasis in lighting and choreography, be unbalanced and made asymmetrical, but no such resources can create symmetry. You are stuck with asymmetry; you can vary symmetry. This doesn't mean that one is better than the other; it is simply important to recognize the condition inherent in your choice.

"AS IF" PRODUCTIONS

Julius Caesar "as if" it took place in a banana republic; *All's Well That Ends Well* "as if" it were happening during the American Civil War; a "mod" *Misanthrope*, a "Rough Rider" *Much Ado*, a colonial Brazilian *Midsummer Night's Dream*—such is the fashion. Such approaches are usually justified these days in the name of "relevance." In the twenties when all this started, the reasons given for period shift were less intellectually pretentious. "The audience is tired of those same old tights and farthingales, and people tripping on swords. Let's give it a new environment, a new set of manners. What would be fun? Let him enter on roller skates, or a bicycle, or smoking a cigar!" The director's desire to explore a new physical milieu, like the conventions of the Kabuki, was allied to a desire to dazzle the public with a new look at an old war-horse.

Nowadays, two impulses seem to set the "as if's" in motion. The first is that placing the classic play in some aspect of today's environment will make a connection between the universal theme of the play and our life today: Human nature has not changed, therefore one should equate the message of the classic with some aspect of today's problems, so that the importance of the play, its relevance to us, will be brought out. The second impulse seems to me to be a byproduct of college education: the notion that if we *compare* things, we understand the nature of each of them better. Take an assignment such as "Compare the author's philosophical position in Goethe's *Faust* with that of Marlowe in his *Dr. Faustus*." There's an obvious and easy task for you. But more clever problems can be set: "Compare Salinger's Holden Caulfield with Dostoevsky's Raskolnikov in the light of Freud's work with the Oedipus conflict." This sort of intellectual exercise—sometimes bordering on the silly—seems to underlie many of our "as if" productions today.

The "as if" production is currently fashionable, but these are, I offer, deep waters. A play is apt to be drowned in such spurious ingenuity, unless greater care than usual is taken.

I find that two chief dangers lie in wait for those who opt for the "as if" production.

The first is that the "as if" may run away with the play, and the audience, coming to see Shakespeare (who is the usual beneficiary of these intellectual attentions), finds itself viewing a tract on Fascism (say, *Julius Caesar*) or a play about Donald Trump (say, *Timon of Athens*) or a play about gang warfare (say, *Romeo and Juliet*) or a play about corporate infighting (say, *Richard* II). These are not trivially suggested "as if's"; each has actually been carried out. The audience members who came to see Shakespeare are outraged or disappointed; those being introduced to Shakespeare meet, not his world, but some "relevant" context with which they are already, alas, familiar.

The second pitfall is that every play, Shakespeare's not less than others, is the product of a particular world, with religious, political, and philosophical underpinnings. This world has social customs and attitudes born of its time. The invention of the railroad, the automobile, the airplane, the atomic bomb, indoor plumbing, the pill, the computer—all these have changed how things get done in the world and what things people talk and think about. Though human nature has indeed not basically changed, I find that a physical environment *later* than Shakespeare's (or any other play's period) brings with it connotations of an inner world that clash with the values that shaped the play's inner world. For example, the religious attitudes that produced Greek tragedy seem to me belied when such plays are presented, without adaptation, in modern dress.

However, they "will do it if they come to it," as the mad Ophelia sings. "As if" productions sometimes draw enthusiastic audiences, and I doubt that my discouraging words will dissuade the relevance seekers in our midst.

Still, a reminder: The director's real task, as I see it, is the truthful and creative interpretation of a play, bridging the gap between written script and live audience. Too often, directing becomes an exercise in cleverness, an exercise in which the playwright's work is merely one element in the makeup of a "theatre experience." By all means, *adapt Twelfth Night*—and call it *Your Own Thing* (which became a successful off-Broadway musical). But if you do choose to *use* a Shakespeare or other classic play as part of a witches' brew of your own, at least take your proper authorial credit—or lumps. "Marlowe's *Edward* II, *adapted* by Bertolt Brecht"—good! Give the audience fair warning.

WORKING WITH THE SCENE DESIGNER

SELECTING A SCENE DESIGNER

In many institutional situations, there is a staff designer who either designs all the productions or is assigned a particular portion of the season to design. In such a situation the director may have little or no say in the choice of designer for the production. On or off-Broadway, the producer may select the designer, sometimes subject to the director's prior approval, sometimes not. In other instances, the director may select the scene designer, either from a pool of student designers, in the case of a graduate directing project, or, in the case of a professional situation, from among freelance designers who are interviewed for the position.

ASSESSING THE DESIGNER'S QUALITIES

Whether you have a choice or not, you must assess the designer's qualities in the following areas:

- Is the designer "painterly" or not? Are his painting skills well developed? Does he draw well? Does he rely too much on his painterly abilities? Do his set photographs look like his renderings and elevations?

- Or is he more of a sculptor or architect? Do his designs excel most in three dimensions, or in two?

- How derivative is his work? Whose designs do his remind you of?

- How is his color sense?

- How verbal a person is he? Does he talk well or is he inarticulate save in the language of the visual?

- What can you sense about his idea of the designer's role? Does he talk well about the play and its structure, story, form, needs? Or does he immediately go to discussing the "look" and other visual matters?

- Obviously, no design interview, no designer–director relationship, can be satisfactory without the director having a chance to see the designer's portfolio. The director must gain a sense of the designer's range and potential, and this can best be done by seeing the work. Designers may talk well or badly, but the proof of the pudding is what gets on the stage. Even if the designer is artistically senior to the director, the director *must* somehow get a sense of the designer's past work. This may mean a trip to the archives rather than, "May I look at your portfolio," but, famous or not, senior faculty or not, the director must know the past work of future collaborators.

IMPARTING YOUR PRODUCTION SCHEME

As I have already suggested, I believe that the basic production scheme ought to originate with the director. It is the director who studies the play's insides, who decides why and how it should be done, what it is to say to the audience, and how it is going to say it. As the director you must convey your scheme in concrete terms clearly enough that the designer can be sufficiently inspired to add constructively to your visual concept, or you must imbue the designer with the *idea* of the production, and then allow the designer to create a visual response to the director's verbal images.

Your notions may emerge in terms of a ground plan—a door here, a platform there; or they may take the form of a verbal description of a style of production—"spaces, pierced by shafts of light," or "pretty painted drops, like a toy theatre," or "nothing but black drapes, white light, and bentwood chairs." You could show the designer photos of real places, or news shots; you might bring in reproductions of applicable paintings. You might even choose to do simple thumbnail sketches, being careful not to draw *too* well.

Whichever method you choose, you must speak first. Don't ask the designer, "How do you see this play?" If you ask the designer to provide the scheme, in the way that an architect designs a building, then *he* has directed the play, not *you*. If you suggest to him which road you wish to go down, and then respond to what you have evoked in him, collaboration is occurring. That's what is wanted.

It may be that you are entirely sure of what you want to see, that your vision of the play has become fixed. This is not good or bad—it may simply be so. In that case, you must tell the designer, "This is what I want." If the designer then says, "Do it yourself," or, "Get somebody else," *do* one or the other. Good productions can occur out of many circumstances, but a *unified* production is an essential. Designer and director *must* work together.

After you have submitted your concept and the designer has said, "I think I can make this work very excitingly," and after you have agreed that this is the right designer—the real work begins.

THE DESIGNER'S RESPONSE

The ball is now in the designer's court, and it is he or she who makes the next response.

There are two separate paths by which he may approach his task, and you.

1. If he is very visually oriented, he may start with how the set might look—just quick thumbnail impressions. You and he may pick one or two of these sketches, and a very primitive floor plan can be roughed out. Then a conversation about material and color might be in order, after which the question of how the scenery can shift will be taken up. Once all this is agreed on, in rough outline, he will go to work on more complete renderings, elevations, and as further accord is reached, perhaps a model, if needed.

2. If he is more structurally oriented, or if structural decisions will dictate how the set will look, he may start evolving a ground plan in consultation with you, moving next to structure, materials, scene shifts, and finally to how the set will look. This approach leads next to a white model, and then perhaps to a full model, probably omitting any renderings or elevations, except to guide the painters.

Either sequence (or some other sequence, as long as all the steps are covered) will work. I happen to prefer sequence one, because I want to know as soon as possible how it will *look*, but I have had excellent collaborations with designers working in both sequences. I do think, once the director has had his say about concept and has chosen his designer, he must accept that designer's preferred way of working, so long as it is thorough.

The director *must*, however, be involved at every step of the way, so that he can speak up the moment anything goes off the rails or takes a wrong turn.

Paper is less costly to tear up than scenery is to throw out. Sketches can even be erased. The director who is involved in the design process and who keeps it subject to constant review saves everyone's time and energy. The director who doesn't—deserves what he gets.

The director must not *pretend* to understand things he doesn't. If you don't quite get how something is to work, say so—it's the designer's job to show you, by explanation or model. The most ghastly admission of incompetence and lack of collaboration in the theatre comes when the director walks onto the completed set and says, "God, I didn't know it was going to look like *this!*"

In the foregoing discussion I have assumed that the director can read mechanical drawings, for that is how the scale floor plan of the set and the structural elevations will be presented by the designer. The director who has not acquired this plan-reading skill in some basic stagecraft or design class (if not along the way in junior high or high school) would do well to do so. Failing this, he will need a model from his designer very badly indeed.

WORKING WITH LIGHTING AND COSTUME DESIGNERS

SELECTING LIGHTING AND COSTUME DESIGNERS

The process of selecting lighting designers and costume designers is much the same as finding the right scene designer. In the costume area, one has both designer renderings and production photographs available to check conception against finished product, whereas the lighting designer can only show complex focus and hanging plots and production shots either in not-too-helpful black and white or in less-than-accurate color. Here are some areas of concern relating to these specific areas.

COSTUMES

1. Can you discern, from the rendering, how the garment is to be cut, or is it just a painter's fantasy? Will the chosen fabrics do what the designer hopes they will do, as far as weight, texture, and material are concerned?
2. Will the designer give you full-color renderings, or will you have to rely on black-and-white line drawings, with swatches attached, for your indications of color and texture? Are the colored swatches presented in size proportionate to the amount particular fabrics and colors will appear in the actual costume?
3. Is the designer's idea of color compatible with yours?
4. Do his views on texture and glitz coincide with yours for the play?
5. Do his ideas about "clothing for the stage" versus "stage clothes" coincide with yours?
6. Does he have a reputation for being *on time*? (Lateness in the scenic and/or costume areas can destroy a production.)
7. Does he get along with actors?
8. Does he have a sense of characterization?

LIGHTING

1. Does he come well recommended? This is almost the only way you can really know much about a lighting designer.
2. Does he seem well organized?
3. Does he have a good practical background?
4. Do his ideas about color and instrument placement coincide with yours? Fads occur in lighting. There's the "white light" fad, in which no color media

are used. There's the "oversaturated" fad, in which many heavy colors are used, making a look some call "rich" and others call "muddy."

5. Do her ideas about brightness agree with yours? Some like it bright, some like it dim.

6. Are you in agreement as to the amount of top and back lighting in relation to front lighting?

As a director, your detailed preparation prior to design should help you to be, not a dictator, but an informed and inspiring leader/collaborator. Designers, like actors, want to be told in what direction they should go. They seek, not aimless latitude, but creative guidance. If you share your vision with them in a way that can release, not inhibit them, designers and actors can contribute unexpected riches as they give form to your dream.

EXERCISES

1. Page 90—What kind of relationship do you want to establish between the audience and the actors? Design a theatrical space for your production that amplifies your concept of the play. What advantages will you reap by staging according to a (1) proscenium, (2) arena, (3) thrust, or (4) environmental arrangement? What challenges does each format create?

2. Page 92—Given your production concept, prepare a budget for your production. You have at your disposal $3,000. Consider costs such as scenery, costumes, properties, makeup, publicity, lighting, and rental of theatrical space. Can you match your production to the fiscal necessities? What priorities should you establish for the production in view of budget constraints? What are your biggest needs?

3. Page 93—What will the production actually look like? It's fine to *talk* about a tree, but what kind of tree will be *seen* exactly? In the text it is described on page 10 as a willow, dead, a brush, a shrub. In Act Two, the tree has "four or five leaves." How many leaves will there be on the tree in your production? Will you have a tree? What kind of tree will it be? What do you gain/lose if you no longer have a tree?

4. Page 93—Draw some sketches of the way you see the play in your mind. These can be very rough. Put them in storyboard arrangement, like a cartoon strip, in order to demonstrate sequence. Or, alternatively, draw one moment in the play, or one image that captures the essence of the play. The sketch should be informational but should primarily evoke your feeling for the play. The sketches could be the basis for a conversation between you and the designers.

CHAPTER 6

CASTING

Directors are dispensable; designers are nonessential. Playwrights are essential in the sense that *somebody* must do that job—but the actor is the essence of theatre. The actor can be his own storyteller, and his own director, and can build the set, too—and, at the last, the actor is the one who meets the audience.

Once you know what play you are doing, choosing your actors is the most important task you will undertake as a director.

CASTING GUIDELINES

STOCK COMPANY CASTING

Shaw was wont to say that he wrote his plays to be played by actors like the ones he saw in the stock companies of his youth in Dublin. The makeup of the nineteenth-century stock company is a good place to start a discussion of casting, since its company of actors was brought together to perform, with a resident ensemble, plays we still regard as the classics of our theatre.

Here are the "lines of business" (an old expression meaning character types) one might find represented in such a company:

Leading Man—35 to 50 (or older, if he ran the theatre), attractive, vigorous, tall, heroic.

Leading Lady—30 to 45 (or older, if she or her husband ran the company), attractive, stately, elegant, ladylike.

Second Man—30 to 45, handsome, less sympathetic, good at villains and light comedy.

Second Woman—30 to 45, elegant, often with a touch of mystery or eroticism about her.

The Juvenile—20 to 30, the young leading man, handsome and boyish.

The Ingenue—18 to 25, the young female love interest, pretty, charming, delicate. (The term ''ingenue'' was sometimes used in England to denote a younger actor of either sex, but in America it refers to a young woman.)

The Character Man—50 to 70, plays fathers and aristocrats, distinguished, authoritative.

The Character Woman—50 to 70, plays mothers and great ladies, often a former leading lady, distinguished and elegant.

BEFORE SUNSET
Schiller Theater, Berlin, 1961
Hauptmann's drama of an old man's last romance offers, in this picture, a view of the range of actors' ages in a true repertory company. Second from the right is the famous actor Ernst Deutsch. Director: Boleslav Barlog.
Photo courtesy German Information Center

Second Character Man—50 to 70, more common, often portly, good at comedy.

Second Character Woman—50 to 70, more common, often stout, good at comedy.

The Low Comedian—30 to 50, a Robin Williams or Red Skelton type, good at physical comedy.

The Soubrette—25 to 40, a coquette, sexy, earthy, good at comedy.

The Character Juvenile—18 to 25, offbeat or funny-looking, good at comedy.

The Character Ingenue—his female counterpart.

Walking Gentlemen and Utility Players—People who played small parts, often aspiring younger actors or less-talented has-beens.

A look at the plays of any period will demonstrate how practical such a list of "types"—despite its apparent datedness—can be. Such basic categories can be useful today, as you begin to think about what kinds of people should inhabit your play. The bad reputation of "type casting" should not prevent you from using it as a tool when you start thinking about casting. "Type" is not dictated by race, nor does it *necessarily* depend on gender or physical attributes.

OTHER YARDSTICKS

There are other yardsticks that can be applied simultaneously, which also have little to do with race, gender, or physicality.

"Square" or "Thin."   Does the role call for a "square" actor/actress (downright, straightforward, direct) or a "thin" actor/actress (temperamentally volatile, high-strung, "spirituelle.")

Sympathetic or Unsympathetic.   Does the role call for a sympathetic empathic actor/actress, or is an unsympathetic quality wanted—or perhaps a hint of the ambiguous in-between?

The "Classic" Actor.   What kind of actor do you want for Shakespeare and the classics? A few years ago, there were very few places actors could go for training in the classics. Most of us so trained had managed to get to England—to the Royal Academy of Dramatic Art, or the Old Vic School, or the Central School of Speech Training and Dramatic Art. We came back speaking stage English, sometimes with the so-called "RADA voice," which in England is no longer the professional seal of approval it used to be. Then, depending on luck and talent, we became the American classic actors. Much later came the Juilliard School's expansion into actor training, along with the development of distinguished conservatory-level acting programs at a number of American universities, producing a new breed of American actors, trained in the classics but also ready for film and television.

These days, there is a bias in certain quarters against British-trained American actors, and against British actors themselves, who used to have a distinct advantage over here. An accepted American speech for classic plays is emerging—not necessarily better than the trained speech of the past, but less British-oriented. The question of what standard should be aimed at, when casting classic plays needing good and uniform speech, is one with which the director will have to deal, either in choosing among trained theatre professionals, or in establishing speech and style goals for his less-experienced performers.

"Personality" versus "Character" Actors.   Another aspect of casting lore I have found useful is the premise that actors divide into two other groups: personality actors and character actors.

"Personality actors" are those actors who always play the same kind of part, no matter how the play's situation and its lines may vary from one show to the next. These actors look the same from role to role, draw on similar emotional resources from role to role, and use the same vocal and physical quirks to ensure that they are "interesting" or "exciting"—to employ two overworked words from the casting director's vocabulary. They may be very talented actors indeed, and often they are stars. Their stardom is not confined to television and film—though these media are especially responsive to personalities—for many an important stage actor has been a "personality" rather than a "character" actor. I am not making a value judgment here, of bad, good, better, best, but pointing out that there is a basic difference in the nature of the two talents, of which the director must be aware and make full use. Even among student actors, the "personality" can be distinguished from the "character" actor. Exposed to the same training process, the difference still remains.

"Character actors" are actors who disappear into their roles. Such personal characteristics as they may possess are subdued and channeled into their performances, so that the actor seems to be a different person in each part he undertakes, irrespective of what makeup changes he may employ to alter his appearance. The actor's own persona may be almost neutral, or even quite nonprofessional and "civilian" rather than theatrical. To this neutral state, when rehearsing and performing, he seems to add the characteristics of his role, so that in very subtle ways—speech and body rhythms, vocal intonations, and appearance—the actor vanishes into the part. This quality is one we see more often in stage than in film actors; however, the screen has its character actors too. Even "stars" have emerged from the ranks of character actors. Examples:

PERSONALITY ACTORS

Screen—John Wayne, Judy Garland, Clark Gable, Greta Garbo, Kevin Costner, Julia Roberts

Stage—John Gielgud, Rex Harrison, Helen Hayes, Kevin Kline

CHARACTER ACTORS

Screen—Meryl Streep, Robert Duvall, Alec Guinness, Dustin Hoffman

Stage—Laurence Olivier, Charles Durning, Peggy Ashcroft, Maggie Smith

THE ABILITY TO CARRY A PLAY

What elements constitute the ability to "carry a play"? The protagonist's role must be inhabited by someone the audience is willing to watch, believe in, and invest empathy in for a whole evening. The director must look for certain attributes in the person who is to do that job:

1. *Authority.* The audience must be in suspense about the outcome of the *play,* how the story is to turn out, but they must never doubt that the *actor* has the capacity to finish the evening. The slightest indication that he is unsteady in his lines, unsure of his moves, inaudible or incomprehensible, physically weak, or in any other way shaky, impairs audience belief. There is danger in the very act of acting, or of walking a tightrope, but the audience does not

RICHARD III
New York Shakespeare Festival, 1957
Old Queen Margaret (Eulalie Noble) confronts Richard of Gloucester (George C. Scott) in the New York Shakespeare Festival's first fully-staged indoor production at the Heckscher Theatre on upper Fifth Avenue.
Photo: Goerge E. Joseph

RICHARD III (WARS OF THE ROSES)
New York Shakespeare Festival, 1970
Here, Donald Madden (Richard of Gloucester) and Barbara Caruso (Queen Margaret) are
in much the same positions as in the earlier production, with David Byrd (Lord Hastings)
looking on. Since this play was played after the *Henry VI*'s, it was important to show how
Margaret had aged and lost political power. Madden was more tormented than Scott,
though equally powerful in his own way, and this shows through. Both productions were
directed by Stuart Vaughan.
Photo: George E. Joseph

want *really* to fear that the acrobat will fall or the actor will disgrace himself. Some actors can walk into an audition room and disappear. Others own the chair they are standing near, or perhaps the space they stand up in. Others own a few feet in a circle around them. Others own the stage, their partner, and the theatre itself from the moment they walk in. Confidence, charisma, sexuality, concentration—it is probably a combination of these and other elements. But authority is recognizable, if somewhat hard to define. The leading actors need it.

2. *Vocal clarity.* The voice need not be beautiful, or noticeably well-produced. It need not be especially low or vibrant. It must, however, be audible and understandable; it must be produced without undue effort, distortion, or affectation; and the actor must provide an illusion of spontaneity—of someone saying these words for the first time.

3. *Intelligence.* The actor must convey enough intelligence in reading the lines and in thinking at the speed of the character to inhabit the inner life of the role. In addition, he must demonstrate enough personal intelligence to convince the director that he can intellectually grasp the nature of the role and learn the lines.

4. *Energy.* The actor must be alive and vibrant on the stage. I don't mean effortfully pushy, but, while apparently relaxed, he must exude vitality. The voice must have "ping," and the body, whatever its shape, must have enough conditioning and grace to encompass easily the physical tasks the role demands.

5. *The kind of sympathy the role demands.* One can think of actors and actresses, overtly attractive and suitable, who give themselves away through subliminal, almost invisible cues, as being conceited, vain, prudish, effeminate, man-hating, pompous, overbearing, remote, cold, brutal, coarse, exhibitionistic, and so on. One senses these negative qualities, although one cannot pin down exactly how one knows. As a director you must learn to trust those instincts and then decide how the qualities you have perceived will affect your casting. Sometimes even the negative qualities can be useful.

6. *Looks.* The actor must be pleasant enough to look at for the demands of the role. Few great actors have been handsome, or great actresses beautiful. Indeed, excessive beauty is intimidating to audiences. Still, people don't want to watch the obviously repulsive all evening, unless it's Charles Laughton as Quasimodo, and even then, theatrical sympathy comes when the Hunchback of Notre Dame is revealed as a creature with tender feelings. Claude Rains was a very short man, although well-proportioned. One night backstage I heard the prop man jokingly ask him, "Mr. Rains, you had them build up the legs on that chair you sit on behind the desk. Why?" I knew it had been done because Rains feared he couldn't be seen over the desk, so I waited for the answer. Rains said, "It's because I have duck's disease, Charley." "Duck's disease—

what's that?'' With a straight face Rains answered, ''My feet are too close to my arse.'' You never felt he was short, though, because he held himself beautifully, and he had enormous authority. Charles Durning, in *Cat on a Hot Tin Roof*, was rotund. He moves, though, like a zephyr, light on his feet, so that which might be unsightly is compensated for admirably.

7. *Mystery.* The best actors give the audience a sense that in spite of all they are seeing of them in the role, there remains something unknown, something mysterious. It is this mystery, sometimes a sense even of danger, that keeps the audience constantly interested, hanging on every word, gesture, look. This kind of actor never satisfies the audience without giving them another question to answer. With them, as Yogi Berra seems to have said, ''It ain't over till it's over.''

ETHNICALLY DIVERSE AND ''COLOR-BLIND'' CASTING

Note that none of the aforementioned casting criteria, including the old-fashioned stock company ''lines of business'' that influenced generations of playwrights, have anything at all to do with racial or ethnic origins, but they have everything to do with the personal qualities to be depicted by those portraying the play's constellation of characters. Happily, our society nowadays accepts ''color-blind'' and ''ethnically diverse'' casting, and such casting has become the ''norm.''

WHEN IN DOUBT

Often, in these theoretical discussions, it may appear that I expect ideal conditions to obtain. I well realize that most directors don't have access to New York's apparently unlimited pool of actors. That pool has sometimes seemed to me more like a shallow puddle, because, believe me, there *are* no ideal conditions. Of the New York productions I have directed, not one was without a last-minute casting crisis over a major role. The trouble is, theatre in New York and Los Angeles, even Broadway, simply cannot pay salaries competitive with film and television. The actor in demand is in demand by everybody, so, when he chooses to be in a play, he is subsidizing the theatre by his presence. This makes for disciplinary and other problems that I shall examine elsewhere, but in regard to casting it puts the director of professional productions in just the same boat as the university or community theatre director is often in—not being able to find the *right* actor when you want him. What, then, is to be done?

Axiom: if you can't find the *right* actor, use the most skillful, the *best* actor available. See that he compensates, with his skills, for what he may lack in ideal qualities. Of course, you will remember never to let him feel, for a moment, that he was not your first or ideal choice. After all, he *is* the Hamlet you've got, and he is probably the only actor playing Hamlet at that moment in a five-hundred-mile radius. Forget the qualities he hasn't got or can't get. Emphasize what he *can* do—because the audience will see only what's *there*. They won't know what you thought of but couldn't bring off. Having cast your less-than-ideal actor (which happens 99 percent of the time no matter how much money you can pay), give him your support, your talent, your energy, your faith.

There is a show business story that *must not* apply here. The producers have cast a young actor, new to New York, in a huge starring role in a new Broadway play. The young man is delighted, but understandably nervous. The producers have him in the day before rehearsals to reassure him. "We trust you," they tell him. "We have faith in you. We'll give you every support, every backing. And if the going gets really rough, and you feel you are really beyond your strength, don't you worry—we'll just get someone else." You *can't* get someone else, you've already tried. So back the actor you've had to go with to the uttermost and beyond.

THE CASTING PROCESS

THE CAST BREAKDOWN

Whether your theatre posts an announcement of its casting call on a bulletin board, announces it in the papers, contacts agents about it, or tells Actors' Equity about it, the director will have to create a "cast breakdown."

This is a list of the characters in the play, with a brief description of the qualities the director wants for each of the parts, including age range, physical type, and other characteristics. This breakdown, if made public, will guide actors in applying, agents in submitting clients, and the casting director, if any, about what actors to call in. Making it forces the director to define for himself how he sees each of the characters and how he sees them in relation to each other.

Lack of preparation, as I have made abundantly clear, is the chief fault among directors. This shows up in casting when, because the director doesn't know what he wants, actors of all shapes, sizes, and types are asked to read for each given role. Thus, instead of deciding in advance that she wants a solid, earthy young woman for Ophelia, an actress with a sense of emotional honesty, the director will see and hear tall Ophelias, short Ophelias, fat Ophelias, thin Ophelias, Ophelias of astonishing beauty who project high-pitched madness, and Ophelias of astounding combinations of any and all of the above characteristics. At some point, the director expects to achieve a glorious insight that will bring him to his feet crying, "*You're* Ophelia!" when someone suddenly strikes a note that seems just right. All too often, though—no insight.

On the other hand, the director who has decided just what he wants can always change his mind. Bob Fosse, with the musical *Pippin*, evidently wanted an old man for the central role eventually played by Ben Vereen. Ben Vereen, on the advice of a casting director, came in (so the story goes) with a creative and surprising idea about the role, and Fosse bought it. When the unprepared director with no casting concepts uses the audition to teach him who to cast, *all* interpretations are apt to look wrong or equally valid to him. Thus—indecision, then seeing more actors, wasting more time and more human energy.

The table below shows a cast breakdown for the production of *The Two Gentlemen of Verona*, New York Shakespeare Festival, Central Park, Summer, 1987.

THE PROCESS BEGINS

The cast breakdown has been distributed in accordance with the policies of the theatre. In university and community theatres, actors generally are expected to turn up *en masse* on the day and at the time and place announced in the casting call. In the professional theatre, agents will have submitted names of clients, and actors will have sent in their pictures and résumés, from which groups actors will be selected for appointments. The director will have a list of people

---

THE TWO GENTLEMEN OF VERONA CAST BREAKDOWN

LOVERS: (20s)
Proteus (must sing)—sensitive, good-looking, not entirely sympathetic
Valentine (athletic)—open, sympathetic, and taller than Proteus

WOMEN: (20s)
Julia—brown-haired to brunette, good legs, later disguised as a boy, virtuous and romantic
Sylvia—beautiful, voluptuous, seems pampered and spoiled at first, but sweet underneath

COMICS: (20s)
Launce (has dog)—naive, childlike, capable of naughtiness but never malicious
Speed—pert, saucy, rascally
They are Abbott and Costello, in a way.

FATHERS:
Duke (50s or 60s)—an absent-minded, dithery Frank Morgan type
Antonio (50s)—burly, impetuous, like Juliet's father

OTHERS:
Lucetta (mid-30s)—witty, attractive, contrast to Julia, a gentlewoman-companion
Thurio (must fence)—pompous, dark, a weight-lifter somewhat gone to fat
Panthino, doubles *3rd Outlaw* (late 30s)—a stocky actor
Host, doubles *1st Outlaw*—older and jolly
Eglamore—"The Lone Ranger," a spoof on a knightly hero, big and stolid
2nd Outlaw—understudy

ADDITIONAL NON-EQUITY ENSEMBLE: (at least six men, six women, more would be helpful)

MEN:
Menservants—both for Antonio and the Duke
Three Lovers of Julia—opening I, 2
Outlaws—including Panthino and Host, a total of five. Two do not speak.
Fencing Master—gives on-stage lesson to Thurio, could be fight choreographer for the production, for there will be a couple of comic fights

WOMEN:
Court Ladies—all court scenes, and *Servants* for Julia and Sylvia

THE TWO GENTLEMEN OF VERONA
New York Shakespeare Festival, 1957
Here is Jerry Stiller (Launce) with the dog we used, a stray who wandered in one day
while we were rehearsing. He was untrained, but he would simply go where Jerry put him.
He finished his days with the Stillers as a valued family member. Director: Stuart Vaughan.
Photo: George E. Joseph

to see, on the basis of personal acquaintance or knowing their work, and they
will be contacted. Too, the casting director or casting department will have
people they think should be seen who will be given appointments. Whatever
the source of the list, the actors to be seen will have each an appointed time,
and casting can begin.

The two main tools of the casting process are the interview and the audition.

THE INTERVIEW

The interview usually takes place in a one-on-one office situation and is not
usually a part of the nonprofessional casting process. I shall discuss it here,
however, because if it is used, it usually precedes the audition.

THE TWO GENTLEMEN OF VERONA
New York Shakespeare Festival, 1987
Thirty years later, Dylan Baker was Launce, and our dog was a high-budget dog complete
with trainer/handler. The dog was less of a mutt than Jerry's dog, and to that degree less
"right." The point of these two pictures is that if you compare both Launces with the
description in the cast breakdown (see table on p. 114), you will see that though they are
very different in type and appearance, they both embody the innocence that is so
necessary. Director: Stuart Vaughan.
Photo: © 1991 *Martha Swope*

The interview is usually a fifteen- or twenty-minute appointment in which
the actor meets the director. A producer or producers may be on hand. The
actor is ushered in by an assistant or secretary who says, "Mr. X, this is Geor-
gina Spelvin," while handing the director the 8″ × 10″ picture, with résumé
on the back, that has already been screened by whoever made the appointment. Both actor and director know that the appointment itself means there is
something potentially right about the actor. The director says something like,

"Thanks for coming in. Please sit down." He then introduces anyone else who may be in the room, and then probably looks at the résumé, saying, "I see you worked recently with . . ." That, or some other conversational ploy, is the actor's cue to be pleasant, relaxed, outgoing, and to hold forth for a bit, while being eyed speculatively by everyone in the room. Some actors actually find it possible to be amusing, vivid, and properly forthcoming on these occasions. The director may well describe the play and the role next. He might even give the actor a script and suggest that a time be arranged for a reading. Or he may simply rise, sooner rather than later, and say, "Nice to meet you. Thanks for coming in."

The office interview is of more use in film and television casting than in casting for the stage, because film and television are more interested in "the real person," making less allowance for acting talent. Still, there are stage directors who want to know *who* they might be working with before they see them work, and for them, the interview has a function.

I remember one office interview during my acting days that served another function. It was for Arthur Miller's A *Memory of Two Mondays.* I was ushered into Kermit Bloomgarten's office, where an aide said, "Mr. Vaughan, meet Mr. Bloomgarten and Arthur Miller." Miller said, "Mr. Vaughan, you're not right for this play, but it was nice to meet you anyway. Goodbye." And that was that—I was shown out. Time and energy saved. When I saw the play, I realized I was indeed all wrong for it, and a brief office interview was exactly the right way for them to pass judgment on that aspect of casting. And, wonder of wonders, though I remember the event very clearly, I had no resentment.

IT'S THE DIRECTOR'S TIME

As the director you must remember that the interview or reading is on your time, to serve your purposes, and the play's. You will, of course, be best served by enabling actors to do their best work. I want each actor who comes in to be wonderful, and to get the job, because then I can stop casting and start rehearsing. On the other hand, once I am certain, for whatever reason, that the actor won't do, then I owe it to myself, in order to save my energies and keep my vision as unclouded as possible, to say, "Thank you very much, Miss Spelvin," and let the assistant show her out.

THE AUDITION

Moving now to the audition, it can be conducted in a number of ways. When I was a member of the resident company at the Erie Playhouse years ago, Newell Tarrant, the director, would sit us all in a circle in the rehearsal room and hear us read the play. He would pass the parts around, so that, as the play progressed, he would hear different people in the roles and different combinations of people in the scenes. Then, as I recall, a cast list would appear on the call board.

Some university and community theatre auditions herd everyone into the auditorium, get each person to fill out a card, and then call people up in groups to read from selected scenes. Everyone gets to hear the competition. After this initial evening, there will be callbacks, with people asked to read specific parts in smaller groups.

There is an Actors' Equity rule (though it is frequently violated) that actors auditioning for parts cannot read together. This means that each actor reads with the stage manager or with someone brought in especially to read. Whether union rules apply or not, I prefer seeing one actor at a time, whether they are reading from the script or giving a prepared audition piece. It is very difficult to focus fairly on more than one actor at a time, and even a particularly bad reading (or a particularly good one) on the part of one actor can distract one's attention from the other. The *director* deserves his chance to assess each actor fully.

Recently in a university situation I saw auditions conducted very sensibly. Candidates were asked to report to a particular room where they were each assigned a five-minute time slot in the order in which they had arrived. Small groups were led to a room adjoining the stage, from which candidates were brought, one at a time, to read from the stage. Only directors of upcoming productions were allowed in the auditorium. This system worked very well, both to satisfy the need to see one actor at a time and to avoid the time-consuming business of setting up individual appointments.

What to Look for in Auditions.   What can I learn from the first round of auditions? What can *anyone* learn about an actor in five short minutes? We can find out:

1. What the actor looks like.

2. What his voice and speech are like.

3. Something about his degree of authority.

4. How he handles the nerves of the audition situation.

5. How truthful his acting is.

6. Something about his movement.

7. How effective is his first impression.

8. Something about his intelligence.

9. How right he is, in relation to all these factors, for the part—whether he should be called back for the next round of auditions.

Audition Material.   I prefer not to hear readings from the script during the first round of auditions for two reasons: (a) I get tired of hearing the script read; more important: (b) I would rather not be put off by a faulty interpretation of the role. In the first round, I am interested in the *actor*, not in how he feels about the part. I want to know whether he is "right" for the part. At a later callback, I can (or cannot) achieve the interpretation I want. At this first meeting, it's the actor's *quality* I need to see, without some possibly mistaken interpretation of his coming between me and his nature. So—to get the best answers to what I can learn from the first round, I prefer the prepared audition, or what a friend calls "the party piece."

I ask the actor to bring in one selection—Shakespearean verse, if what we're doing is Shakespeare, prose otherwise. The speech should be no longer than three minutes. If we're doing a comedy, the speech should be comedic. Indeed, the selection should bear some resemblance to the role the actor is auditioning for. If the audition is a general audition—for membership in a repertory season, or a company—I will request two selections: one verse, one prose, with the prose selection from a relatively modern play. Also, one of the two selections should be comedic. When the actor brings in a prepared selection of his own choice, he is demonstrating how he sees himself, and that can be useful information.

The Place.   As to the physical situation, I prefer to hold auditions in a theatre approximating the size of the space where the production will be done. Adequate lighting is essential, for the sake of seeing the actor. I prefer to be centered in the auditorium and to have the actor brought on from the wings. My object is to meet actors, insofar as possible, as the audience meets them, acting.

The Process.   The assistant says, "Mr. Vaughan, this is George Spelvin." I say, from the house, "What are you going to do for me, Mr. Spelvin?" He'll say, "Hamlet's first soliloquy," let's say. I'll say, "Go to it." All this prevents the actor from sailing up to me, shaking my hand, and starting a conversation. You may say, "But don't you want to set the actor at ease?" And I would say, "He's not there to be at ease; he's there to work. If he's *prepared* to work, he isn't any more eager to talk about the weather than I am."

In a well-organized audition, I will have been given a sheet with the time slots indicated, the actors' names typed in, and enough space next to each name for any notes I choose to make. I will also have the photos and résumés in hand, stacked in order of appearance, so I can remind myself of the actor's background during the audition.

The Actor "Using" the Director.   If the actor begins by playing him speech straight at me, I usually stop him and explain that, while some directors may want you to look them in the eye, I don't, and he should start over. Sometimes the *actor* will ask (and it is good to do so), "Do you mind if I use you to play to?" I will then explain why I'd rather they didn't.

1. If they act at me, I will feel I should react, as an actor, to them. If I do, I'm not really seeing their audition as a director, which is my job.

2. If I go about my business as they audition, looking at their picture, making my notes, and only looking at them now and then (as is my habit), they will be thrown and distracted instead of doing *their* job.

3. If, instead, I look at them pleasantly, wearing my "audition mask," a poker face which gives away nothing, I will feel uncomfortable, and I still won't be able to make the notes I need to make.

So—I'd rather they'd play over my head, or to a chair, or toward the wings—anything but to me.

The Director's Notes and Symbols.   One has to make notes in order to remember the actors and their auditions. I abbreviate the play title and character they have chosen. I may describe them physically: "blonde, gawky," "tall, weight-lifter," "sexy brunette." I may note "good speech," "Southern," "hard r's," and so on. And finally I grade the audition, using a set of symbols I won't give here. As a director you should devise your own secret set of symbols. Here is my scale:

Outstanding professional, deserves to be cast

Very good, possible

An adequate professional actor, usable sometime

Not adequate

Unfit for any stage

I have one other symbol, the one for "crazy," which can be used in addition to any of the above.

Why use symbols? Casting notes are sometimes filed by secretaries, assistants, and casting departments. They can be lost, thrown away after the show is over, filched, or otherwise come into the wrong hands. I myself once came across some notes about an audition I had given, a long time after I became an employee of the institution in question, and the nature of the note didn't make my relationship with my employer any easier. In addition to the symbols, I have also developed a "casting handwriting," which is almost indecipherable. My set of symbols I borrowed from a friend who had been casting director for a film company. However you do it, it is very important to preserve confidentiality about your opinion of someone's audition. After all, as has many times been said of casting, "You start out wanting Laurence Olivier and end up with Joe Doaks," and you certainly don't want Joe ever to find out what you thought of him first time around.

Audition Nerves and Forgetting Lines.   Actors sometimes forget lines in auditions. So what? A director is used to seeing actors forget lines, isn't he? Actors will sometimes stop in the middle, for no discernible reason, and ask, "May I start over?" I always say, "Please do." These are not black marks. Neither is nervousness—short of terror. Nerves just mean the actor cares, and God save us from the actor who is too "laid-back" to care.

When actors seem terribly nervous and yet possibly worthwhile, I remind them that "the theatre is a very small world, and that this is not a crucial moment but simply the first time we have met and have worked together—for an audition is part of the work. Today our work will be very brief; soon it may be for the longer span of a rehearsal period. Still, it is all just work—the beginning of a working relationship. It may continue with this play or resume later with another play." Actors too often get caught up by the feeling that an audition means either total acceptance or total rejection. The director can help dilute this tendency.

The Director's Reaction.   If, at the end of the audition, the actor has created a positive impression, the director may choose one of several things to say. The simplest is, "Thank you, that was very good. You'll be hearing from us." The actor will expect to be called back, and he'll leave happy. The director may, though, have some questions. Perhaps the actor's selection was so well done that it seemed "canned," or for other reasons you want to know more about his flexibility or how directable he may be. You can say, "Now, I'd like to try it again. What you did was good, and no doubt correct, but let's do something else, just for the hell of it." Then pick a very different approach, and ask him to try it. Hotspur, telling the King, "My liege, I did deny no prisoners . . ." (*Henry IV, Part One,* Act I, scene 3) is usually angry, hotly protesting. He could, however, be genially asking, in a man-to-man way, "What would *you* have done?" Get him to try it "the other way." One can even ask for a deliberately "incorrect" interpretation, to see if the actor can unbend enough to bring it off. Juliet's horrid imaginings before taking the potion *could* be done as a series of increasingly funny notions. Can the actress detach herself from her preconceptions? Macbeth, instead of being amazed and mesmerized at the appearance of the "air-drawn dagger," could be scoffing incredulously at it. Encourage the actor to test the limits of your bold or outrageous choice if you want to assess his flexibility.

You will probably, after a successful audition, want to have that pleasant five-minute exchange of words with the actor (the beginning of "getting to know you") which you avoided by placing yourself in the center of the hall when he was brought in. If you do, you will help establish the cordial working relationship you'll need for the callback.

Some actors *expect* to be worked with at the audition. I only do it if they've sparked my interest. I remember a young lady some years ago who was sent a script through her agent and given an appointment for a reading. (In New York, the burgeoning film or TV star sometimes has no prepared audition pieces.) Three times she called and changed her appointment. Finally she appeared. The reading began, and it soon became clear that she hadn't a thought in her head about the character—it was virtually a sight reading. I stopped her and said, "Miss X, you've had the script for two weeks now. I would have supposed you might have become a little familiar with it—might even have some ideas about her." "Oh, Mr. Vaughan," said she, "I want *you* to tell me what to do. I'm just an empty vessel. Fill me!" Rude thoughts occurred to me, and perhaps she meant them to, but all I really could say to her was, "I know what I can do; this meeting was for you to show me what *you* can do. You did. No vessel-filling today. Thank you." She left, and I made sure her agent was informed that she had come in totally unprepared.

If the actor has not succeeded with his audition, and you know why and feel moved to help by telling him—don't! A pleasant "thank you" hints what needs to be hinted, but if you say directly to the actor, "That didn't work, and I'll tell you why, for the future," the actor will only hear that he has failed. Your well-meaning advice will be lost on him—drowned in his feelings of defeat. If you feel strongly about helping him, call him in later to give him your advice—he'll see that as a compliment and no doubt will learn something. At the end of the audition, all you can do is let him down gently and get on with the next person.

There is a phenomenon about casting that protects the actor, at least where I'm concerned. In New York, one may see five hundred actors for one play, and I find that if someone is competent but simply "not right" I just forget them. There is no way an actor can "blot his copybook" except by behaving badly or being an "empty vessel." I may remember meeting the actor, if reminded, but the slate is always clean for a good impression to be made as each new role comes along.

CALLBACKS

The callback is the next step in the casting process. I follow the same appointment procedure, with the same stack of pictures and résumés and the same kind of note taking, except that I usually allow fifteen or twenty minutes per actor this time. Also, the second time around, I usually want to hear readings from the script. One makes sure the actors have access to the script and know what scenes to look at. If the character has several phases, it is good to ask the actor to look at scenes representative of these various qualities. Someone will be on hand to read with the actors. That someone will be instructed to sit or stand well downstage, so that the actor auditioning is the one we watch. The director may want the actors to sit, stand, or roam about at will. Whatever makes them comfortable is usually all right with me. Not only acting, but aspects like height, weight, coloring, and vocal quality are important at this juncture, for the director is beginning to find, not just which actors are right for the play, but which actors are right for each other. At this time, a bit of work with each actor *is* important. If someone is missing an element in the scene, help them out. "Go back. Let's try it this way." Suggest the right intention or tone if they are going in the wrong direction. Don't hesitate to give them every hint as to how you see the role. This is particularly important for those you will want to see for the final callback, because they can take your ideas home and come back next time with a deeper idea of the part.

Special Skills, Special Problems.   Sometimes a role will demand special skills, such as singing. Hear them sing. Dancing? See the actor dance, or at least move. Fencing? Get a sense of it. For my sins, I "directed" (that was my title—director) Douglas Fairbanks, Jr., in an evening of Thurber sketches assembled into a musical revue and called *Out on a Limb*. He wanted to insert a vignette of the famous cartoon captioned "Touché!" in which one duelist has just decapitated the other one. I said, "Fine. I can choreograph it," happy to draw on my thirty years of fencing. "No, no, old boy," said he. "I'll do my own. All those films, you know. Coached by Dick Caven." "Good, good," I agreed. So we had some weapons brought to the rehearsal hall. The moment he picked up an épée, I knew he had never had a serious fencing lesson in his life. All the decent fencing in those films must have been done by doubles. Recently, glimpsing a tight shot from the rear of some terrible swordplay from a film on TV, I said to my wife, "I think that's Fairbanks." Next shot, a close-up from the front—sure enough, there he was, whacking away at the other fellow's sword with all the science of a guy beating a rug. The story goes that a whole musical version of *The Corn Is Green* was created on the premise that Bette Davis, who was the star, could sing—but nobody involved had the guts to ask to *hear* her sing, and then they found out, too late, that she couldn't. End of musical. See them fence, ask them to dance, hear them sing, make them play the piano. I believed an actress who said she could play the piano, and I organized a set of scene changes around her going to the instrument several times to play a few bars. Oh, she really could play—but it turned out that she was seized by debilitating stage fright the moment she sat down in front of the keyboard. Accept no excuses—make them do it, whatever it is.

Check them out, too, for ailments—bad backs and trick knees come to mind. If there are things to lift, Cordelias to carry, smoking required by the text—be quite clear about it so you aren't surprised by, "Oh, I can't do *that*!" Fear of heights may come between you and your desire to have your leading lady picked out by a pin-spot on a tiny platform twenty-five feet above the stage. I cast myself as Oberon and then let the designer sell me on being lowered from the flies for my first entrance. We played it for fifty performances and my heart was in my mouth every time they dropped me in—but at any rate, I had only myself to blame. If nudity will be required, say so up front, so to speak. Surprise not the actor with unexpected demands, lest you yourself be surprised!

FINAL CALLBACKS

Generally speaking, a second callback is all that will be needed. By that time, it may be that you have reached a decision about one or more of the actors. It may prove helpful to have those actors you are sure of read with those you are still considering. At this point, the chemistry of people together may be the deciding factor. In any case, by the third callback, you will probably have eliminated all but two or three people for each role. Some you will want to work with a little more, some you will want to talk to, to know them better. Some you will simply want to be reminded of, once again. At the third callback, I use the script to read from, but I ask the actors to prepare a new set of scenes, so that I can see them in yet other aspects of the roles.

CHOOSING

Now comes the moment of choice. You may want to make *pro* and *con* lists—those qualities each has in his favor, against those qualities that are negative. You may, on the other hand, have arrived at strong, intuitive choices for certain roles. My best advice is, once you have chosen, be prepared with alternates. Even now, something can happen to take your final choice out of the running. For example, would you believe falling off a horse and breaking both legs? It happened. And it will probably not be a simple matter of just moving up the alternate, but of shifting people around. "He isn't available to play Y. My next best actor is already cast as X, so I'll have to move him into Y, and that moves the guy playing Z into X, so who plays Z? Back to the drawing board!"

There is another kind of casting pitfall ahead, too. Axiom: the larger the cast and the less professional the production, the more cast changes you can anticipate during rehearsals among the smaller parts. When people are being paid, it seems to hold their allegiance, but university and community casts suffer serious attrition among the attendants and soldiers. Illness and fading interest strike hardest among those who have the least to do. In other words, keep your audition lists around; you'll be needing them.

What about casting understudies? Professional productions (Equity) are required to have them. In nonprofessional productions, finding someone who can carry the show with a minimum of rehearsals is often impossible. A long run (several weeks or more) means the chance of illness is greater, and, in the case of productions involving hazardous physical activity, the chance of accident looms larger. I would be guided, in the matter of providing understudies, by my best judgment as to length of run versus the difficulty of the role.

The final step in the casting process is posting the cast list, with a request for initialed acceptance, or phoning actors or their agents to make offers of the roles. In the professional theatre, unless everyone knows the salary level up front, this is the signal for some negotiating about pay, billing, and other variables. These negotiations are conducted by people on the management side of the theatre, and even if the director is involved on the business side as well, it is advisable that third parties conduct discussions about business matters. The director and actors must remain artists together, in spite of business details that may still be under discussion.

Not until contracts are signed and acceptances are received can the director be sure that the play is at last cast.

EXERCISES

1. Page 114— Are the parts interchangeable in *Godot*? Do they require types? If so, what are they? List the qualities of the characters that you wish to emphasize in production. How do those qualities relate to the actors that you know? Are you bound by the text and by your interpretation to cast four men in the roles? Defend or attack the idea of "nontraditional" casting for *Godot*.

2. Page 113—Consider the following casting options for the role of Vladimir: an actor who is extremely talented but because of a prior commitment must miss the first week of rehearsal (the entire rehearsal period is five weeks); an actor who is not as talented as the first actor but whom you know to be extremely dedicated; an actor who looked very good at the audition but whom you have never seen before. The other roles are already cast in your mind. Choose one of the options above to complete your cast, or suggest an alternative. Rationalize your decision.

3. Page 123—In a callback situation, what scenes would you choose to read from the script of the play? Is that important to you? How would you maximize your time in order to get the best results? What else might you elect to do besides reading from the script? What does reading actually reveal? Based upon your experiences, what are the limits of an audition experience? As a director, how do you interpret and make allowances for the necessary limitations? How do you improve your chances of casting the right person for the role? Compare the theatrical audition to the job interview experience. How might your experiences as a job applicant aid you as a director?

4. Page 124—A recent New York production of *Godot* at Lincoln Center featured Robin Williams, Steve Martin, F. Murray Abraham, and Bill Irwin. What type of production did this casting guarantee? Cast an ideal production of your own and assume that budget is no concern. Then, cast your production among your peers. How do the two cast lists correspond?

PEER GYNT
Schauspielhaus Düsseldorf, 1985
Here, note the striking use of distance, level, and paths of alternate light and dark to
create a sense of emotional remoteness.
Photo courtesy of German Information Center

CHAPTER 7

STAGING

Two columns of the director's promptbook are filled before assembling the design team and bringing the production scheme to life. Filling those two columns—the intentions and the adjustments—completes the analysis of the play's internals, and that helps, too, with making the casting decisions. After the play is cast and the ground plan is designed, one can work with confidence on the externals—the activities, the actual blocking and staging of the piece—with the actors in mind who will be executing that staging.

The design of the set—where doors and stairs are, where furniture is, where the actors sit down, the nature of the space they have to move in—in large measure determines the outline of the staging, with moment-to-moment decisions left to be made about the positions and moves throughout the play. Should all this be pre-blocked—worked out by the director in advance—or should the staging, within the limits already imposed by the scene design, be worked out only in rehearsal in collaboration with the actors?

TO PRE-BLOCK OR NOT TO PRE-BLOCK?

One can certainly come to rehearsals with only the first two columns worked out (the internals) and the set designed. The cast and director together can then work through the script, trying this and that, until they arrive at a staging that pleases them. I must say that I usually come to rehearsal with the main physical action worked out in advance. Both methods can produce satisfactory productions. Anybody with the visualization skills to pre-block is certainly capable of improvising workable movement in consultation with the actors. However, each time I have been forced, for lack of time, to come to rehearsal without a detailed plan for the staging, I have felt at a disadvantage. I prefer to work out the blocking in advance for the following reasons:

1. It gives me a chance to test the effectiveness of scenic and furniture decisions without at the same time having to orchestrate the personal dynamics of the actors' team effort. One's study is a neutral atmosphere.

2. I can make decisions (always subject to change) without having to deal with individual actors' egos. Accepting or rejecting actor suggestions always involves the parental "no" or "yes"—with attendant consequences.

3. I can avoid the whole question of whether the actor "feels" like moving—or sitting, or standing, or kneeling—and see first what is right for the *play*.

4. I can save the actors' time by working things out ahead of time. Instead of spending a week putting the play on its feet, I can have a walkthrough in two days.

5. I can help the physical departments work efficiently, in that achieving an early run-through by means of pre-blocking enables them to anticipate problems in time to solve them.

6. Even though I have pre-blocked, I can always undo any movement decision, can always respond to any actor's needs, can always improvise something new. There is a notion that the director who pre-blocks deprives the actors of some of their chance to work collaboratively with him. I think all the actors are deprived of is their chance to see the director floundering.

My advice to the director taking on, early in his career, multiscened, large-cast plays or musicals, is: *Always* pre-block. As your experience grows, you may find that small-cast plays, or particular kinds of plays, respond very well to a more improvisational approach, or that you need the stimulus of the actors' presence more in the staging of certain kinds of plays. I do know that you will gradually find an answer to this question of "how much pre-blocking," tailored to your own mind and needs. In the beginning of one's career, though, becoming deft with the basic skills is all-important—the scales, the chords, the finger exercises, the arpeggios. The director's basic skills are exercised to the full in the rigorous and thorough preparation of the promptbook, pre-blocking included.

SOURCES OF MOVEMENT

From what does movement on the stage originate? From the same place every-thing else originates in the theatre—from the play you are doing! Staging should be created, not in pursuit of beauty, or excitement, or originality, or to keep things lively, but for the sake of supporting and enhancing the play's meaning, conflict, and progression.

Three slants on the movement question deserve mention here. Louis Jouvet, the great French actor-director (1887–1951), was fond of saying, "There's no such thing as staging!" This is from a man who designed sets and costumes meticulously for the plays he directed and starred in. He meant, "No physical effect is so precious that the play will go under if you can't achieve it. It is wrong for the director to cling tenaciously and against all odds to some particular bit of picturization when he can always invent another." The director wants the character to sit at a particular place in the speech. The actress tries, sincerely, to do it that way and is miserable and uncomfortable. For heaven's sake, let her try it as many ways as it takes until she finds a position in which she feels all right and which you find effective.

The second movement principle comes in a story told by my mentor Harold Clurman some years ago in class. I am reasonably sure names and facts are apocryphal, but the story itself has the ring of true theatre. David Belasco, famous American director-producer-playwright (1854–1931), is directing a scene from a Civil War drama in which the Union soldiers are about to shoot a young man as a Confederate spy. The heroine comes forward and cries, "Don't shoot!" Otis Skinner, famous American actor, is a guest at rehearsal. They run the scene. She cries, "Don't shoot!" Belasco says, "That's not strong enough—*that* wouldn't stop the soldiers from shooting. Again." She does it again. "No—not right. They'd just shoot him. Again!" And again, and again. Finally, Belasco shouts to the exhausted actress, "Yes, that's fine. I believed that. Do it again!" And she does. Belasco comes forward from the house with, "Well done. Break for lunch." As the cast left, Skinner joined Belasco in the aisle. "David, that was wonderful," he said. "You really got something grand from her. But—what would you have done if she just couldn't get it?" Belasco chuckled. "I'd have had her grab the flag from the soldiers and throw it over the boy," he said. "The soldiers wouldn't shoot the American flag!" Moral: There's always another way to skin your cat.

The third tidbit came from Clurman, too—during an acting class when no-body had a scene ready to show. After he finished being cross about our general laziness (the class included Colleen Dewhurst, Mildred Dunnock, Nina Foch, Vincent Gardenia, and Robert Loggia) he said, "Well, then I'll talk about directing *Tiger at the Gates*." This was the elegant Giraudoux play with Michael Redgrave that was then on Broadway, based on the Trojan Wars. Indeed, the

French title translates as *The Trojan War Will Not Take Place*. It is a witty, thought-provoking reworking of ancient material. Clurman talked about the classic basis of the play, its modern attitudes, the costumes, the language, the intelligence, the humor—and then said, "And this is why I decided the set shouldn't have any places for the actors to sit down!" I had seen the production, sensed that something was wrong, and now he'd told us. All the interesting and good things he'd said, including his complete sympathy with the author's attitude toward his sources (which was irreverent), revealed that the set should have had *loads* of places for the actors to sit down. Giraudoux's people shouldn't have been forced into "classic acting" postures, at odds with what they are saying. Their thought and language is modern, so their movement and bearing should be based on modern reality, not on the stage conventions of a bygone day.

Moral here: The director's intelligence must include choosing the right *theatrical* tools to send the message he wants to convey. All movement decisions originate from the play, but they must be based on a sound *theatrical* judgment of that play.

STORYTELLING THROUGH MOVEMENT AND PICTURES

Basic principle: If hundreds of uncaptioned still pictures were to be taken of the ideal production, each one of those pictures would embody, in composed images, the unique content and conflict of that particular moment in the play, and the play's basic story would be told without any dialogue.

As a director you must learn and control the art of storytelling through movement and pictures if you are to sustain audience involvement and understanding in the course of your production.

STAGING TERMS

Defining a few terms will help clarify the rest of this chapter.

Movement as used in the theatre generally means getting from place to place, or large actions like sitting, standing, or jumping.

Activity generally means the flow of human behavior accompanying life on the stage.

Independent activity means an ongoing task such as washing dishes or jumping rope that continues as the character is carrying out some other internal intention.

KING JOHN
New York Shakespeare Festival, 1988
Here are two kneeling figures, close together, in the midst of a great dark stage. King John
(Kevin Conway) is huddled at the foot of his throne as the Bastard (Jay O. Sanders) tries
to rally his courage. Note how the composition supports the nature of the scene.
Director: Stuart Vaughan.
Photo: George E. Joseph

Business usually refers to the specific use of particular props: lighting cigarettes, cleaning eyeglasses, loading a revolver.

Staging refers to all these, along with stage pictures, choreography, composition, etc.

Blocking has two usages: (a) It can refer to the basic positioning of actors
on the stage, as in, "The blocking was awkward," or "Writing down the
blocking comes after working out the internals." (b) It can also refer to the
process, as in, "We are blocking Act Two this morning." The terms *blocking*
and *staging* are used almost interchangeably.

Indeed, as I have complained before, our technical vocabulary as regards
the acting and directing crafts is woefully inexact, and it is apt to remain so
unless we appoint some commissar to lay down the law—an unlikely and unde-
sirable event.

FOCUS

Think of a production as existing, not just in space (on the stage, in its set, in the actors' movement) but in *time*—as a series of tiny segments of audience attention. As a director you must control and target that attention, during each of your moments of time, so that the story you want to tell gets told. The audience must collectively look where you want them to look and hear what you want them to hear, in a sequence you have selected, at a tempo you have chosen.

MOVEMENT VERSUS SPEECH

The first law of focus, stated simply, is that *audience attention goes first to that which moves*. If movement and speech are occurring simultaneously, the audience will attend more fully to what it is seeing than to what it is hearing. *Movement defeats speech*. It follows that we *listen* best during stillness. In film, the camera can come in on whatever the director wants to emphasize—a face, an eye. On the stage, such a "close-up" can be achieved only by keeping everything unmoving and still except the face we want the audience to watch. Lighting, of course, is a useful tool here, too.

Another law relating to focus is: *The important thing comes last*. The actor points at the door and says, "Go, never darken my door again." Gesture first, line last makes the *line* most important. Actor says, "Go, never darken my door again," and points at the door. Line first, gesture last makes the *gesture* most important. Actress holds filled glass out to guest and then says, "Please, have a glass of wine before you go." Here, the hospitable invitation—the line—is last and hence receives more importance than the gesture of offering the glass. If she says, "Please, have a glass of wine before you go," and *then* holds out the glass, the focus is immediately on the gesture. Will he take it? Why does she want him to take it? Is the wine poisoned?

This leads to a question the director must ask himself as he begins to stage: "Is this a listening play or a watching play?" In other words, the staging lays down the ground rules for audience attention—it conditions the audience toward the visual or the aural. In still other words, if you are doing a play of language that demands a high level of audience attention to what is said, hold down the amount of movement. If the play is a farce or melodrama depending upon a lot of physical activity, begin with and maintain a vivid barrage of stage business.

Look at the opening of *The Importance of Being Earnest*. Notice how from the first moment, the focus is on what is heard.

SCENE

*Morning room in ALGERNON'S flat in Half Moon Street. The
room is luxuriously and artistically furnished. The sound of a piano is
heard in the adjoining room. LANE is arranging afternoon tea on the
table, and after the music has ceased, ALGERNON enters.*

> Algernon: Did you hear what I was playing, Lane?
>
> Lane: I didn't think it polite to listen, sir.

In contrast, here is the opening of *The Happiest Days of Your Life*, a farce by
John Dighton. Notice how the focus is on what is seen:

SCENE

*When the CURTAIN rises the stage is empty. One side of the French
windows is open and the sun is shining brilliantly. The Common Room,
if not luxurious, looks bright and airy. After a moment the double doors
are barged open from outside and DICK TASSELL enters. He is a tall,
cheerful young man of about twenty-six, laden with a suitcase, a cricket
bag, a bag of golf clubs, a tennis racquet, and a net bag of tennis balls.
He staggers with all these to the table C. and drops everything on it. He
looks around with an air of resignation, then moves to the double doors
and calls.*

> Tassel: (calling).   Rainbow. (He *moves to the locker above the fire-
> place, opens it, and glances in. He is surprised and pleased at what
> he sees.*) Good Lord! (He *pulls out a dusty-looking mortar-board
> and gown. He blows the dust off the mortar-board, puts it on to
> avoid holding it, and starts to shake the gown.*)*

ACTING AND MOVEMENT

If the basis for movement, the kind of movement, and the amount of movement can be discerned from the play, the actual movements themselves arise
within the play from character—from the acting.

There are so many kinds of plays and so many different ways of mounting
them that, once again, your best preparation as a director is to arm yourself
with a battery of *questions* and *principles* that prod you toward creative answers
for each new set of problems.

---

*John Dighton, *The Happiest Days of Your Life* (London and New York: Samuel French, Ltd., 1951),
p. 1.

At *whom, or at what, can the actor look—and therefore speak*? One might respond, "Silly question—at an infinite number of places!" No, happily, the question doesn't have that many answers. There are *five* possible objects for the actor's (character's) attention.

1. His partner or partners in the scene—other characters on stage—speaking to them directly, looking them in the eye.

2. Himself, usually looking at the stage floor, or out a window, or into the fireplace, or at a side wall of the auditorium. A character can talk to himself this way even with other characters on stage.

3. An object, as at a pencil, or a book, or a picture on the wall, as if it were a partner in the scene. This, too, can happen with others on stage.

4. God, or the whole world, or the infinite, as in prayer or general defiance, usually looking up toward the auditorium ceiling, or into the flies over the stage, or toward the front lights from boxes or coves.

5. The audience, looking right at them in direct address.

In the presentational production, all five objects of attention can be put to use, and in the same speech. Take this soliloquy (*Hamlet*, Act III, scene 1):

Hamlet: (*To self, looking at floor*) To be or not to be:
(*to audience*) that is the question:
(*To self, looking at side wall*) Whether 'tis nobler in the mind (*Looking to other side of audience*) to suffer
The slings and arrows of outrageous fortune
Or (*drawing dagger, looking at it*) to take arms against a sea of troubles
And by opposing end them? (*To God, looking up*) To die, (*to self, eyes closed*) to sleep; (*to God again, looking up*)
No more—and by a sleep to say we end
The heartache and the thousand natural shocks
That flesh is heir to, (*to self, eyes closed*) 'tis a consummation
Devoutly to be wished. To die, to sleep; (*eyes open, head up slowly*)
To sleep: (*looking straight at audience*) perchance to dream: (*sweep audience with eyes*) ay, there's the rub: (*etc.*)

Or take this segment from a realistic play, to be presented representationally—Ibsen's *Ghosts*, in a version I adapted for The New Globe Theatre's production starring Kim Hunter. Note that in this representational production, speaking directly to the audience was out of bounds.

Pastor Manders: (*Looking at Mrs. Alving*) Now I must speak
to you, not (*looking down at briefcase on chair*) as your advisor

and business manager, (*to her again*) not as your friend from
childhood (*glancing around room*) and your late husband's
friend (*lifts head to look her in the eyes*) but as your priest,
exactly as I spoke to you at the turning point of your
life, when you had lost *your* way.

Mrs. Alving: (*Looking at and fingering the "advanced" book still
on the table*) What has the priest to say to me?

Pastor Manders: (*Drawing breath, to himself looking up to the
ceiling*) Let me first evoke some memories. (*To her again*)
It's a fitting moment. Tomorrow is the tenth anniversary
of your husband's death. (*Turning to look out the window towards the orphanage*) Tomorrow his memorial will be dedicated. (*Gesturing towards the orphanage*) Tomorrow I shall
speak to a gathering assembled to honor him. (*Turning his
gaze on her*) But today I must speak to you alone.

THE "HOW'S"

As with all aspects of the production, movement must submit to the questions
"why" and "how." In other words, *we must ask, "What is the character's intention in
looking, sitting, walking, running, etc.?" and then, "How does he do it?"* Well, the overall
intention for the given beat is well in hand, written in the promptbook, column
1: "to win her over," "to batter him into submission," "to tread water," "to
string him along," or whatever it is. The adjustments (promptbook, column 2)
have to do with carrying out the intention, word by word, phrase by phrase,
all keyed by number to segments of text. The activity (column 3), the subject
of this chapter, is derived from the adjustments.

There is an old but correct axiom about speaking: "The audience knows
that the actor has changed his thought *only* if he changes pitch." Its counterpart
in regard to movement is, "*The audience can see the actor's changes in intention and
adjustments only by changes in position, accompanied by changes in tempo and rhythm of
movement.*"

Here is an example of a common stage direction: "Juliet crosses center."
Crosses . . . let us presume—walks. Now, let us examine intention and adjustment through movement, using "walking." We cannot catalogue here every

kind of walking, but we can suggest the nature of the inquiry that must be made of every movement.

WALKING
  Toward something
    to take it away from someone
    to use it (as to sit on a chair)
    to examine it
    to read it
    to hide it
    to demonstrate it
    to break it (etc.)
  Toward someone
    to intimidate them
    to embrace them
    to greet them
    to speak confidentially
    to take them someplace
    to sit by them
    to show them something
    to stroke them (etc.)
  In what manner
    tentatively
    decisively
    pouncing
    creeping
    cautiously
    firmly
    stalking
    casually
    unconsciously
    sidling
    strolling
    unwillingly
    as if mesmerized, drawn (etc.)
  In what tempo
    rushing
    deliberately
    striding rapidly
    marching
    step by step, inexorably
    tiptoeing, slowly
    hastily (etc.)

Questions that define:

the movement (walking, running, sitting, kneeling, rising, lying down, etc.)

its object (person or thing)

in what manner it is to be done

in what tempo it is to be done

can be used to test, particularize, and enrich whatever physical tasks present themselves in the production. The director and the actors must always ask themselves: "He doesn't just do it—*why* does he do it, and *how* does he do it?"

BASIC COMPOSITION FOR THE PROSCENIUM STAGE

The proscenium stage is still the standard space in which plays are performed—actors at one end of a room, mounted up on a shelf, with spectators sitting in rows down the length of the room, all looking in one direction. Because the proscenium was invented to be a "picture frame," some of the compositional principles of the two-dimensional picture plane work for it. However, the stage has a dimension in space as well, so what the painter does with perspective, the director can do with actual distance and three-dimensional objects, as well as incorporating the painterly illusions when it seems appropriate.

TERMS FOR THE PORTIONS OF THE STAGE

The set of terms used to describe the stage's geography is in wide general use, at least for the English-speaking stage. R (right) means on the actor's right hand as he faces the audience. For the director, facing the stage, Stage Right (the actor's right) is to the *left*. This simple reversal has led, and will yet lead, to an endless number of directorial confusions: "Move a little to the left on that line—no, no, I mean *right—your* right." After forty-plus years of directing, I have stopped saying "right" or "left" and simply say, "Move *that* way a couple of steps," or "Go down there beside the chair on that line," avoiding the trap altogether. Anyway . . . left, thus, means the *actor's left*. Up means away from the audience, as in *upstage*, so identified because on the early proscenium stages, when perspective scenery was a new thing, the stage floor was built so that it actually sloped toward the audience, from back to front, making a more realistic vanishing point for the scene painter's drops. *Down*, then, means toward the audience, as in *downstage*. *Above* someone means upstage of them, and *below* means downstage of them. *Center* means just that, so *up center* and *down center* are self-explanatory. The various areas of the stage are abbreviated as follows:

DL means down in the (actor's) left-hand corner.

DR means down in the (actor's) right-hand corner.

UC means upstage center.

DC means downstage center.

DLC means down left center, and refers to a position downstage not in the center and not in the corner.

DRC means down right center, and refers to a position downstage not in the center and not in the corner.

ULC means upstage on the left side, not in the center and not in the corner.

URC means upstage on the right side, not in the center and not in the corner.

Figure 7.1 diagrams all this.

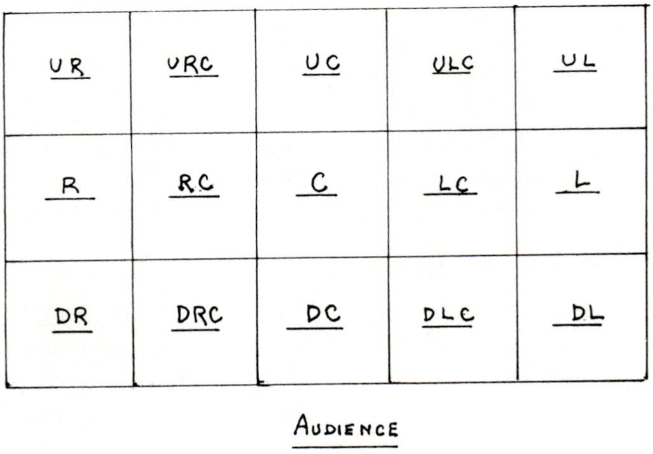

UR	URC	UC	ULC	UL
R	RC	C	LC	L
DR	DRC	DC	DLC	DL

AUDIENCE

FIGURE 7.1

Thus, if the director says, "Move down right center on that line," the actor, wherever he is onstage, should understand where to end up.

DYNAMICS OF STAGE SPACE

Achieving emphasis and focus in the space and frame of the stage is an important part of the director's task. The stage itself has certain dynamics, relative strengths and weaknesses, which are there to be used. So too have the actors' spatial relations to each other within that space.

The relationship of upstage to downstage must be grasped. An actor in an upstage position is generally in a stronger (more emphatic) position than those downstage of him, who will have to turn away from the audience in order to face him. The farther upstage he is placed, the more the others will have to turn their backs to the audience. In the days of the old stock companies, with short rehearsal times and less directorial supervision, a "dirty trick of the trade" was to upstage the other actor in the scene—to move back slightly, in order to be more visible and make him turn his back. Realizing what was going on, the second actor would himself move back, and gradually the whole scene would work its way back against the back wall. Such practices have, alas, not wholly died out.

Diagram of "upstaging"

Figure 7.2

When the actors are *sharing* the scene equally, they are standing level with each other, as in Figure 7.3. Neither is stronger, if they are center stage.

Diagram of *sharing*

Figure 7.3

The Royal Game
The New Globe Theatre/NIU Theatre, 1978
These actors (J. Kenneth Campbell as Henry VII and Patricia Falkenhain as Dowager Queen Elizabeth) are sharing the scene equally, but the positions in relation to the trunk make for a strong composition. Written and directed by Stuart Vaughan.
Photo: Northern Illinois University/Barry Stark

Note, however, that in a proscenium house, the *sharing* position cannot be achieved, away from the center, by having the actors stand in a straight line, as in Figure 7.4.

Diagram of *straight line*

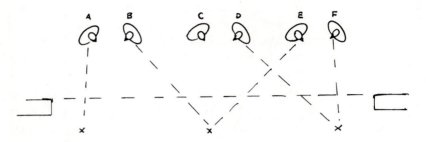

FIGURE 7.4

In A–B, for most of the audience, A is most visible.

In C–D, for most of the audience, both are equally visible, because they are center.

In E–F, for most of the audience, F is most visible.

So, in terms of *sharing*, think of the proscenium line as a curve. (See Figure 7.5.)

Diagram of "curve"

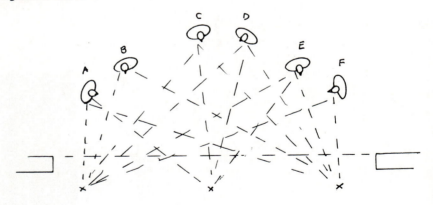

FIGURE 7.5

Now, in each set of actors, both participants share the scene.

To *share* a "two-scene" (a scene between two characters), follow the "curve" diagram. To *give* the scene to one of the characters, follow the "straight line" diagram, and be sure the one you want to "give" the scene to is on the *offstage* side (toward the wings, not the center). It follows that when your pair is in the center, the one to whom the scene is to be given must be, to some degree, upstage.

When an actor, standing on one side of the center line, must play an important speech to a partner on the same side of the stage but farther toward the wings, the actor with the important speech, to be seen, must be quite far upstage of his partner (Figure 7.6).

Diagram

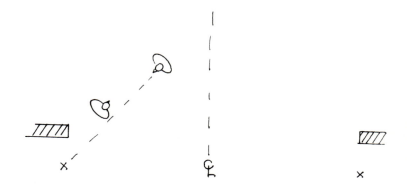

FIGURE 7.6

If the actor with the important speech must play it to a partner on the same side of the center line, but nearer to the center, then the partner with the important speech must be, while still upstage, careful that sight lines to the opposite side of the house are clear, as in Figure 7.7.

Diagram

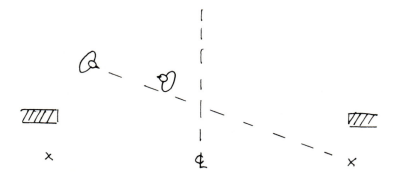

FIGURE 7.7

All this becomes simpler (not necessarily better) when the partners are on opposite sides of the center line, as in Figure 7.8.

Diagram

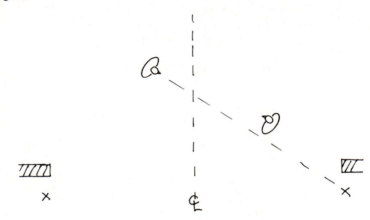

FIGURE 7.8

Remember, in these discussions, we are dealing with, not good choices versus bad choices, but the basis for making movement and visual choices.

RELATIVE STRENGTH OF ACTOR POSITIONS

The actor's relative strength, in terms of visibility, can be affected, in addition to his upstage–downstage adjustment, by his position on his own axis—by how much of himself he turns toward the audience. The available positions, with their relative strengths, are shown in Figure 7.9.

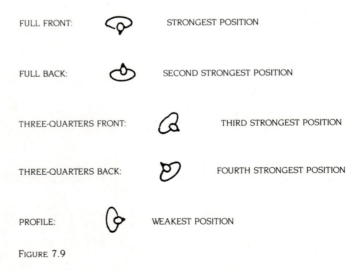

FULL FRONT: STRONGEST POSITION

FULL BACK: SECOND STRONGEST POSITION

THREE-QUARTERS FRONT: THIRD STRONGEST POSITION

THREE-QUARTERS BACK: FOURTH STRONGEST POSITION

PROFILE: WEAKEST POSITION

FIGURE 7.9

KING JOHN
New York Shakespeare Festival, 1988
Constance (Mariette Hartley) gets focus here because she is on a level above King John (Kevin Conway), because she is well SR of him and both are SR of center, and because she is full-front and he profile. Director: Stuart Vaughan.
Photo: © 1991 *Martha Swope*

Emphasis can also be achieved by judicious use of *level*—body position in relation to height. On a flat floor we have various levels available. (See Figure 7.10.)

FIGURE 7.10

OUR TOWN
Repertory Theatre, New Orleans, 1967
Focus and sharing in a conventional two-scene at a table. Dr. Gibbs (Herbert Nelson) is tactfully admonishing his son George (Michael Goodwin).
Director: Stuart Vaughan.
Photo: Frank Methe

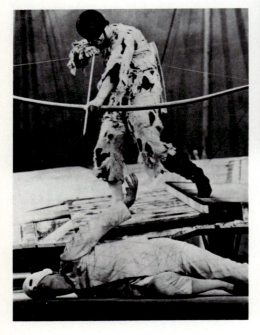

PHILOCTETES
Residenztheater, Munich
In Heiner Müller's adaptation of Sophocles' drama, the hero with his wonder bow stands over Odysseus. Note the masks and the commedia-like costumes. The photograph is printed here because of the strong use of the vertical figure of the archer and the interesting look of the drawn bow echoing the lying figure.
Photo courtesy German Information Center

One might think that standing is strongest and lying is weakest, but "it ain't necessarily so." See for example, Figure 7.11.

FIGURE 7.11

Here, the lying figure gets the focus.

THE LIFE OF GALILEO
North German Television, 1968
Director Egon Monk has staged this moment from
a televised version of Brecht's play just as he might
have for the theatre. This shows yet another
relationship between two figures and a table.
Photo courtesy of German Information Center

DEATH IN BERLIN
(Theatre not credited)
Still another strong relationship between
two figures, one sitting and the other
standing, both visible. Director:
Ernst Wendt.
Photo courtesy of German Information Center

Sitting would ordinarily seem weaker than standing, but in Figure 7.12 the sitting figure gets the focus.

FIGURE 7.12

DISTANCE BETWEEN ACTORS

In the stock companies of the nineteenth century, the old-time barnstorming stars would come in for an afternoon's rehearsal with the local company before playing that night in whatever vehicle, usually Shakespeare, the star was "out" in that season. Aside from quickly reviewing exits and entrances, for of course everyone had played in the play before, if not with each other, the star would usually say something to the company like, "Just keep at arm's length from me, one step downstage, look at me when I talk, and everything will be fine!"

These days we have a somewhat less rough-and-ready approach to the distance question.

DON CARLOS
Schiller Theater, Berlin, 1964
Distance is used here to create formality, along with a feeling of antagonism between the two men.
Photo courtesy of German Information Center

Try this experiment. Have two actors stand next to each other on the stage. You sit in the house, at various locations—close, middle, back. Ask them, for each location where you sit, to back slowly away from each other, on cue, one going to the right, the other to the left. Note at what point, for each location, your eyes must choose which one to stay with—the point at which you can no longer focus on both actors. When they are close you will be able to see them in a "two shot," but soon, as they move apart, you will follow one, and the other will become a blur.

Your directorial decision, in regard to distance, has to do with which actor you want the audience to see clearly at each given point. The effort the audience has to make when characters speak to each other from positions widely separated in space must be considered. To choose an extreme case: an argument between two characters, one placed DR and the other placed DL, means the audience will be able to see only one of them at a time, probably the speaker, so their attention will be split, like spectators at a tennis match who turn their heads from player to player at each shot. David Hare, directing his own interesting play *Secret Rapture* in New York, consistently placed speakers ten and fifteen feet apart, breaking what would seem to be a fairly realistic and seriously thoughtful play about the nature of love into a series of set speeches, like a staged Socratic dialogue. Once again, the question is not about what's bad or good—the question is, what effect do you *want* to create? Hare had made an artistic choice. Was it the *right* choice? Here we have only good taste to guide us. "There's no accounting for taste," said Mrs. O'Leary as she kissed her cow. With a wider range of choice and more experience of the world, *would* Mrs. O'Leary have kissed her cow? Ah, this is why textbooks are written and perhaps read and digested.

The degree of distance one wants between actors is affected by the size and conformation of the theatre itself. In a tiny house with a twenty-foot opening, two people standing side by side in close contact (not embracing) can look comfortable. In a huge theatre, two people at the same close quarters would look silly and crowded (unless they were embracing.) See Figure 7.13.

Diagram

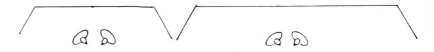

Figure 7.13

See how the various distances represented in Figure 7.14 strike you in theatres with proscenium openings of different widths.

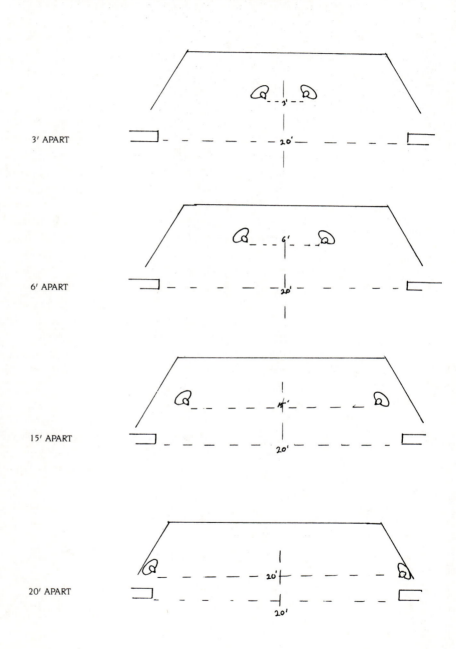

3′ APART

6′ APART

15′ APART

20′ APART

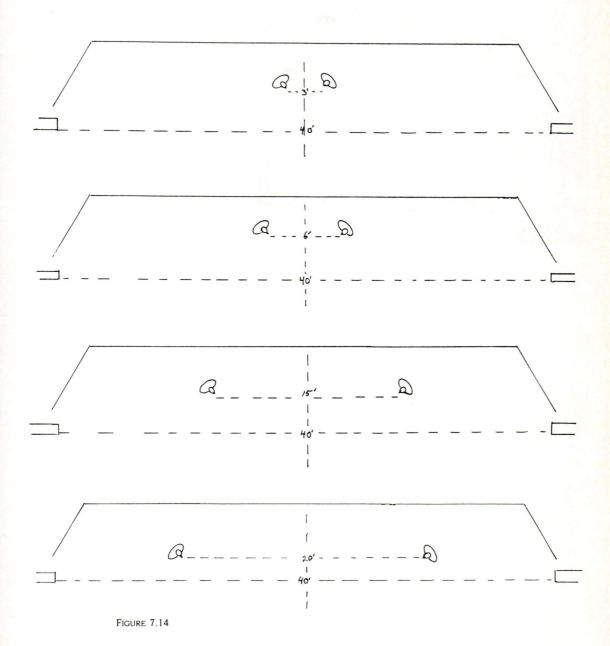

FIGURE 7.14

149

THE RIVALS
Repertory Theatre, New Orleans, 1967
Bob Acres (Don Perkins) admires his new
clothes, with the approval of Sir Lucius
O'Trigger (Dillon Evans). As staged, both
actors can be seen with maximum effect.
Director: Stuart Vaughan.
Photo: Frank Methe

Note, in passing, that the wider the stage and consequently the wider the audience seating area and sight lines, the more difficult it becomes to see both people when two people stand very close to converse.

On the vertical plane, with one person upstage and the other down, the audience can see both people in the same "shot," as in Figure 7.15, so long as the person downstage is not "covering" or "blocking" his partner too severely.

FIGURE 7.15

Underlying all this discussion of actor placement is the premise that every spectator should have a clear and unobstructed view of the action and of the actors, even though all seats are not equidistant from the stage. When such a clear view is impossible, as on a thrust stage where the audience sits on three sides or an arena stage where they sit on four sides, the actors must be kept in motion so no actor is blocked from view for more than a moment at a time from any seat.

Theater für Kinder, Berlin, 1978
In a "theatre in the round" situation, here is a vital solution to keeping everyone in the
scene visible.
Photo courtesy German Information Center

THE TWO GENTLEMEN OF VERONA
New York Shakespeare
Festival, 1987
Sylvia (Deborah Rush) confides in
Sir Eglamour (James Lally) from
her balcony. Besides ilustrating an
effective use of verticality, this
picture gives a good idea of
Robert Shaw's delicate and
decorative permanent set.
Director: Stuart Vaughan.
Photo: © 1991 Martha Swope

The deeper the set (the greater the distance from the front of the stage to the back wall of the set) the more advantageous it is to have rising levels upstage, either employing steps and platforms, Shakespearean upper level, or "inner above," or using a raked stage floor (sloping from high at the back to low at the front.) (See Figure 7.16.)

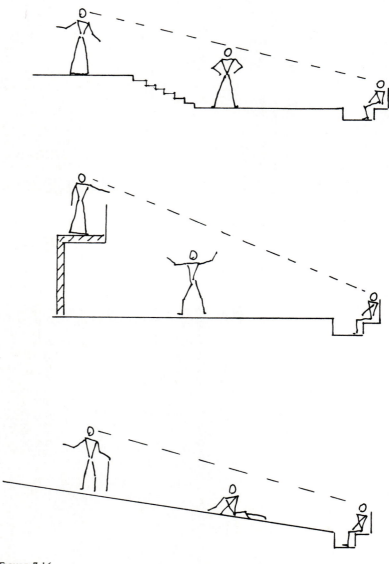

FIGURE 7.16

In interior settings with furniture, some raised areas of floor, the presence of stair landings and balconies, and the relationship between standing and sitting figures provide a variety of levels that can assist in maintaining clear sight lines, as the examples in Figure 7.17 demonstrate.

A. SOFA

B. CHAIR & FLOOR

C. FIGURE ON PLATFORM

D. ENTRANCE FROM
   SHORT STAIRWAY

FIGURE 7.17

CANDIDA
The New Globe Theatre
Prossy (Anne Thompson) is shocked by the outspoken
frankness of Marchbanks (Michael Arabian). Here is a
typical use of the behind-the-sofa position in
performance. Director: Stuart Vaughan.
Photo: *Northern Illinois University/Barry Stark*

JULIUS CAESAR
New York Shakespeare Festival, 1988
Marc Antony (Al Pacino) addresses the "mob" over
the body of Caesar (John McMartin). Levels, distance,
intense side- and down-lighting, and the two white
togas (Caesar and Antony), help to achieve focus in
this composition. The "mob" (as large as the budget
would allow) carried off into the "voms" at the side
and to some extent across the front, so that their
silhouettes would blend into the theatre audience.
Director: Stuart Vaughan.
Photo: *George E. Joseph*

GROUPINGS

When more than two people are on the stage, the director's means of telling stories through pictures become more elaborate. We should never, of course, be simply in pursuit of beauty, though something beautiful may, in passing, indeed be achieved; we must unceasingly try to embody the conflict of each particular moment in each particular play in a vivid and exciting and forceful composition. There are pictorial clichés of the stage that are often appropriate but always boring because we have seen them so many times. They don't express any particular moment or any particular play. Figure 7.18 shows one that comes to mind:

FIGURE 7.18

Note the semicircle, with equal distance between its members. The central figure, in this all-purpose configuration, could be dancing, saying a speech, singing . . . oh, he or she might even from time to time address a chorus member, or walk back and forth. In a situation like this, the director should strive to create relationships between members of the group surrounding a principal. This opens up possibilities for interesting, story-supportive staging. Immediately, members of the on-stage audience will have at least two directions in which to relate: the principal, and their immediate partners. Figure 7.19 shows what I mean:

FIGURE 7.19

THE ROYAL GAME
The New Globe Theatre/NIU
Elizabeth of York (Sharon Laughlin) fails to identify Dickon (Mark Cheney) as her missing
brother. Here the two watching figures complete the triangle and point up this crucial
moment in the play. Written and directed by Stuart Vaughan.
Photo: Northern Illinois University/Barry Stark

In addition, having broken the on-stage audience into small groups, the groups
themselves may interrelate, with some individuals perhaps moving from group
to group.

Figure 7.20 offers another staging cliché.

FIGURE 7.20

We can see that someone is cross with someone else and that perhaps a fight
is about to break out. Or maybe they are making peace. Or maybe they are
about to start a basketball game. There is an equal number of people on each
side, and on each side everyone is looking at the opposite side. Boring. They
are standing equidistant from each other. Boring. Most people are in profile.
Weak—and boring.

But, in Figure 7.21, see what happens.

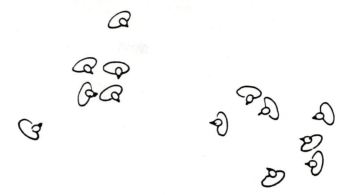

FIGURE 7.21

This group accomplishes the same task, but provides everyone with more to do in the scene. It is visually more interesting. The greater tension in the staging provides stronger focus on the principles, and a story emerges.

This arrangement points up an important principle: Sharing a scene equally between characters or groups should not often take place. Compositional storytelling works better when there is one major center of interest, with secondary and tertiary centers, each supported by groupings designed to give them the proper degree of focus. The major center of interest can then be shifted, by changing the picture, as another character begins to lead the scene. "Share" by giving your principals an appropriate amount of time as the center of interest, rather than always sharing the center of interest between them.

Now, in Figure 7.22 we have a cliché Shakespearean throne room.

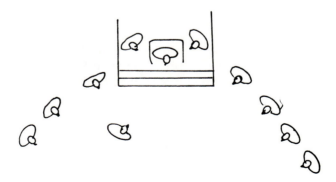

FIGURE 7.22

This is a variation of the "chorus and principal" conformation with which this section started. However, this is a king, with guards, courtiers, and a messenger, or Sir Walter Blount. Poor messenger or Sir Walter—the king has all the focus. Oh, it probably looks fine—banners, windows, shafts of light, maybe a crowd of costumed and salaried Equity members. But the only person who can act in this scene without "cheating down" (standing in a phony position so the audience can see his face) is the king.

In *Henry IV, Part One*, Act I, scene 3, Hotspur, speaking to King Henry, defends his actions after a recent battle in flouting the king's messenger. If the king were placed upstage, Hotspur's speech, the best speech in the scene, would be spoken toward the back wall. This scene, like most throne scenes, would benefit from placing the throne at the side. Indeed, I placed the scene in a room without a throne, giving the king emphasis by having him the only one seated, but at the side, so Hotspur could take stage with his speech. (See Figure 7.23.)

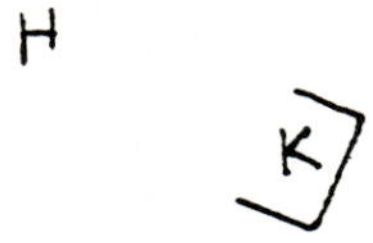

Figure 7.23

After the speech, Hotspur was brought downstage, and the king could rise and move to the center when needed. (See Figure 7.24.)

Figure 7.24

Or, take the coronation of Richard III, in Act IV, scene 2. The balance of the scene consists of Richard speaking confidentially to people who approach the throne, punctuated with several public pronouncements. If the throne were to be placed up center, Richard could come downstage for his confidential chats, but a recently crowned king, and particularly this one, just wouldn't. With an up center throne, the confidential chats must be loud, and the assembled court would have a difficult time convincing the audience that they could not overhear. In the 1970 Central Park production, part of the three-play *Wars of the Roses* repertory, I put Donald Madden, as Richard, on a dais five feet tall, down right center, facing three-quarters upstage. Those with whom the king spoke confidentially came down to the downstage sides of the throne. The

king, in turning toward them, faced downstage, and in this way the audience received the full benefit of conversations successfully kept from the court. (See Figure 7.25.)

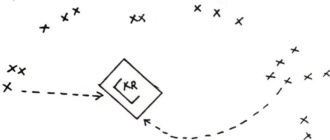

FIGURE 7.25

This worked for the acting and was visually arresting.

Plays set in realistic interiors have their clichés too. Figure 7.26 gives an example.

FIGURE 7.26

The furniture here is conventionally placed for the drawing room play. Are they having tea? Plotting a murder? Dividing up the spoils? Discussing a divorce?

Possibly. Neither furniture placement nor character relationship suggests anything *particular*. All is merely appropriate and conventional. In addition, the furniture arrangement allows for little variety of actor placement.

Figure 7.27 shows a formal furniture arrangement for a formal room that at least provides opportunities for a variety of relationships.

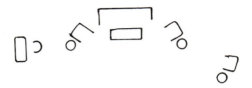

FIGURE 7.27

The placement of doors and windows around such a seating arrangement provides variety in traffic patterns.

Unidentified Play by George Tabori
This irresistible picture is a wonderful demonstration of how the most conventional furniture placement (a downstage center park bench) can be used to delicious effect.
Photo courtesy German Information Center

Figure 7.28 shows a less symmetrical furniture placement offering other interesting possibilities for actor placement.

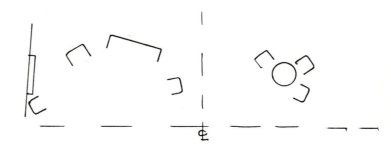

FIGURE 7.28

Straight lines on the stage are to be avoided. (See Figure 7.29.)

FIGURE 7.29

The actors cannot see and address each other, emphasis is impossible, and moving to another place in the group is awkward.

Semicircles are boring, as noted earlier.

But the *triangle*—the triangle is the stuff of which good pictures and movement are made. Figure 7.30 shows a variety of ways in which triangles may be used for emphasis in staging.

Take a simple triangle:

FIGURE 7.30a

A has focus—A is leading the scene. Then A crosses, and now we have:

FIGURE 7.30b

B is now emphasized. Then A turns, and:

FIGURE 7.30c

C is emphasized. Perhaps then, A crosses again, from L to R, turning to face them; and C moves in:

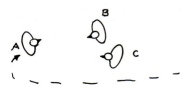

FIGURE 7.30d

B and C have joined forces against A.

KING JOHN
New York Shakespeare Festival, 1988
Cardinal Pandulph (Moses Gunn) tries to
impose the will of the church on King John
(Kevin Conway) and King Philip of France
(Richard Venture). A triangle! Director:
Stuart Vaughan.
Photo: George E. Joseph

DIE KATACOMBE
Theater für Kinder, Frankfurt, 1978
Yet another triangle—this time with an
interesting prop.
Photo courtesy German Information Center

CHARLEY'S AUNT
Repertory Theatre, New Orleans, 1966
Charley (Rex Thompson) and Jack (R. Scott
Thomas) capture Fancourt (Steve Perry).
Another triangle! Director: Stuart Vaughan.
Photo: Frank Methe

163

There are triangles and triangles (Figure 7.31).

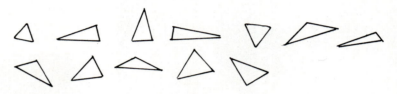

FIGURE 7.31

And they can all be turned inside out at will. Too, there can be satellite triangles *ad infinitum*, depending on cast size and the nature of the scene (Figure 7.32).

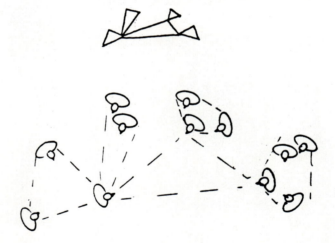

FIGURE 7.32

Now introduce *levels*, and begin to exploit triangles in the vertical plane, along with the lateral.

OUR TOWN
Repertory Theatre, New Orleans, 1967
Two triangles: the three ladies (Eugenia Rawls as Mrs. Gibbs, Jane Rose as Mrs. Soames, and Barbara MacMahon as Mrs. Webb) comprise one. The other triangle, inverted, is made up of the women in the center and George (Michael Goodwin) and Emily (Anne Thompson) at the upper corners. Director: Stuart Vaughan.
Photo: Frank Methe

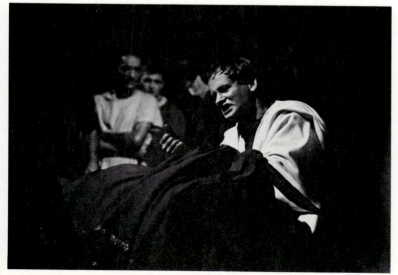

JULIUS CAESAR
New York Shakespeare Festival, 1959
Donald Madden (Marc Antony) is here seen over the body of Caesar, with a triangle of faces behind him. Stuart Vaughan directed. Madden later played Hamlet for The Phoenix Theatre under Vaughan's direction, for the longest run any American actor has yet had in the role. Alas, no pictures of that production are available.
Photo: George E. Joseph

165

SOME AXIOMS ABOUT MOVEMENT

1. No character should ever move on the stage without an internal reason.

2. Crosses *to* someone or something can be of any length, because the audience will easily understand the purpose of the move. "Internal" or "thinking" crosses, on phrases like, "Well, I don't know—" should be *short*, generally not more than three steps, or the audience will begin to lose what the character is doing.

3. The actor, when still, must be and seem ready and able to move at any moment; the moving actor must be and seem ready to stop at any moment.

4. Absolute stillness takes focus; avoid it unless focus is what is wanted. Unnecessary movement is attention-getting, and, if unnecessary, distracting.

5. The more verbal and poetic the play is, the more the actors' bodies should be positioned full-front. This permits them easily to look front and move forward as they discover the poetic images—talking to themselves, or to God, or the audience. Body full-front, the actor can always *look* toward his partner. In these plays, the verbal images come quickly, and full-front avoids moving the feet every time there is a change of thought.

6. Actors must not hang on to chairs, tables, skirts, swords, or other actors. Touch people or things only for genuine story purposes.

7. Kissing is not a spectator sport. *That* a kiss takes place advances the story. The *duration* of a long stage kiss is a stage wait—a pause in the action.

8. The actor should be encouraged to move a little as he begins to speak. This helps the audience know where to find the speaker.

9. "Gesture"—as in operatic, pictorial, balletic, oratorical—should be avoided. D*o* something, by all means—just "Do not saw the air too much with your hand, thus."

10. Don't let the audience wait in silence while someone crosses to a door. There is always an earlier line to cross on, so the exit line can be placed near the door.

11. Every time a character enters or leaves, all the characters on the stage must adjust their physical positions. With an arrival or departure, all existing relationships change.

RELATIVE STRENGTH OF STAGE AREAS

Most of the "do this; don't do that" rules of the stage relate to how audiences see and hear. The play, remember, happens in their minds and imaginations, not on the stage.

One element in audience attention has to do with where people generally look first. In Western societies, people read from left to right. Translated to the stage, this means audience eyes are accustomed to swinging from stage right to stage left. We look to our left for the beginning of signs, book pages, newspapers, billboards, the titles in foreign films, and so on. Then our eyes follow the message as it carries them to our right. Our expectations are conditioned to looking for things to start at our left and resolve on our right. Therefore it can be said, remembering that onstage we are talking about the *actor's* right and left, that down left center is the strongest place on the stage—the place toward which audience eyes, looking from *their* left to right, will tend.

JULIUS CAESAR
New York Shakespeare Festival, 1988
"The lightest light next to the darkest dark" occurs where Antony's shoulder meets the stripes on his costume and the cloak over Caesar's body. Antony—Al Pacino, Caesar—John McMartin. Director: Stuart Vaughan.
Photo: © 1991 *Martha Swope*

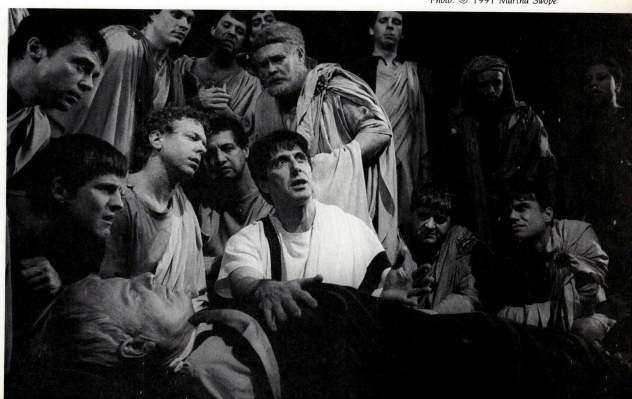

This observation may be of some use. There is a lot of other accepted lore that deserves challenge. In that generally valuable book, *Fundamentals of Play Directing,* by Alexander Dean and Lawrence Carra, the authors attempt to define the basic emotional tone of areas of the bare stage and what sort of scene should be played where. For example, down right is judged suitable for intimate love scenes and long stories, whereas down left is deemed better for conspiracies and business dealings.

In my view, such "mood values" depend entirely on level, furniture placement, door placement, and above all, on where the light is. No unlit area is as strong as a brightly lit one. Concentration of light will put the audience's attention where the director wants it, and the color and direction of the light will determine the mood of the scene. Even a scene played far upstage can seem intimate if the space between audience and actors is destroyed by making it a black void.

One "law" from the graphic arts will help you here: "The visual center of interest is where the lightest light meets the darkest dark." Remembering that concept will help you achieve strength and focus wherever you want it.

THE THIRD COLUMN IN THE PROMPTBOOK

The foregoing discussion of staging comes at this point in this book because that part of your preparation that involves working out the blocking in advance comes at this point in your work as a director—the last creative task before actual rehearsals.

The director's promptbook requires a form of blocking notation that parallels notations about intentions and adjustments with the text, across the page. What must be completed comprises a conductor's score, as for an orchestra, where all aspects of the work are spread before the director at one glance, as he takes in the page.

Some directors work out the blocking on a scale ground plan or model, moving scale figures about (toy soldiers, chessmen, cut-outs) to test the choreography. If you need or want that kind of visualization tool, fine. You still will have to record your decisions in a form that you can translate rapidly for transmission to your cast in the blocking rehearsals.

I offer here my own scheme for recording the blocking. It is not nearly as precise a tool as Laban-notation is for dance, but stage managers who master it can take down accurate blocking notes with it as fast as the play goes by. For the director, this method provides the time-saving, space-saving, precise-enough notes one needs to conduct an efficient rehearsal.

Sample pages from an actual promptbook are provided in Appendix B demonstrating the system's use in practice, but the basics of the system can be easily described.

Character identification: Just as in recording intentions and adjustments, I use the first initial of the character's name—H for Hamlet, C for Claudius, G for Gertrude, etc. When the author has inconveniently created two characters with the same first initial (Hamlet and Horatio), I abbreviate the less prominent of the two using the first two letters of his name—Ho for Horatio. Thus: for Orsino, O; for Olivia, Ol. For unnamed characters, before the roles are cast: for Soldiers, S1, S2, S3, etc. For Ladies, L1, L2, L3. Once the parts are cast, the actors' own first initials can be used.

In setting up a scene from *Hamlet*, the characters' positions might be indicated as in Figure 7.33.

FIGURE 7.33

When a character crosses from one place to another, an "x" is placed *over the word in the text* on which he moves. If there are other crosses in one speech, I would write "x1," "x2," "x3," etc. Take this example:

Ophelia: ^{x1} There's fennel for you, and columbines; there's ^{x2}
rue for you, and here's some for me; we may call it herb
of grace o' Sundays. O, you must wear your rue with a
difference. ^{x3} There's a daisy. I would give you some vio-
lets, but they wither'd all when my father died. They say
he made a good end,—

In the activities (third) column, the moves would be indicated as in Figure 7.34.

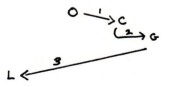

FIGURE 7.34

Furniture can be indicated as in Figure 7.35.

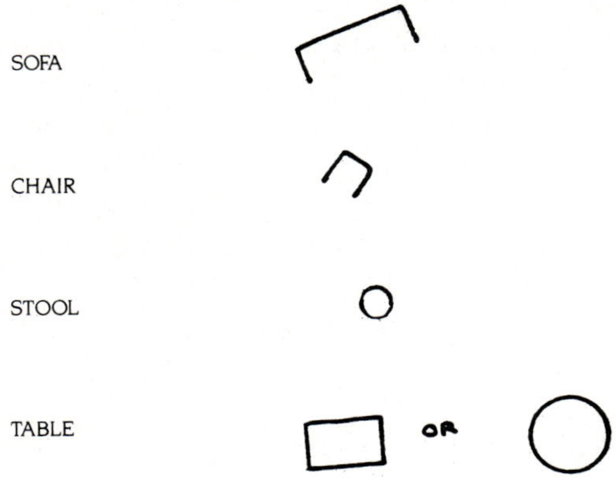

SOFA

CHAIR

STOOL

TABLE

FIGURE 7.35

If a character is sitting and rises to cross, over the operative word of text, I write "rx"

Oswald (Walks around the room):   Regina would have done it.

In the activities column this would be shown as in Figure 7.36.

FIGURE 7.36

Crossing to sit would be shown as in Figure 7.37.

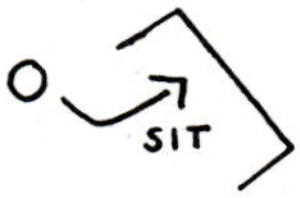

FIGURE 7.37

Crossing to put foot on bench would be shown as in Figure 7.38.

FIGURE 7.38

The entire set need not be shown for each notation. Say one is using a conventional "Stratford, Ontario" Shakespeare unit set which, in full, could be indicated as in Figure 7.39.

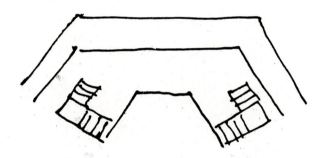

FIGURE 7.39

For someone coming downstairs on such a set, one need only use arrows, as in Figure 7.40. Other actions are represented in Figure 7.41.

FIGURE 7.40

FOR A CENTER ENTRANCE

AN ENTRANCE ABOVE

A CHASE AROUND A BENCH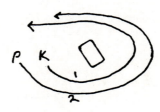

A MELODRAMATIC EMBRACE

DROPS HER

JUMPING OVER A BENCH

SITTING ON STEPS

THROUGH A DOOR

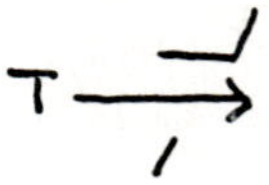

ENTERING, CLOSE DOOR

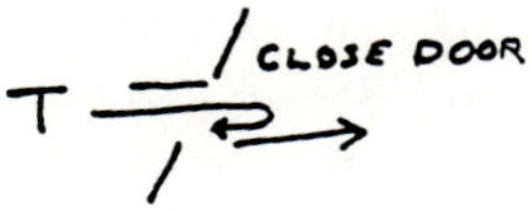

LEANING ON SOFA

SITTING ON FLOOR BY CHAIR

POSITIONS AT A TABLE

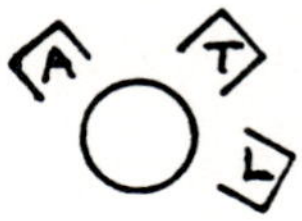

LEANING ON PROSCENIUM

FIGURE 7.41

Devise your own symbols and notations. It is unimportant whether anyone else can read them. They are *yours*, for your own use. Use mine, if you like. They work. As a Broadway assistant stage manager, I learned them from another stage manager. They were easy to learn, because they make sense. There is nothing obligatory about them; they are merely a useful personal shorthand.

You must remember, as you work through the movement of the play and record it in your promptbook, that each decision you make must be *chosen from among other possible moves and positions*. As Bertolt Brecht puts it, the character "says, not *this*, but *that*." Well, the character *does* not "this" but "that." Remember that you are not just visualizing movement but are *making selections*. You must use the areas of the stage with variety, not playing everything "down center," for example; not having the same two people always sitting or standing in the same way when they meet in the play. You must take full advantage of depth, distance, balance, level. Above all, you must remember that all decisions you make in your study can be unmade if they prove wrong on the stage. The director who prepares is always ahead of the director who does not prepare, even if the preparation is imperfect—as, indeed, it is bound to some extent to be.

And if, because of some time emergency—illness, change of schedule, a last-minute call to replace another director—you find yourself without time to work out the entire play in advance, you should work out whatever you can, for just getting started will aquaint you better with the spatial problems the set asks you to solve than if you were to arrive at rehearsal with no preparation at all. Time limitations should not change the director's *method* of work; they merely reduce the time for making choices.

EXERCISES

1. Page 130—Examine the opening pages of the play (prior to the entrance of Pozzo and Lucky). To what extent do the beats aid your efforts to stage the play? What does this breakdown tell you about relationships in this play? Assigning intentionality to dramatic character makes what assumption(s)?

2. Page 137—On pp. 46–47 of the Grove Press edition of *Godot*, there is a lengthy sequence of stage business concerning Lucky's hat. Will you be a "mechanic" who follows the directions and supplies a third eye for the actors and allows them to perform the actions cleanly; or will you, as director, flesh out Beckett's diagram to fulfill his meaning; or will you be an "artist" who creates something new and different but manages to convey the "spirit" of Beckett's directions? Which do you understand your job to be as director?

3. Page 137—If you will deviate from the explicit directions in the text, why not change the lines in the text as well? Aren't there a lot of expressions in the text that are difficult for an American audience to understand: knook, dudeen, Macon country and Cackon country, bullocksed. To whom are you responsible?

4. Page 137—Does a Beckett text present any special problems to you in your role as an editor?

5. Page 137—Write a policy statement concerning directorial editing of dramatic texts.

6. Page 166—What tool does a director forsake in any stage configuration other than a proscenium? How might a director compensate for this lack?

CHAPTER 8

JUST BEFORE REHEARSALS

Every Broadway producer who ever put together a show has probably at one time heaved a sigh of relief and said, "Well, I've raised the money, secured my stars, found a director, revised the script, got a designer, booked the theatre, found a cast—all that's left is just putting on the play!" Yes, that's all. In fact, that's all it's really about, and the producer's attitude, as described above, is one reason so many seemingly well-conceived projects go off the rails. The producer thought about everything but putting on the play.

The director who has followed a preparation scheme like the one outlined in this book still has some important steps to take before the play can actually be "put on."

A rehearsal schedule must be devised; light plots (for the designer), music plots (for the composer), costume plots (for the designer and the shop) and property plots (for the designer and the prop department) must be developed; and a stage manager and assistants must be engaged and put to work.

THE STAGE MANAGER

The stage manager is one of the most important members of the collaborative team, but we have not yet discussed his function. This job begins only at this point in the work. Equity stage managers go on salary one week before rehearsals begin. At that time, they help create the rehearsal schedule, organize prop lists, make contact sheets containing cast, staff, and management addresses and phone numbers, find rehearsal props, get rehearsal furniture together, and lay out the ground plan on the rehearsal room floor or the stage, whichever is to be used for rehearsals. Should the stage manager be available earlier, either as a permanent staff member or as a volunteer, the director can use him as the casting assistant who makes casting calls, posts lists, handles auditions, sets up callbacks, and handles all the other mechanical details of the casting process.

The stage manager is second-in-command to the director and is the person in charge when the director has completed rehearsals and later, during the run. The stage manager is the liaison person between director and designers, director and cast, cast and costume department, and between the director and all other departments: props, set construction, composer, sound, press, business management, and so on. The stage manager posts notices on the call board, distributes schedules, is in charge of company discipline (lateness, inattention, unnecessary noise, etc.). The stage manager also distributes technical information and rehearsal notes to the various departments, keeps track of any rehearsal overtime, is on top of union regulations, anticipates schedule conflicts, coordinates costume fittings with the rehearsal schedule, sets up photo calls and press interviews . . . does everything possible to make for the efficient organization of time, people, and space.

During rehearsals the stage manager and the assistants keep a record of the blocking and its changes and permutations, keep track of script changes, do the prompting of actors, stand in and read for any absent actors, maintain phone contact with cast members in case of lateness or illness, and run certain special rehearsals (fight scenes, line rehearsals, music rehearsals, dance calls) when the director is simultaneously rehearsing some other part of the show.

During performances, the stage manager calls the show. Either from backstage, or, more usually these days, from a booth at the back of the house, the stage manager is in head-set communication with the assistant stage managers backstage right and left, with the light board, with the sound operator, and with any operators of scenic effects, such as winches, curtains, tracks, travelers, flies, etc. Except in very few instances, every cue for every operation should be called by the stage manager, so that the timing of the show's separate elements is firmly in the control of one authoritative source.

When I started in the theatre, stage managers were people who wanted eventually to direct in their own right. Stage managing was a stepping-stone to a directing career. I think this was because "the road" and "the long run" were still mainstays of the Broadway theatre, the only significant professional theatre we had. During the long run and on the road, the director seldom appeared more often than once a month or so, and the artist-in-charge, the person who gave notes to stars and bit players alike to keep the show "up," was the stage manager, whose word was law. On Broadway, the stage manager still exercises this authority. "Keeping the show tight" is the stage manager's most important job, and this is a job that is directorial in nature.

More and more, however, in regional and nonprofessional theatres where the staff director remains in evidence, stage management falls to technicians, people who often have lighting design as a second string to their bow, since so much of calling a show has to do with our increasingly complex lighting coordination. These people can run the staff and call the show efficiently, but very often they are not actors, are not interested in acting, and are not skilled at prompting or keeping the actors "up." They may record the substance of the blocking clearly, but, not being actors or directors themselves, they may not comprehend the logic or spirit behind it. Thus, they may fail to remind actors of important details of movement, which can then be lost, or they may interrupt to correct unimportant variants from the directed pattern, which a directorial eye would evaluate correctly.

I would like to see stage managing restored to its position as an important step in director training. I urge you, as a would-be director, to spend a year or so stage managing (or assistant stage managing) under directors you respect. You will probably not be able to endure more than a season or so as a stage manager, but in that period you will, from a safe seat on the sidelines, learn a great deal. You can watch the interaction between director and cast and see what works and why. You can silently match wits with director and cast as they set about solving the play's problems. You will rarely be at the center of the artistic battles which can envelop director, producer, writer, designers, but you will be privy to them. You, almost alone, can remain objective. In fact, all sides may use your shoulder to cry on. You can, indeed, be an important and steadying influence, just by quietly employing those directorial skills of tact and encouragement which you will use far more visibly when you do your own directing. And I would urge any director, choosing a stage manager, to select an aspiring director, if one is available. Such a person will be of far more use and get much more from the experience than a "technician" stage manager. A flow of intense, interested energy from the stage management table can help actors and director feel that what they are doing is worthwhile and that someone cares.

THE SCENE BREAKDOWN

One of the first lists the director and stage manager must prepare is the scene breakdown. This is a chart showing which characters (and actors) are in each scene. The stage manager can work this up alone for a simple play without unspecified nonspeaking roles. With Shakespeare, however, or a big musical or outdoor drama, or any play demanding the deployment of soldiers, ladies, servants, guards, doubling, and other directorial inventions, the only source for this vital information is the director's prerehearsal blocking. The use of these forces *must* be defined by the director for the stage manager in advance so the right actors will be on hand for the right scenes at the right time, and so the right number of costumes can be designed and built for them.

Here is a sample scene breakdown:

THE TEMPEST
SCENE BREAKDOWN

I–1: Master, Bosun, Gonzalo, Alonso, Ferdinand, Trinculo, Stephano.

I–2: (a) Prospero, Mirando; (b) Prospero, Ariel, 2 Spirits (Mark, Will), Miranda, Caliban; (c) "Dumb Show": Prospero Double, Alonso, Gonzalo, Antonio, Adrian, Sebastian; (d) Ferdinand, Ariel, Miranda, Prospero.

II–1: Alonso, Sebastian, Adrian, Antonio, Gonzalo, Ariel.

II–2: Caliban, Trinculo, Stephano.

III–1: Prospero, Miranda, Ferdinand.

III–2: Caliban, Stephano, Trinculo, Ariel.

III–3: Gonzalo, Alonso, Sebastian, Antonio, Adrian, Prospero.

IV: All in show, including Spirits.

V: All in show, including Spirits.

THE COSTUME PLOT

From the scene breakdown, the director's costume plot can be easily derived. This plot tells the designer at a glance not only who is in what scene, but how many scenes separate a character's different appearances, or an actor's doubling, so that change time and changing problems can be estimated.

Such a costume plot, along with a costume list, for *King John* will be found in Appendix C, p. 335. It may not, at this early stage, be possible to include in the costume plot exactly what each character will be wearing in specific scenes, but such scenes as battle scenes, requiring armor, or coronation scenes or other ceremonial scenes, scenes requiring certain special garments such as outerwear or nightgowns—these can be indicated for the designer's information. The stage manager needs *director* input here; just reading the play will not reveal enough.

THE REHEARSAL SCHEDULE

Now, director and stage manager can turn to developing the most significant of these planning guides, the rehearsal schedule.

Margaret Webster, in her comments to the cast after the first reading of *The Strong Are Lonely*, said something that has been very useful to me over the years. "My schedule," she said, "—how I use my time, how much time I devote to each phase of rehearsal—is one of my most valuable tools. Please do your part in helping me keep to it. I mean, learn your words on schedule, be ready

A MIDSUMMER NIGHT'S DREAM
Schlossparktheater, Berlin
The director, Boleslav Barlog, clearly had a concept about Bottom's ass-head which the costume designer fulfilled. The transparent buckram let the actor's features be seen. More important, his voice could come through unimpeded. An elaborate and realistic mask usually makes Bottom sound as if he is speaking in a bucket. This doesn't help the jokes.
Photo courtesy German Information Center

to take each new phase in stride at its alloted time, and allow me to control the length of discussions."

My own period of rehearsal on a play breaks down into the following units:

1. Reading and discussion
2. Blocking, followed by a run-through
3. Detailed work-through, scene by scene, followed by a run-through
4. Second detailed work-through, followed by a run-through
5. Time permitting, a third work-through
6. Run-through period
7. Technical run-through without actors ("dry tech")
8. Tech/dress rehearsals
9. Previews through to opening

Given a typical professional rehearsal period, using Equity's seven out of eight and one-half hours (the hour and one-half is for lunch), a rough outline of what happens week by week when rehearsing a five-act Shakespeare play follows:

FIRST WEEK:
Day 1. Read the play. Show set and costume sketches. Director's discussion.

Day 2. Read the play slowly; stop–start for basic discussion.

Day 3. Continue reading play slowly, as above.

Day 4. Block Part One (Acts I, II, III).

Day 5. Block Part Two (Acts IV, V).

Day 6. Finish blocking, if things have gone more slowly than above. First run-through, carrying books.

The seventh day is Day Off. Since Monday is usually the "dark night," professional rehearsals generally start on Tuesday, with Mondays off.

SECOND WEEK: DETAILED WORK-THROUGH, SCENE BY SCENE. NO BOOK CARRIED, BUT UNLIMITED PROMPTING ALLOWED.
Day 1. Act I (with each scene called at a specific hour).

Day 2. Act II (as above).

Day 3. Act III (as above).

Day 4. Run Part One. Then, Act IV (as above).

Day 5. Act V (as above).

Day 6. Run Part II. Then run through play, no books.

THIRD WEEK: DETAILED WORK-THROUGH AGAIN, BASED ON NOTES TAKEN DURING PREVIOUS RUN-THROUGH.

DAYS 1 THROUGH 6: LIKE PREVIOUS WEEK.

FOURTH WEEK:
Day 1. Detail work as needed. Run-through.

Day 2. Detail work as needed. Run-through.

Day 3. Detail work as needed. Run-through, add music if possible.

Day 4. Tech/dress.

Day 5. Tech/dress.

Day 6. Two dress rehearsals.

FIFTH WEEK:
Day 1. Scene work. Dress rehearsal.

Day 2. Scene work. Preview (first public performance).

Following days: Same pattern of scene work, performance as union rules permit, until press opening.

Appendix A, p. 315, provides a schedule for evening and weekend rehearsal covering a use of time similar to the professional schedule given here.

On such a schedule, all actors (speaking and nonspeaking roles alike) should be called for the first day of reading and discussion. They get to meet each other, they get a sense of the whole play, they see the model and sketches, and they hear the director's comments on the nature of the particular production.

For the next two days of the first week, days of reading and discussion, I usually call only the speaking actors, because people without anything to say will eventually become bored, and being bored will fidget, and, fidgeting, will distract the others.

For the blocking rehearsals, it is a good idea to call the entire company for all of the days involved, since it is hard to know how efficiently a particular group or a particular play can be moved along. If the director is ready, two days will suffice for blocking, but it is helpful to keep half of the third day as a cushion. The first run-through of a two-and-one-half hour production will take about four hours, in a rather bumpy ride. To end the first week with a run-through, however chaotic it may be, is to send the company away for their first day off with a sense of accomplishment and self-satisfaction.

By blocking efficiently, you will have let them know that you respect their time and have used it and filled it well. They will respect the director all the more for giving them a sense of the objectives to be attained.

What, I hear someone muttering, a day off? There will be some readers, unaffiliated with unions, who have the option of working on the play every single day, from first reading to opening. They should resist the temptation to exploit this opportunity. Actors must study. They can never *really* get a day off, except from the director, when the seventh day holds no rehearsal.

Part of my own particular strategy, to which the ''day off'' contributes, includes getting the line learning over with quickly. I would be grateful if all the actors knew the words before rehearsals begin! If you let them know you approve, your Hamlet or Medea or Mrs. Alving will certainly learn their roles ahead of time, because they will be well aware of the size of their job.

I make it quite clear that as soon as a scene is blocked, actors should learn it. In Week Two, when the detailed working through begins, each scene is to be done without book, as they come to it. With skill and tact, by the end of Week Two the director will have a cast that not only knows its objectives from a week of slow and careful work but also knows its lines.

How long should you schedule for the detailed work-through of each scene? I count on about one hour for five pages of Shakespeare or three pages of a modern prose play, during this first go-round. Spend the first few minutes just running the scene for the lines. That usually gets rid of that particular anxiety. This leaves forty-five or more minutes in which to do something about intentions and adjustments in an already blocked and learned scene.

The run-throughs of Parts One and Two scheduled for the middle and end of Week Two are review times, to give the actors a chance to fit together what they've spent the week pulling apart. These partial run-throughs also help to reduce anxiety about the end-of-week run-through. The run-through at the end of the second week, what with objectives in view, intentions clarified, and lines learned, should begin to look like something.

At this run-through, the trouble spots, scenes that don't work, individual actor problems, script and casting anomalies, should be emerging. Those problems will be the basis for the detailed work of Week Three. Week Three is the time for reblocking scenes that don't work in their current shape. It is the time to listen to actors, who now have a pretty good idea of what serves them and what doesn't. The director, too, will have made discoveries that call for reworking. By Week Three, ''going back to the drawing board'' can be profitable in the extreme. In terms of time spent on scenes, Week Three resembles Week Two.

Week Four is the week when the production pulls together. The first part of each day gives the director time to give attention to those parts of the whole play that still need moment-to-moment tinkering. The last part of each day contains a run-through, and each of these should feel easier for the actors and take minutes off the running time. At some time during this week, music cues will have been recorded and the sound tape made, so that the stage manager, on a rehearsal tape deck, can integrate music and sound with the show so actors can get used to the actual sounds and timings.

Proper pacing, builds, variety of mood and tempo from scene to scene—these must be achieved during the working rehearsals and run-throughs of Week Four.

No note-giving sessions are scheduled, because general notes can be given at the end of each run-through, and individual notes can be dealt with in the working rehearsals.

The tech/dress rehearsal schedule speaks for itself, and, like all phases of rehearsal, will be dealt with more fully in chapters that follow.

The question of how much rehearsal schedule to hand out to the acting company at one time has various answers, depending on the specific situation in which the work is being done. Director and stage manager must have the full schedule in mind in order to allot the time properly. On the other hand, enough flexibility must be retained to permit adjusting to emergencies or to unforseen problems that require a reordering of time. What the director wants to avoid is announcing a necessary schedule change and being met with, "The schedule said I wasn't needed on Tuesday and Wednesday, so I've already bought my plane ticket to Chicago."

Certain premises governing schedules must be made absolutely clear at the beginning of rehearsals:

1. The director has every right to call each actor all day, every day and make him sit around until needed.

2. Not doing so is a courtesy to the actor, and it also relieves the director of having a lot of unnecessary people underfoot.

3. Schedules *can* be changed to accommodate actor conflicts, but the show comes first.

In regional or university theatre situations, the detailed schedule can be announced two weeks in advance with impunity, because everybody generally knows what is on his personal docket for two weeks ahead in those communities. Schedules can be posted in detail, so students with class responsibilities can work them out around posted schedules, and actors can be called when they are needed. Calling students for rehearsals at which they must sit all day and never set foot on stage—when they have a paper due the next day—is not good for cast morale.

Professional productions in New York, Chicago, and Los Angeles, though, require different tactics. Actors will have auditions, voiceovers, television commercials, soap opera commitments, or film dubbing assignments, all of which make it possible for the actors to take theatre jobs. In these entertainment markets, the sad truth is that actors subsidize theatre work through other work, and theatre producers and directors must adjust to that reality. In addition, the theatre's own costume fittings, fight rehearsals, dance rehearsals, and press interviews all have to be fitted into and around the rehearsal day. Most stage managers working under these conditions prefer to announce the details of next day's schedule at the end of the preceding rehearsal day. Those who are not around to hear the announcement will be telephoned by the stage management, giving them the schedule. All this is easier than it was in the days before the telephone answering machine, now an essential part of every professional actor's equipment. This day-at-a-time issuing of calls means that director and stage manager must confer each day, usually at the lunch break, to be sure of what the next day will hold.

This means that the stage manager, at the onset of rehearsals, must know exactly what actors' schedule conflicts the management has accepted prior to signing them. It must not come as a surprise that the actor is on a soap. When unexpected conflicts develop, such as the actor wanting time off for an audition, director and stage manager have no other obligation to the actor but common courtesy.

Should the director try to schedule scenes in sequence, proceeding always from Scene 1 to Scene 2 in an orderly way? I generally do, because it helps the actors understand their roles in sequence. When, however, the play has main plot and subplots, it can be useful to rehearse those plots in their separate sequences—leaving out the intervening material. On the other hand, a sense of the way the play alternates between plots may dictate rehearsing in the play's sequence. Perhaps one week could be in chronological sequence, and the next week each plot could rehearse separately. You must vary your tactics to suit your needs.

I try always to *block* in sequence, so the actors can get their movement patterns straight from the start. Remembering the sequence of scenes, particularly in Shakespeare, is difficult enough anyway, and if one has to block out of sequence, confusion tends to dominate the first run-through. An alert stage management, in this instance, can do much to alleviate confusion by warning actors in upcoming scenes to be ready.

Having allotted, say, two hours for detailed work on *Romeo and Juliet*'s balcony scene (an adequate amount of time for one session), how does the director stay within the time limit? With one eye on the clock! Avoid *unnecessary* discussion, and keep necessary discussion from wandering. A fine-tuned sense of time gradually develops. Part of the bargain about scheduling must be put to the actors this way: "Making a schedule is a courtesy. I will *try* to be on time, ending one scene and moving on to the next. But you—*be* on time! You may, on occasion, have to wait for me—but don't make me wait for *you*!" In case of continued infractions by actors, a last resort is to scrap the schedule and call everybody for the entire rehearsal each day. They will quickly realize the advantage of making the hour-by-hour schedule work.

MUSIC, AND THE MUSIC AND SOUND PLOT

As you prepare your production scheme, the role of music in it will become clear. Some realistic plays will need only a few bars of mood-setting music before the curtain rises, to capture the audience's attention and to cover the lowering of house lights and the beginning of the play. Some episodic plays, like Shakespeare's or Brecht's, call for incidental songs and dances and will benefit from music bridges. Some plays are so stark that even pre-curtain music would be an intrusion. The director's taste and the nature of the play in question will determine whether music is to be used or not. Once the decision to use music is made, the nature of the music must be defined precisely. The quality and precise duration of each cue must be established, and, if music is to be specially composed for the production, its function must be organized in time for the composer to do the job and get the results on tape, if it is to be recorded, in a satisfactory fashion. In situations where copyright is not monitored closely, a music score for a play can be put together from snippets of prerecorded music drawn from commercial recordings. Assembling a score from these sources involves much the same kind of organization as having an original score composed.

ORGANIZING THE MUSIC

The following elements are involved in planning a music score/plot for a play:

1. The function of the cue—overture, bridge, offstage band, etc.

2. Its location in the script:
   Page
   Act and scene
   Cue number

3. A description of its mood and nature

4. Speaker location

5. Duration

I define a *cue* as one start and one stop of the tape deck, if the music is recorded, or, dealing with live music, each time the orchestra plays.

A cue may, thus, consist of one musical selection: say, the overture, or a dance, or a song accompaniment.

On the other hand, one cue may consist of several musical parts, if it bridges from one scene to the next. Such a cue could start with a "play off" or "button" or "period" to end the previous scene; it could continue with a transition covering a scene or light change or to denote passage of time; it could end with a "play on" or a mood-setting passage leading into the next scene.

In the plot, I could write such a cue in this manner:

CUE 4:

A. Comic button, for exit

B. Harp arpeggios, as revolving stage turns

C. Bright walking music for entrance

In a recording session for original music used this way, each section of such a cue may well be recorded separately, since musicians will be called to record all the cues they are involved in at one time, to save time and/or money. In other words, the harpist in item B above may not be there when sections A and C are recorded. The sections of a given cue must be musically compatible as to key, so that when the cue is constructed as above, by editing, it can play continuously as one piece of music.

Each section of each cue will have to be timed in rehearsal by the stage manager with a stop watch to be sure the length of the music, when composed or selected, will suit its stage function: the duration of the procession, the timing of the exit, how long it will take the revolve to turn (inspired guesswork is called for here), how long it takes the curtain to open, and so on. Early in rehearsal, these timings will vary widely, but gradually they will become consistent. Even timings for music composed to end precisely at the end of a given speech can be relied on to become consistent to within a fraction of a second.

One caution: Let each cue and section of a cue come to a logical musical end and have a precise timing. *Never* rely on a manual fade at the board to take out music as a scene begins or ends, because the chance of operator error is too great. If, indeed, the effect of a fade is what is wanted, build it in during the recording process, so that the operator of the tape deck has only to stop and start the machine and hit the required levels. The manual board fade is reliable only for a long, continuous drumming or continuous rain or waves on one deck while other cues may occur on another deck. Get the music written for the best average timing the stage business takes, and then make the stage business adjust, if necessary, after the music has been recorded.

WORKING WITH THE COMPOSER

Composers, and those who select music from existing sources, should the director delegate that function, will be grateful for descriptive words, however elaborate, defining the nature of the music requested. For example:

Angry waspish trumpet bursts, punctuated by urgent snare drums

Haunting, languishing, viola notes—a sigh

Boisterous "drinking song" music, as Toby staggers on

A solemn, funereal anthem

The play itself will suggest, to director and composer, how to organize the music. One way to give the music coherence is to assign to each principal character a musical theme, which can itself be varied: (a) by means of instrumentation; (b) by being played in major or in minor key; (c) by slow versions or fast versions; (d) by happy versions or sad ones; or (e) by playing characters' themes contrapuntally.

Shakespeare's *Twelfth Night* can serve as a useful example of how a musical shape can be found using character themes.

This raises the question of instrumentation. Most plays are too intimate to suit, in scale, accompaniment by a full symphony orchestra, even if one could afford such a score. Music for a play is like a frame for a picture. The music must support and enhance the play, not distract from it. Budgets permitting the composing of original music will usually be small enough to encourage a modest instrumentation. Note, however, that if music is being selected from prerecorded sources and budgetary constraints do not obtain, the question of scale still arises. A modestly sized musical aggregation is usually a better sound for plays using unamplified actors' voices.

For *Twelfth Night*, an amiable romantic comedy, one might select strings and woodwinds. Suppose our instruments were to be flute, oboe, bassoon, clarinet, violin, cello, and harpsichord. This would give us the principal voices, high to low. Feste, with luck, will be able to accompany himself on the guitar. Using these instruments in relation to the characters, the director and composer might request the following themes and instruments for the following characters:

Orsino—Violin. A lyric, soaring melody.

Viola—Flute. A haunting, gentle tune.

Olivia—Cello. A graceful, flowing song.

Toby and Andrew—Bassoon and oboe. A grotesque drinking song.

Malvolio—Clarinet. An impudent, irritating march.

Feste will have his own guitar to contribute when needed, and with the harpsichord used both as *continuo* and solo instrument, this combination of themes and instruments could produce a very useful musical structure for the play. Remember, key and tempo can be varied, and the music can take its identity from either the locale (whose house we're in), the characters who enter or exit, or what characters are together in the scene. In the case of *Twelfth Night*, an added resource is the presence of songs in the script, the melodies of which can also be used for scene setting.

The Shakespeare history plays resolve themselves naturally into "trumpets and drums," plus ceremonial music for coronations, processions, and religious services, with occasional dance music or other domestic music. Marching soldiers can sing marching songs. There can be church bells, alarm bells, drum rolls, and marches with drums. The history play's instruments often turn out to be a brass choir with percussion: trumpet, French horn, trombone, snare drum and tympani. The plays usually end in battles, and it can be supportive if the opposing parties have musical identities, one side identified with trumpets, another with horns, and even a third with the trombone. Occasionally, strings or a harpsichord may be wanted for domestic cues. Synthesized sound can be combined with acoustic instruments in interesting ways to broaden the musical palette. Live musicians, including the composer, can even improvise along with the rehearsal to produce an effective and continuous accompaniment. This approach requires, above all, that the composer and musicians be creatively sensitive to the rehearsal process. I am not advocating any particular kind or use of music, but simply suggesting ways for organizing the musical task.

Those who want traditional music composed (music that can be written down and requires arranging) must remember that, in addition to creating the music, the composer must orchestrate it, get the parts copied, hold recording sessions, and supervise the editing of the tape. The director and stage manager must organize themselves so the composer gets the time he needs.

After director and composer have agreed upon the nature of the music and after the music plot has been prepared, the composer must then write the basic themes and review them with the director for approval. These can be short sessions near a piano or can even be conducted over the telephone, so long as the director hears the actual themes. Then the composer can construct the actual cues, after which these, too, must be played for the director's approval. Once the cues are composed and the director has approved them, the next time the director will hear them is after they are recorded and edited. For good or ill, the budget will probably dictate that re-recording sessions are impossible, though cutting and editing are always available. If the music works out well, it will be a credit, not only to the composer's creativity, but in great measure to the director's organizational skills and the stage manager's accurate support.

SOUND EFFECTS

The *sound effects* cues and the music cues will be on the same show tape (or tapes if two decks are used) if both are recorded. If live musicians are used, the sound tape will be a separate matter. If the music is recorded, then any recorded sound effects must be ready when the music tape is edited, so they can be inserted in their proper sequence into the show tape.

There are two types of sound effects:

1. Manual, or live: These are traditionally operated by either the prop crew or the stage management. They might consist of gun shots, door slams, shouts and crowd noises off, bells, thunder from a thunder sheet, and so on.

2. Recorded: These are put on tape and run from the tape deck by the sound operator, and can include effects such as thunder, rain, crowds, birds, artillery, automobiles, sirens, bells, waves, synthesized electronic sounds, or any other sound known to human ears. A wide range of sound effects can be purchased on tape, on record, and on CD's. Sometimes, as in the case of crowd noises, recorded sound can be blended with live sound. Two or more decks can be used to blend sounds back and forth or to play sounds one on top of the other or to control the length of a sound by cutting in with the next sound on cue.

How does one decide which sounds are to be live and which recorded? Choices are made in relation to scale, fidelity, and control. Recorded sound can have all the size of which the system is capable. Thunder, waves, artillery, crowds in a stadium—sounds like this, for their reality, their larger-than-life dimension, and the need to regulate their volume carefully, commend this sort of sound for recording. Single offstage pistol shots are both easier to time and in better scale to the onstage action if they are live, from blank pistols. Door-slams, too, are best live. Some sounds are hard to achieve in the theatre. For example, I have yet to hear an acceptable offstage automobile starting, leaving, or approaching, or an acceptable car door closing, in a play. The recorded effects sound false, and no production I have been around has been able to use a real car in suitable proximity.

Whether the sound be live or recorded, you must list the sound effects you will need, and, if recorded, where in the music tape they will occur. Your next responsibility regarding sound effects is to hear the sounds selected by the sound department early enough so they can be improved upon if not satisfactory. Sound cues should be selected under conditions similar to those of performance—if possible, in the theatre and on its sound system.

The sound plot itself follows the same outline as the music plot: page number, act and scene number, cue line, description of cue, speaker placement or source of sound, and duration.

A sample music and sound plot, as prepared for an actual production, will be found in Appendix C, p. 335.

THE LIGHT PLOT

The director and the lighting designer will already have had a concept discussion. Agreement in principle will already have been reached on color, location of instruments (areas, sky, specials, down lighting, booms, front-of-house positions, and so on), use of follow spots, and special effects. The lighting designer will still need from the director a chart showing when cues come, of what they consist, notations about which areas the acting happens in for particular scenes, when specials come up and down, when and where follow spots are used, and other such precise information about how the lighting is integrated with the show. This plot is not so much about how the lighting *looks* as about how it *moves* for the show. The director is the person who decides how the light must serve the production; the designer achieves the director's goals and makes it all *look* better than the director ever could.

The director's light plot will be in two parts. The first, the *lighting ground plan*, covers the spaces of the stage, shapes of areas as they will be used, including notations of ideas about location of specials, washes, and special effects, all identified in language keyed to the second part of the light plot, the *cue plot*. This is not the *working* cue sheet for the show; that will come from the designer after the concept is translated into instruments and circuits.

This *cue plot* is much like the music plot, in that it involves page numbers, act and scene numbers, cue numbers, the cue line, a verbal description of the effect wanted, a notation of what happens in the cue (what areas go up or down, what specials are involved, which washes, etc.) and the duration of the cue—the number of counts or seconds it should require.

Sample light plots, director to designer, for an actual production, will be found in Appendix C, p. 335.

Even for the simplest of realistic comedies, such a plot gives the designer something concrete and thus avoids misunderstandings. The more complex the production, the more essential the director's light plot is as a communication tool.

How the designer uses the tool varies with individuals. Two recent experiences with highly experienced and talented New York designers illustrate the point. The productions were equally complicated, with a similar number of cues. Each designer received plots with detailed information appropriate to the play. Each sincerely voiced appreciation for the amount of information provided. They used almost the same words to express how glad they were to know so much up front and how often they are expected to "fly blind" before they can see a rehearsal.

One of these designers completely surprised me with the *look*, although she accomplished everything I had asked for. Her solutions were extraordinarily original. After I became used to what she had achieved (in the course of a couple of technical rehearsals in which I kept silent about her area and simply let her work while I solved problems of my own) I realized how wonderful it was, a truly splendid piece of lighting design, utterly different from what I had imagined but superbly apt. The other designer turned on the lights at his first technical rehearsal—and there it was, just as I had dreamed it, only much better! Each designer was creative in an individual way. Each turned in a splendid job; I look forward to working with each of them again.

Occasionally, though, I have given such a plot to a lighting designer who has said, "If this is what you want, *you* do it. You've designed the lights already." Then I have to say, "No, I've spelled out my minimum requirements. If this seems to you to be the whole job, then you aren't creative enough *for* the job, and I'll have to find someone else."

THE PROPERTY PLOT

The property plot for most productions has two phases:

1. Those pieces of furniture and objects used in the play that can be anticipated before rehearsals, from the script itself and as a result of the director's preparation.

2. Objects added during rehearsals, as the need for them emerges.

Every play has two kinds of props:

1. Set props: furniture (chairs, tables, benches, rugs, etc.); and objects that help set the scene and function like furniture (cannon, barrels, crates, suitcases, etc.). Most set props are preset, by crew members, before the curtain opens or the lights come up. Some, however, like Mother Courage's wagon, stretchers, sedan chairs, sometimes thrones—these objects work like set props, but are brought on by actors during the scene.

2. Hand props: articles which, as their name suggests, are handled by actors: spears, swords, guns, fans, pens, letters, cigarettes, pencils, dishes and flatware, food, and so on. Most of these objects are preset by the crew on prop tables backstage right and left, from which actors pick them up and return them. There is also a category of props called "personal props," which are those objects the actors may prefer to carry and keep in their costumes: pocket watch, handkerchief, jewelry, fountain pen, wallet, purse, etc. Perishable props, usually food, must be kept under sanitary conditions and their supply renewed periodically.

There are two kinds of prop lists:

1. *The director's prop list.* This list enumerates and describes, scene by scene, the set and hand props required for the play. This list is created so the correct objects can be located or constructed.

2. *The running prop list.* This, compiled by the stage manager, includes all the props used in the production and shows where they "start," which side they come in on, and where they exit, plus to what location they must be returned. This list contains diagrams of prop table setups and diagrams of onstage table arrangements, bookshelf arrangements, and the like, so the crew (even a replacement member) can tell at a glance how to set the props.

The director's list must be as comprehensive as possible. Not only should the objects be named and the number of each stated—10 halberds, one English coronation throne with Stone of Scone, 20 wooden wine goblets, and so on—but a description, including size and period of the object, should be provided, along with a sketch, or a photograph or a picture from a book or magazine of the way the director would like the thing to look. It is not enough to say "small, drop-leaf oval table." One must be specific: "18th century mahogany drop-leaf Pembroke table, approx. 3'6" long in its open position, and 30" wide." Then give them a picture! Do not assume, for example, that they will know what you want when you say "gauntlet." Do you want a leather one, or one from a suit of armor, or a leather glove with a metal cuff, or simply a pair of cuffed driving gloves? Goblets can be metal (they shine and rattle), glass (they break), wood (they are primitive and thump when dropped), or horn (hard to find). What kind of pistol do you mean—make, period, type—and is it to be "practical"— that is, does someone fire it, or load it?

What the director must create is a reference sheet—one that informs fully and also documents the production's needs. Good technical people will delight in knowing exactly what the director wants and having that information on paper. Be warned, however, about technical people who resent the written word. If given plots and lists, they seem not to read them. The time to spot these types is at the first prop or light or sound conference. One of them will ask, say, "What kind of a throne do you want?" The director must say, "It's on your plot." When they extricate their plot from its resting place and peer at it, saying, "Oh, *yes*, I see what you mean," their secret is out; this is the first time they've looked at it. The director's next step must be to read over the entire plot with them, word for word, sketch by sketch. The detailed prop list, with dimensions and pictorial aids, puts responsibility for an equal precision on the technical staff. Yes, it is a chore, before the fights are blocked or the banquet staged, to figure out just how many rapiers and daggers, how many plates, knives and goblets will be wanted. But if the director can't be bothered, who else will care? That which is not planned cannot be built!

Phase 2 of the property plot, those props that emerge from rehearsing, require self-discipline on the part of cast and director. If it is only a matter, in the week before dress rehearsal, of putting one more ashtray on the side table or ten more documents in the briefcase, then "ask and you shall receive." If, however, someone says, "Wouldn't it be funny if . . ." and "if" turns out to be parade of servants carrying a bird cage with parakeets, a monkey on a leash, and a cart piled with luggage, the director is the one who must consider the outrage with which this request will be received by the property department and try to guide creativity into channels practical for a late stage of rehearsal. Small props can be added, within reason, into Week Three if the property department has been warned in advance that improvising will occur and if the stage manager has kept them apprised of each day's "improvements." But an effort should be made to anticipate the bulk of the prop list at the outset, unless working time and budgets are unlimited—which, now I come to think of it, sounds more like a definition of hell than of heaven.

An example of a director's prop list from an actual production will be found in Appendix C, p.335.

E X E R C I S E

1. Page 87—Assume that you have a five-week production schedule for your production. Draft a preliminary rehearsal schedule for the entire period from first rehearsal to opening night. The schedule should at minimum include actors called, technicians and designers called, what's to be done, time beginning and ending, and location. A typical schedule might include read-throughs, blocking rehearsals, working rehearsals (scenes), run-throughs, technical rehearsals, and dress rehearsals. How does the schedule impose a structure that will allow you to achieve your production goals? Justify the time you spend, the hours you require of your cast and crew, the number of run-throughs, the number of days off. How does your schedule reflect your style as a director?

PART TWO

THE DIRECTING
PROCESS

CHAPTER 9

REHEARSALS—
THE FIRST WEEK

THE FIRST DAY

I always have "nerves" the first day—anticipation, anxiety, eagerness, dread. How is the chemistry going to be? A cast becomes a family during rehearsals. What kind of family will it be? The first day can be "love at first sight," or the beginning of a rocky road. As director you must set the tone. You are parent, host for a four-week party, kindly guide, stern taskmaster.

"How diplomatic you are," I've often been told. "You're a wonderful politician," has also been said. "No, on both counts," I must reply. "I am a skilled manipulator, dealing with a group of people who have come together agreeing to be manipulated and hoping to be manipulated well." Diplomats and politicians certainly manipulate, but they must never be seen to do it. Everyone involved in the production of a play knows that the director's *job* is to manipulate. All they ask is that it won't hurt too much—the sort of thing we expect of our dentist.

It's the first day, and the journey through the play is about to begin.

The stage managers are the first to arrive, at this first rehearsal and at every rehearsal. Each has a promptbook, which each will keep up. There must always be more than one promptbook—promptbooks can be lost, even stolen. Each will keep his book in his own way.

The stage managers will set up the rehearsal space for the first reading.

REHEARSAL ROOM OR THEATRE?

This is a good place to discuss the advantages and disadvantages of rehearsing for the whole period on the stage itself. Rehearsing on the stage is usually regarded as a good thing, even if the reason rehearsals are held there is because it is the only large space available. If so—so be it. Given a choice, however, I would actually prefer to start in a rehearsal room, so long as it is a good one. It is essential that it be a room large enough to lay out the entire acting area on its floor. It is good, too, if the director can sit ten or fifteen feet back from the setting line, in order to be to that extent ''outside'' the scene. Too, there must be some other room that can serve as a ''green room,'' or actors' lounge and waiting room so that their conversation when offstage can be isolated from the rehearsal. Also, the rehearsal room must be insulated from outside noise and yet be well ventilated, and properly heated or cooled.

Given these necessities, I prefer to start in a room. There is an energy and concentration difference between rehearsing and performing, just as there is a difference in acting energies for different phases of rehearsal. Someone has pointed out that the words for ''rehearsal'' in German, French, and English indicate quite different kinds of rehearsals. The German *die Probe* means literally ''the trial,'' with a sense of experimenting, trying different effects. The French word is *répétition*, with a sense of going over and over things to get them right. Our English word ''rehearsal'' translates, after a moment's thought, into ''hearing again,'' with an emphasis on language. The difference in those words tells us something about German, French, and English theatre, but all the words imply that rehearsals are work, and all plays need all three kinds of rehearsal. The playhouse is a place of showing, of ''playing'' in the sense of pretending, for and to the public. Performing is something actors should not be encouraged to do until they are ready. One of the worst criticisms actors can make of a director is, ''This one expects every rehearsal to be a performance!'' Early rehearsals that take place in the theatre can lead people into ''acting'' and talking loudly too soon.

The rehearsal room will probably be scruffy, a place where one wears work clothes. There will probably be no place where guests and fellow actors can watch (and judge) the work without themselves being observed. However large, it will still probably not be a place where the actor will be comfortable playing full out, so it will encourage contained and focused rehearsing. There will be an atmosphere of the makeshift, the temporary, and this will help the actors concentrate, so they can bring into being things that have to be *imagined*.

BUILT-IN ''LIFTS''

The production that begins in the rehearsal room gets a big lift from moving into the theatre. I like to see this adjustment occur at the beginning of the third week, although it usually comes when the technical arrangements make it possible. By the beginning of the third week, decisions have been made, and the actors are ready to test and expand the "how's." Now vocal projection can have its place, for there is now something in the mind to project. The jolt that comes on moving into the theatre is good: the realization comes that things which in the rehearsal room seemed private have to be shared in public. Filling and fulfilling now have their place, as the actors expand to occupy the new space.

Some other lifts are built into the rehearsal schedule which each will give the production a surge of progress. One lift comes when the stage lighting takes over from the general work light, for with the stage light and the accompanying darkness in the auditorium come heightened concentration. The actor's sight and thought are now confined within the light, creating better listening and an intensifying of relationships. The next lift arrives with costumes and set. The costume rounds out the character and supports the actor's inner reality with an outward confirmation. The set supplies a physical world in which the events marshaled in the actor's imagination can take place. The last, and greatest, lift comes when the final collaboration occurs—when there is an audience present whom we invite to share the magic life we have created.

The director can take greatest advantage of this series of energizing lifts by starting in a rehearsal room.

TOGETHER FOR THE FIRST READING

Coming back now to the first day, I think that as director you should make it a point to be the first person in the room after the stage managers, so you can help them arrange the room. They are your "team," and they will prefer to see you share in readying the space, rather than making a star entrance after everyone else has come.

The "star entrance" was a reality in the old days—for the star, I mean. The first day always seemed to be a contest between the actors as to who would arrive last. Perhaps cast members lurked in doorways spying out the terrain, but usually no one would be on time that first day but bit players. Gradually, though, all would filter in, almost in exact pecking order (billing and salary). Then, precisely half an hour late, Ina Claire or Jane Cowl or whoever it was would sweep in, furs and all, and finally things could get started. I sometimes wonder what about the good old days was good.

Anyway, I like to be pottering around, opening windows or putting my script and notepad on the table, so that I can greet the actors by name as they arrive—not the easiest of tasks if the cast numbers over thirty and one has met some of them only twice. I try to see that they are introduced to one another as they arrive. The theatre is a small world, wherever in it a given production is being done, so there is every likelihood that some members of your cast have worked together before. This makes it easier, for the director's function as the first day begins is rather like that of the host at a cocktail party, circulating to make sure the guests have met one another.

If the management is generous and the stage management thoughtful, there will be coffee, tea, and suitable sweet rolls and goodies provided at a side table as a first-day treat. This helps to create an informally hospitable atmosphere.

The stage manager, on a cue from the director after all cast members have turned up, should start the proceedings by asking everyone to sit down.

Chairs should already be arranged in a semicircle, placed so everyone can see everyone else. The director's place will be center, seated at a small table, with the stage managers off center, at another table. Card tables are fine. Other tables should be placed so actors can rest books, belongings, coffee, etc., on them.

At the outset, I have the stage manager announce that smoking will not be permitted in the rehearsal room and point out the location of the designated smoking area.

Next, the stage manager distributes the contact sheet, with names, phone numbers, and addresses of company and staff, plus any other documents the company needs. In a professional company, these include insurance and withholding forms. These are either filled out on the spot or handed in later.

Next, in Equity companies, comes the Equity Deputy election ritual. For this, the director, even though he may be a member of Equity, must leave the room, since he is part of management. The stage manager presides over the election, from among the actors, of the person who will serve as Equity Deputy (shop steward), filing reports with the union on rehearsal hours and conditions, overtime, and any disputes over union matters that may arise. Upon election, the deputy will be given a packet from Equity containing the rule book and copies of weekly forms to file. The stage manager then passes around the election form, which company members sign, verifying the election of the lucky member.

Cast arrivals, coffee, and union business may take from half an hour to an hour, depending on the amount of talk. Before the actual rehearsal begins, the stage manager will perhaps call a short break. At last, though, the stage manager tells the director to "come out now." Now, the real business of the day can begin.

THE DIRECTOR BEGINS

I use this moment to introduce the stage management, who by this time probably need no introduction, and to identify members of the design or business staff who may have come to hear the reading. Anyone in the room must be introduced, because, of all days, this is the day the actors are most nervous and self-conscious. Next I ask that they refer to contact sheets, and then I ask the actors, in the order they happen to be seated, to say their names and roles loudly enough to be understood, to make doubly sure that they have had a chance to know who they're working with. That done, I announce that before we read the play I have a few brief points to make:

1. Don't stop to ask questions; just read straight through, because we will be trying to get a rough timing of the play.

2. Even though it is a first reading, read loudly enough for the rest of the cast to hear you. All we want is a sense of the play and the voices. Don't worry about "acting"; just don't "hide" by being inaudible.

3. No one will read stage directions, and, if it's Shakespeare, just let one scene follow directly on the other.

4. If necessary, I rearrange the seating so people who have scenes together may see each other easily.

5. Then it's, "Let's go—when the stage manager says, 'Curtain!'"

Warning: the director would be well advised not to say anything *significant* before the first reading; the actors won't remember it. All they are thinking about is, "I hope the director will like all the fine things I've thought up to do," or, "I'll show those other guys," or, "I hope nobody notices me at all," or, "I hope I like the people I have to work with." The director, at this time, cannot produce words of sufficient wisdom to get past these concerns.

THE FIRST READING

The director, at any rate *this* director, has some of his worst moments during the first reading. Although he has himself cast the play and has realistic expectations of his actors, his own understanding of the play is far beyond theirs. In his mind he already hears the text supported with the subtext he has imagined. After all, he has been working on it for weeks. The actors, even those who have studied and those who are ideally cast, cannot read the director's mind. At best, they will confirm why they have been cast; at worst, you'll wonder why you ever did. Don't judge them by this first reading, however excruciating it may be. Naturally, there is a disparity between what they do now and what they will grow into later.

During the first reading you *can* take note of how combinations of actors work out. You can listen to the music of combined voices. You can watch for the balance of sympathies—will the audience be rooting for the right people?

Above all, you can use the time to read your promptbook notes as the actors read the play. You can, in this way, begin to see, moment by moment, the size of your task. How do their instincts, if any, compare with your choices?

How strong and clear do your choices seem as they collide with the reality of the actors' personalities? This can be a valuable learning experience, as opposed to just sitting there, watching and listening helplessly as wrong readings go by. If I review my promptbook, I am doing something creative at every moment. If they look up to see how they're doing, instead of seeing my polite "audition" face, they'll see me busily occupied with the script, already working. This, I think, diminishes their need to "prove something" by "performing."

No matter how persuasively the director urges the actors to give a relaxed but audible first reading, he will get readings at each of two extremes, with all gradations in between. One extreme is the actor who hides. He may be one of your most able actors, but he has made no decisions yet, and he feels "unfairly" called upon to read his part aloud when as yet it means nothing to him and he has nothing to act. He takes refuge in slumping and inaudibility, with his script in his face, possibly chewing gum or sucking throat lozenges. The other extreme is the actor who has worked, often hard and well, and who wants the director and everyone else to know it. His conscientiousness, his ego, and his desire to "prove himself" drive her over the edge into loudness, overplaying, spurious emotion, and "indicating" all those values which he may well be able to play later with power and truth. He, too, may be one of your best people. These particular bad habits at first readings are annoying in the extreme, and to everyone. Nobody can relate to the hider, and the bravura one is so overboard there is a sense of collective embarrassment. These habits emerge at their worst when actor and director work together for the first time. Working with the director over time will give the actors confidence to "come with what they have," rather than yielding to self-consciousness and fear, of which these two extreme responses are the symptoms.

At least one ten-minute break should interrupt the reading, at an appropriate spot—an intermission or a scene end. Sitting more than one hour without a break is bad for the attention span. Take care, when you stop, to say, "That's wonderful!" or "What a good cast!" or some other strong and general compliment. Unless someone is disastrously on the wrong tack, like giving Hamlet a Danish accent, it is best to say nothing, *nothing*, negative. No doubt the director can find something to say to the designers or a need to make a phone call during the break to avoid the "How'm I doing?" conversations that some actors will want to create. Of course, if the production contains a "vehicle" role, like Lear or Cleopatra or Blanche Dubois, it is necessary for that actor's morale that the director say a private word of praise in passing during the break. Otherwise, save it all until the play has been read.

When, after the break, the reading comes to an end, it is likely that the stage manager will have some announcements to make, and that the cast will be told that after lunch the afternoon will consist of a showing of the scenery and costume designs and the director's comments. If, for any reason, the director has little to say and the designers' "show and tell" is brief, there is much merit in just reading the play again. Such a second reading is usually much more relaxed and, for that reason, useful. Ordinarily, though, the full afternoon will be needed for the director's comments.

"SHOW AND TELL" AND DISCUSSION

First thing after lunch is a good time for the designers' showings. If there is a model, so much the better. In any case, the designer can talk from the renderings about set changes, entrances and exits, platforms and walls, so the actors can begin to visualize the production. The costume designer, in turn, can show his sketches and swatches. The actors should be allowed to get close enough to see models and sketches clearly. Questions can be solicited. Actors should be encouraged to confine their questions to matters that might affect everyone. Questions that concern individuals can be dealt with privately, particularly costume questions, especially if the actor finds himself unhappy with the design for his own character.

When the design showing is finished, the director takes the floor, seriously, for the first time. What you begin with will depend on how well you and the company know each other. If you are a guest director, or a director who has pulled together a company from wide-ranging auditions just for this particular play or for a new season, you may find yourself starting a new set of artistic relationships. In this instance, you can help the actors know what to expect by describing your work process, giving a brief outline of your own background and training, and giving a brief sketch of what the next rehearsal weeks will be like, how rapidly blocking will be done, and when lines should be learned. Next comes the play itself. The matter of what is good about the play and why it is being done must be discussed. The style of production must be described. The spine of the play should be spelled out and enlarged upon. Any special acting tools the play requires must be defined: the kind of speech required for the play; verse speaking, should the play be in verse; the nature of special period movement, should that be involved; and specifics of comedy, tragedy, and melodrama, as they affect the production, should be taken up. You are preparing the ground for detailed work, during rehearsals, in the areas you outline.

At the same time, you must be careful not to tell people more, on the first day, than they may be ready to hear. You must whet their appetites, and engage their interest. You must raise questions without attempting to answer them fully. If you are working with professional actors, you must always take the position, whether it proves to be justified or not, that you are reminding them of things they already know, and, among the many skills they have, talking about the particular skills that will be helpful for this production.

One thing everybody learns at this point in a production of mine, if they haven't already realized it during auditions, is that I have my reasons for doing the play and a way already in mind in which I want to do it. Sometimes a director sets up a rehearsal atmosphere in which he, as enthusiastic group leader, says, "Gosh, how do we all want to do this play?" Those rehearsals are creative in the sense that everyone helps invent everything. My rehearsals are interpretative experiences in which each participant has a clearly defined area in which he can exercise his creativity. Each will be asked to do his assigned task in a controlled interpretation of a clearly conceived whole. The actors will be glad to know early on which kind of rehearsals they will be coming to. This talk by the director tells them that, and this may well be the most important thing that comes out of the first day.

The last phase of my talk on these occasions takes up each character in turn, with a brief description of how I see them. The actors must be helped to feel that the director has chosen them above all others because of qualities they bring to their roles. Each character's super-objective can be touched on here. The actors can be introduced to how the characters relate to the spine of the play, and to how each character functions in the scheme of the play. By talking about the characters last, the director can end the day by bringing the focus back to each actor's task, so he can take these remarks about his role home with him and think about them in relation to next day's effort. This brings the first day to a close. The stage manager repeats the next day's call—and that's that; the juggernaut's momentum has begun. Each day's goals are clear; each day leads to the next. The adventure is in progress, and it will be all the more exciting because its course is clearly charted.

THE SECOND AND THIRD DAYS—THE SLOW READ-THROUGH

Now the director's promptbook is the star.

Everyone who speaks in the play should be on hand for the whole of these two crucial days, because the foundation for the production's internals will be laid down at this time. Also, the director, during these two intense and difficult days, conditions the acting company to being interrupted, to being directed, to being actively led.

I begin by explaining my promptbook. Some acting teachers, especially in New York, encourage their students to interleaf their scripts and create a workbook for their roles on exactly the same principles I have recommended to the director in this book. Those actors say, "Why, that's what I was taught to do." These actors will already understand the purpose of the promptbook. The others will need to be informed and reassured.

They need to learn that the director is prepared and how he has gone about his preparation—so I talk about my three columns and what they mean, and about beats and intentions, so I am sure we begin to share a common language. They need to grasp that the director's preparation, far from creating rigidity, brings the confidence that banishes defensiveness and insures flexibility.

TECHNIQUES FOR THE SLOW READ-THROUGH

As the reading starts, explain the mood of the first moments of the play. Set up the staging and lighting, verbally. Then, when they begin to read—the director must participate!

Your participation will vary with your sense of how much the actors can absorb. I usually say something like, "I've done all this work, and I want to share it with you," and then something like, "Just listen and try to find my wavelength. As the director, I want to get there first with my ideas. Your ideas will come as you see how they fit in with my ideas. I've conceived the production; casting you is part of that conception. And if you want to take notes on anything I say—I certainly won't be offended." A company of very experienced and professionally prominent actors will probably become wary and defensive if the director intervenes at every phrase at the beginning of this first working day. Conveying a sense of mood, pointing out transitions, suggesting a different tone if the actor seems headed in a dangerously wrong direction—these are ways to test the water. As the reading progresses, you will find you can intervene more often and more specifically.

With a bright company of student actors most of whom I have had in acting class I have on many occasions said, "Draw your three lines on the opposite page. Be ready to draw in the beats horizontally as we define each new beat." And then, beat by beat, I have given each character what I have worked out as his intention and also, line by line, the adjustments as I have prepared them. The actors have written them in their scripts, as I have them in mine.

This method *works*—with motivated and dedicated *students*. It teaches them how to build a scene, gives them actable tasks to work on, points them in the right direction for the play, implants in them the basics of an approach to work, makes them apply in practice what may have seemed theoretical in class, and produces an organic, tightly knit and extraordinarily clear production.

I have worked in this detail, almost as fully, with a company of resident professional actors, when we have a track record of successful productions together, after mutual trust has been created, and after they understand my process and how it can serve them.

In a professional production where most of us are just beginning to know each other, I have to feel for that special middle ground between *laissez-faire* free-for-all and dictating my entire promptbook to them. I have to learn how much each particular group can handle without becoming defensive.

Here is a bald version of the problem:

Actor: "But I've barely read the line aloud once. You
   don't know how I want to do it."

Director: "That's true, but first of all, for today, I'd like
   you to think about how I see it."

They'll think the director is "giving line readings" to "get a result." What the director must convey is, "Don't worry about being *good* or making final choices—we're just starting to diagram the play. Just mark it, trying what I suggest, and see how it works." *Mark it* is a useful old expression that means simply, "Go through the motions without acting," and that's how I like these two reading days to be handled. It should be like making a line drawing in preparation for a painting.

The director's concentration, patience, and persistence the first day of serious work will pay great dividends. The actors will quickly discover that you are not *correcting* them; indeed, you must never do so. You must *encourage* them to try your suggested choices. Instead of saying, "Don't do . . . ," say the same thing couched positively. "Let's take that again, and this time try . . ." Your tone should not be emotional, or exhorting, or even persuasive during these "exploration of the text" rehearsals; you must be objective and kind. At this stage, you will not need to resort to reading the line to convey your meaning; you can suggest the tone of the scene by means of paraphrase and tone of voice.

These rehearsals focus on the words of the text—what the author wrote. The director will be dealing with the speeches as tools to carry out intentions, and will chart the actors' paths by pointing out the various sections of the speeches and relating those sections to the necessary adjustments. The actors will begin to get a sense of the architecture of speeches and scenes, and *they* will start to approach the play objectively, rather than subjectively.

The director who starts working intensely in the reading rehearsals is, where experienced actors are concerned, setting himself against years of reading rehearsals with few interruptions from the director and relatively little talk about the show. In such productions, the reading rehearsals, if any, achieve little but familiarity with the play. There is no need to waste time in this way. As proper reading rehearsals progress, the actors will relax and gradually give themselves more freely to the process. It is truly gratifying, at the end of the week, to have a veteran leading player say, "It's wonderful to have accomplished so much. I feel as if we've been rehearsing, not one week, but three." When breaking into a scene or into the middle of an actor's speech, try to speak *before* the line, or in later rehearsals, *before* the move about which you are commenting. Two things will be achieved: (a) time will be saved, because the actors won't be saying the lines twice—once before you stop them and then again when they resume; and (b) especially in the early rehearsals, the actors cannot possibly feel criticized or corrected when they haven't even said the lines yet. Remember, the director is talking about the *play* or the *character*, not about the *actors*.

That is why I like the Brechtian "third person" when addressing the actor. Brecht held that the actor should not say "I," identifying with the character, but that he should say "he," referring to the character always as separate from himself. I like to phrase my remarks in this fashion: "Bill, I think when he crosses to her, he should pull her close to say that line." I don't bother actors if they say "I" when they refer to their character, but it seems that my using the third person helps create the atmosphere of objectivity that I seek.

EARLY SPEECH DECISIONS

These reading rehearsals give the director a chance to standardize pronunciations in the play: characters' names, place names. The accent in which the play is to be played should be discussed, too. If the play is by Coward, Wilde, Shaw, Osborne, Pinter, shall English accents be used, or shall the play be performed in mid-Atlantic or American standard speech for the stage, as exemplified by Edith Skinner and her disciples? If the play is by Shakespeare or Congreve, there is another dimension with which to deal—that of period speech and vocabulary. American plays offer their dialect questions, too. *Our Town* is specifically New England in the same way that *Cat On a Hot Tin Roof* is distinctly southern. What about classics in translation—say, the plays of Chekhov, Molière, Ibsen, or Pirandello?

Let me share the way I have thought about these questions. Plays by Shaw, Coward, Wilde, Pinter, Osborne, and the like are all written for British sounds and cadences. The plays work when correctly spoken—and acted with truth. If they can be cast with uniform appropriateness, I like these plays to sound British, and with the proliferation of the products of British television available to us, everyone senses the difference between good British and fake British. If the acting company can't be British, then they must aim at mid-Atlantic, or if they can't do that, then decent, well-produced American stage speech (nonregional in sounds and pronunciation) may perhaps do. But there comes a point at which one must say, "If this group can't produce a more authentic sound, then I'd better do another play." That criterion must also be used for American dialect plays. The New England play can be adequately cast in New York. The southern play *can* be adequately cast in New York, if care is taken—but fake southern is no more acceptable than fake British. Outside of New York, the question you must pose is, "Will the balance of the regional audience (wherever you find yourself) accept the sound I can achieve with the available actors?"

The translated classic brings up the question of class distinctions as reflected in speech. American speech differs, by and large, on regional and not on class lines. In all European languages, a person's social class can be identified from his speech, and a necessary step in transcending class distinctions for the upwardly mobile European is to learn upper-class speech. The only class distinctions readily available in our language come when we adopt a British standard. So, do we play Molière in British? If we do, do the servants use Cockney? Here is where "mid-Atlantic" or American standard stage speech is so useful. Speaking in that way, one avoids the danger of telling a British story on top of a French story. I think a cast playing Ibsen in upper-class British sounds affected, unless they *are* British. Still, when class distinctions are important, as in Chekhov, some way must be found for the lower-class characters to sound *rougher*. Hard "r's" and an added nasality can move such characters toward a rural or country sound. The British jokingly call such an all-purpose country dialect for the stage "Mummerset."

Another issue that involves speech is national temperament. Speaking English with a foreign intonation tends to bring out the appropriate national mannerisms: Italian hand-waving, French shrugging, German heel-clicking, and so on. This is all very well, if the worst clichés are avoided, when the foreign character is speaking English to English speakers in the play. But should everyone in an Italian play use an Italian accent to remind us that they are supposed to be speaking Italian? I think, no. If they are presumably all speaking Italian, then they would speak it without a foreign accent, and therefore the audience should be hearing unaccented English, since the play is translated. If the director wants to invest the production with physical indications of national temperament and manners, common sense and good taste seem to me to indicate that these effects should not be allowed to infect the company's speech.

Shakespeare still gives us problems in the speech area. We Americans are all too aware that he was an English writer. Yet, he wrote, "not for an age, but for all time." Class distinctions are very much with us in his plays, since his characters range from royalty to the lowest of the low. There seems to be little point in an American cast adopting an "Oxbridge" accent for the upper classes in Shakespeare, since that accent was not even in use in Shakespeare's day. I encourage Shakespeare casts toward ''mid-Atlantic'' or American standard stage speech, so that the sounds are well-produced (to keep the voices intact) and pronounced clearly enough for the audience to comprehend what is being said. When lower-class speech is involved, an American version of ''Mummerset'' seems to do very well, so long as the speech is not too broad and effortful. What must, I think, be absolutely avoided is any American regional accent, Brooklyn or western or southern, which would suggest cultural associations alien to the play's content.

In any case, the reading rehearsal is the time for establishing the speech ground rules.

THE PRODUCTION LIBRARY

At this point I like to introduce the cast to the production library. A copy of a good International Phonetic Alphabet pronouncing dictionary should be available. I use *An English Pronouncing Dictionary* by Daniel Jones.* A good Shakespeare glossary, like Onions,** should be around every Shakespeare rehearsal, as well as a copy of Eric Partridge's *Shakespeare's Bawdy*, for research into Shakespeare's dirty jokes.† Books on the history, politics, and general culture of the period of the play (for modern plays, too) should be assembled and placed in the care of the stage manager, so that, when people are offstage, they can look up questions of interest that the play has evoked. Illustrations from the period will help with questions about posture, the wearing of clothes, and general behavior. The presence of such books will help create an atmosphere of inquiry and will stimulate curiosity and imagination.

EXAMINING STRUCTURES

As the scenes are read and a start is made on interpreting the play, the director should take the opportunity to alert the cast to structural devices in the writing: a series of short lines characterizing a scene, characters answering each other with long speeches of equal length, alliteration, poetic images, contrasts, comparisons, internal rhymes, builds, and so forth.

Writing habits of the playwright can be noted. Ibsen uses many broken speeches, which are usually printed ending in three dots: ''Do you mean . . . ?'' In his case, speeches are broken to indicate that characters interrupt one another; the broken speech is a device to keep the play going, to keep the pace up. If the actors think that the broken speech means the character stops for thought and finally, after a short pause, one actor answers, ''Do you mean'' with, ''Yes, I do,'' just imagine how the faulty interjection of these pauses can distort the tempo the author meant to convey.

---

*Daniel Jones, *An English Pronouncing Dictionary* (New York: E. P. Dutton & Company, Inc., 1943).
**C. T. Onions, *A Shakespeare Glossary* (Oxford: At the Clarendon Press, rev. ed., 1966).
†Eric Partridge, *Shakespeare's Bawdy* (New York: E. P. Dutton & Company, Inc. 1960).

The structure of speeches can be pointed out here. Shakespeare and many other writers of long speeches use an outline for such speeches that goes like this:

Introduction: usually a connective link with the preceding speech

Theme: a brief statement of the subject of the speech

Variations 1, 2, 3, etc.: examples, illustrations, and developments of the theme

Restatement of theme: a summing-up, reminding the listener of the subject of the speech

CHARACTERIZATION DECISIONS

It is during these days of slow reading that many general questions and answers about character will emerge. In *Twelfth Night*, for example, the actress playing Olivia is going to want to know early on how the director feels about some major questions; for example: is she a foolish, willful flibbertigibbet who, scorning a good man's love (Orsino), is punished by falling in love at first sight, like Titania with the Ass, with the inappropriate girl-disguised-as-boy Viola, or (b) might she be a serenely sensible person who values control in her life and who has successfully worked out her extended mourning for her brother as a device to evade the importunate and unacceptable Orsino, only to lose control by falling in love at first sight—unpredictable and all-powerful Love being the controlling element in the play? Is King Lear to be a senile dotard making a foolish decision and only too late learning what he should have valued, or might he be the strongest and wisest man in his world, who, as a limited human being, makes a human mistake, and is finally able to learn humility and forgiveness? Is Sergius in *Arms and the Man* just a fatuous ass or is there something heroic about him after all? Is *Pygmalion*, in spite of what Shaw says, really propelled by the sexual attraction between Higgins and Eliza?

Large questions like this, resolved of course by the director in preparation and already to some extent by casting, must be worked through with the actors step by step as the scenes and lines that led to the director's interpretation come up in the reading.

Questions about what is funny, what is moving, what is appealing will be broached and positions taken, to be expanded upon later in rehearsal.

In sum, every interpretative question posed by the play should be touched on during the reading period. Some questions may even be answered fully. Some bones of contention will be discovered. Still, by the end of the slow reading of the play, both director and cast should be working together toward clearly stated and understood goals, with a good idea of the nature of the task ahead.

THE FOURTH AND FIFTH DAYS—BLOCKING

By the time the cast arrives for the blocking rehearsals, the stage managers, who always arrive thirty minutes before the cast, will have removed the reading arrangement of chairs and tables, and the necessary rehearsal furniture and set-props will be in place.

When all cast members are present, the stage manager should assemble them facing the set. Then the director should walk the set for the actors, explaining where doors, stairs, platforms, and other elements of the set are and interpreting the tape marks on the floor. When two or more sets are indicated on the floor by different colors of tape, the floor is indeed a confusing maze. Fortunate are those who are in a situation where the basic platforms and stairs can be provided for rehearsal. Most actors have trouble visualizing scenery, and the more nearly the physical environment of early rehearsals resembles the real thing, the easier the adjustment to the actual set will be. It is disheartening to everyone when, in the fourth week, adjusting to the real platforms and stairs means reblocking the show.

For the blocking rehearsals I find I work best from a chair centered directly in front of the actors with a card table in front of it for my script. The stage managers can be at other tables to one side of me. I will need to move easily from my table into the acting area to demonstrate things and get back to the table again to consult my book. The stage managers' tables must be far enough to the side that I can move freely. Sneakers or rubber-soled shoes that don't "clump" will help me keep these moves unobtrusive. I like to have chairs at the far right and left to mark audience sight lines. Actors should be encouraged to walk *behind* the director and stage managers, never between them and the set. In any room with dance mirrors on the walls, the mirrors should be obscured. Brown wrapping paper taped to them works wonders.

BLOCKING—EVOLVED OR IMPOSED?

Anyone who has persevered to this point in reading this book knows that I think blocking is something the director works out in advance. Remember, however, that many actors have to work, and perhaps most often work, in another kind of situation, one like the first winter stock company in which I was hired as an actor.

After the director had walked the set for us, he would say, "Now, let's put Act One on its feet. *You* come from that door, and *you* are already seated over there. Let's go."

Now, this director was a talented man. He picked the plays, hired the company, designed the scenery, was his own business manager, wrote the press releases, and I think even took the photographs. This didn't leave him a lot of time for preparation. When he said, "Let's go," we did. We wandered around, with a lot of reference to what the Samuel French stage directions had to say about standing or sitting—all of us, except the character man. He had a good deal of weight to take off his feet, so he would head for the chair nearest to center stage, sit down, and stay till his exit came. This made for a certain monotony in the staging, so he was eventually uprooted, but it usually took a couple of weeks to do it. Otherwise, the blocking that we evolved from our wanderings was all the blocking we got.

This way of work—letting the blocking just happen—goes along with the atmosphere in which everybody says, "What luxury it is to have four weeks to rehearse!" So, they read for a week, and get up and wander around carrying the book for two weeks ("Isn't this comfortable!"), and then at the beginning of the fourth week somebody notices the poster out in the lobby and realizes that the thing opens in a week. Then panic ensues, the play finally gets blocked somehow, lines are crammed down by dint of much midnight oil, and the production that opens is essentially the summer-stock production they could have put on in a week, if that was all the time they had.

This evolution of the blocking by guess, by gosh, and by accident is often referred to as "organic," meaning emerging from the play and the actors as they grow to know it, rather than "imposed." Well, with three months to rehearse, I would be quite willing to be "organic" and go through with living actors those trial and error struggles that I confine to my study. The realities of the American theatre impose more efficient methods of work.

At the end of the first week of rehearsals or the beginning of the second, the actors cannot yet know what they want to do. They don't know enough about the play or themselves in it to say with any validity, "It doesn't feel right to sit on this line," or, "I feel I ought to do this speech lying on the sofa." For heavens' sake, they may very well end up doing the speech on the sofa, but they are in no position to boast valid feelings so early on.

THE BLOCKING PROCESS

What I ask the actors to do next is to acknowledge that we're just at the beginning, so that they are under no obligation to "feel" anything or to judge its artistic merits. I want them to accept that, for me, these days of blocking and the run-through that follows are simply mechanical and technical affairs.

I make it clear that all I expect them to do is read the lines clearly and write down as precisely as possible where I ask them to go and at what moment—and then go there. This works out best if each actor has a pencil. If not, the stage manager will provide one. No pens should be used, as changes will inevitably come that will require erasing.

Then, the blocking can begin. The time will be most efficiently used if the director, especially when blocking, remembers to speak *before* the move the actor is to make and before the line is read in which it comes. Two-thirds of the total rehearsal time is wasted if the actor reads the line, the director reads it again saying, "Now when you say . . . move to the chair," and the actor reads the line yet a third time as he moves to the chair.

The director should block as rapidly and efficiently as possible, but taking care *to give the actors all the time they need to write things down.* Insist on the writing down; some people will feel the instructions are so simple they cannot help but remember them, but it is just when things seem simple and obvious that they *must* write them down to avoid confusing one moment with another.

Treating the blocking as merely a technical matter of walking through and writing down what the director has already worked out has another advantage besides efficiency. It cools the actors off; it helps them deal with the play objectively. They quickly realize there is no way to be "good" when the director is interrupting all the time with things that must be written down. The actors, indeed, have *no* responsibility, except for reading the script clearly, writing legibly, and going where they are told. Not only are they not required to "act"; the conditions of the rehearsal make it impossible.

Once a scene, or ten or so pages of script, has been blocked, it is wise to go back over it. Just run it again, and when an area of confusion is uncovered, get the actors to write it clearly and correctly this time. This review gives the stage managers a chance, too, to get their own notes straight. Then, having reviewed, press on. No coffee, no cigarettes, no food should be permitted on the set in these or any other rehearsals. Spilling coffee, shifting cigarettes in order to write, fooling with ice cream—all this is time-wasting. Methodical, steady, unpressured progress is wanted here.

Half the play can be blocked this first day, although if things are a bit slower than that, there is no cause for concern. As director, cast, and stage management get used to one another, the pace will pick up.

The cast must be reminded during these blocking rehearsals that the blocking is just a sketch of the final product. They must be assured that gaps will be filled, changes will be made, and improvements will come in due course. They must be reminded that getting the show on its feet and seeing that first run-through is important for designers and the director, too, in terms of the whole production.

THE RUN-THROUGH AFTER BLOCKING

The director will do well to remember that "whole learning" is more effective than "part learning." In accordance with that well-established psychological principle, the run-through after the blocking actually speeds the learning process, although it feels like trying to take the play at one gulp. The prospect of this first run-through brings on panic in some actors. Insist that they carry the script and read, even though some of them will know many of the lines. Remind them that you are not looking for a performance but merely checking on the overall shape of the blocking, and that this, for them, must remain a mechanical and not an artistic task. Keep repeating, "Don't rush, don't act, take it easy, just mark it." And then be sure, if you give any notes, to confine them to matters of choreography and mechanics. It is "dirty pool" to ask them not to act and then give them interpretative notes. Save those notes for later; they won't get lost.

Indeed, at the end of this first run-through, all my notes are for me. Axiom: *All important notes and all notes that break new ground must be rehearsed, not merely given out verbally. The only note given verbally without rehearsal that has a chance of being executed is a reminder of something that has been rehearsed earlier.* So, at the end of this first run-through, I say loudly, "That was very good! You can all go home now—see you next week!" Someone is sure to sing out, "What, no notes?" I say, "Lots of them, and all for the director!" They want notes, of course, as an acknowledgment of their effort in "getting through." One reason not to give any is because, though something important on a mechanical level has taken place, nothing subjective calling for reward has happened. I want to keep the actors focused on *process*, not on results or on pleasing the director. A great deal has been accomplished, but not yet on the level of, "You were great!" More about notes, anon.

EXERCISES

1. Page 206—Prepare a "show and tell" for your production with the goal of exciting and stimulating the creative energies of your cast/audience. Things that you might want to consider are: why you are doing this play; why it is important to do now; what it means to you; how you are going to approach the text; how you are going to stage the play. Pay particular heed to the "showing" aspect of the presentation: drawings, renderings, pictures, sketches, floor plans, models, slides, film. The manner of presentation, as well as the contents, should represent your artistic vision as a director. Don't leave out music as a possible inspiration.

2. Page 211—Beckett was an Irish writer who wrote all of his plays in French. He prepared the English version of *Godot* after it had premiered in Paris. How do you think the transmission of the text reaches an American ear?

3. Page 216—You have two hours in which to block as much of the play as you wish. How do you wish to use that time? Show what you get as a result of your rehearsal. Justify why you did what you did.

CHAPTER 10

ACTING

T his book has proceeded chronologically through the director's tasks, and, though this chapter on acting may seem like a diversion from that outline, it is at exactly this point in the production that the director begins to deal with the art and craft of the actor. This subject deserves a chapter of its own at this point because all the rehearsal time between the second week and the beginning of technical rehearsals will be spent on solving acting problems.

THE "ENSEMBLE" IDEAL

The ideal for most serious American theatre people for years has been to create an acting ensemble whose members are activated by identical artistic goals and whose training embraces common principles and skills. Few of us have had a chance to create such ensembles, and almost none of us has built an ensemble that has endured. In *The Fervent Years*, Harold Clurman describes the waxing and waning of the Group Theatre. The Actors' Studio never achieved a company. I began the Seattle Repertory Theatre on the premise that a company could be created in Seattle that could stay together and learn to work in a unified way. Rotating repertory was to be the device on which our stability would depend. During my tenure there we did succeed in keeping productions on from one season to the next, but actors came and went seasonally, as actors have always done, which put an end to the notion of any *permanent* ensemble. Later, after my departure, Seattle abandoned rotating repertory and then abandoned the company idea. Actors were simply ''jobbed'' for one or more plays, a custom that eventually dominated the regional theatre scene. As I write, the ''company'' idea is coming back, but more as a response to budgetary than artistic considerations, since jobbing means one cast on salary playing one show and another cast on salary rehearsing the next show, and is thus more expensive than keeping one company that rehearses one play in the afternoon and plays another at night.

I now think that, to achieve a true ensemble, one would have to start with actors early in their careers, training them in the desired mode and then somehow insulating them from opportunities in film and television and theatre elsewhere until their work habits were thoroughly set. I suspect that our society and the theatre it fosters may be marching to a different drummer.

Our work with actors then must, willy-nilly, be such that we can create satisfactory productions with actors trained in whatever ways they come to us, selecting them because of their talent, their fitness for the play, their flexibility, and their cooperativeness.

ACTING THEORIES AND REHEARSAL

All directors inevitably develop their own theories about acting. I have, but I urge that discussions of acting theory be avoided during rehearsal. It is true that one of the chief tasks of the director is to function as acting coach, dealing with truth, connections from moment to moment, tensions, mannerisms, and the kit-bag of personal impedimenta that every actor brings to acting. Of course the director will *have* theories about acting. In rehearsal, though, you should focus on *process*. ''This is how we'll block; this is how long we'll read; this is when the lines should be learned.'' But ''method,'' Stanislavski, Brecht, Strasberg, Meisner—all that should be left for classes. In rehearsal, you should simply work in terms of your theories, without discussion. Ask for what you want done, and get it from the actor as best you and he can, but do not justify yourself by quoting theory or authority. *What you want the actors to do* will very likely be received by them with conscientious willingness. The *theory* you put forward to support your choice may well prove to be *the red flag that creates resistance.*

Another side of this question has to do with how the actor achieves his effects, what he is ''using.'' Suppose, say, that the character receives a piece of terrible news. In *Abe Lincoln in Illinois*, Abe has to deal with Anne Rutledge's death. Suppose that what the actor does who is playing Abe is very moving. Suppose he is able to repeat it and it becomes part of the production. ''What is he using?'' ''Don't ask,'' is my advice. If it is working, just be grateful. Describing things that are working often kills them. ''If it works, don't fix it.'' On the other hand, if the actor has trouble making the moment work, the director's questions or probings about what to ''use'' can be productive—general suggestions for looking in areas of sense or emotion memory that may not have occurred to the actor. Even then, you should keep your suggestions general and let the *actor* do the real inner work.

A horror story comes to mind, featuring a director who, for obvious reasons, will remain nameless. When directors do this sort of thing, the story gets around.

This one concerns A *Midsummer Night's Dream* and comes directly from the actress playing Titania. After a run-through, the director's principal note to her was, ''You aren't appalled enough when Oberon removes the charm and reveals what you've been in love with.'' He was referring, of course, to Bottom, transformed into an ass. ''Here's this little paper bag. I want you to carry it around with you from the time when you meet Bottom till Oberon takes off the charm—and then look into it.'' Taking the bag, she obeyed. The great moment came. She was to open the bag and receive the shock that would inform the moment forever after with ''emotion memory.'' She opened the bag, and here I quote: ''The damned thing was filled with dog shit. So I just walked down front and threw it at him and walked out. He's probably still standing there.''

Such ''tricks'' are apt to rebound. I think the director must work with the actors to achieve the desired production by the most practical and direct means, avoiding tricks and didactic lectures and simply acting implicitly in terms of whatever theories apply.

''ORGANIC'' VERSUS ''TECHNICAL''

The battle between advocates of ''living the part'' and proponents of external acting based on vocal and physical effects seems to have been going on for centuries, as one can see from Diderot's having written a piece as early as the eighteenth-century, called *The Paradox of Acting*. The chief codifier of modern realistic acting was Constantin Stanislavski. His disciples Maria Ouspenskaya and Richard Boleslavsky brought his doctrines to the United States in the twenties, where they influenced the aforementioned Group Theatre and the later Actors' Studio. Thus was spawned a line of teachers of an American version of Stanislavski's early ideas, popularly known as ''The Method.'' The Stanislavski influence has spread to England and throughout Europe and is now worldwide. New research and forthcoming new translations of his works will bring us closer to his mature vision.

Stanislavski wrote and taught in reaction to nineteenth-century European "ham" acting, which must have been superficial and broad. In reaction to Stanislavski's psychological realism, other performance theories have sprung up, including those of Brecht, Artaud with his theatre of cruelty, Gorotowski with his "poor theatre," and Peter Brook, with his restless experimentation.

Unless, like Stanislavski with the Moscow Art Theatre, Strasberg and Clurman with the Group, Brecht with his Berliner Ensemble, and Brook with his Paris base, you have your own theatre with its own funding and audience, you will have to be eclectic, taking your influence from all "schools," as you find them useful in working with your eclectically trained actors.

I reject definition by extremes. I don't accept that "organic" acting is good acting and "technical" acting is bad acting. I don't accept the opposite, either. I don't accept that "instinctive" is necessarily warm and honest and that "intellectual" is necessarily cold and false. Neither do I accept actors' descriptions of how they act, be they Olivier or Jack Nicholson, because invariably they have an ax to grind relating to publicity or image or philosophy. What they reveal can be only partial—interesting, but never the whole truth.

A DIRECTOR'S IDEAS ABOUT ACTING

First, I want to expose "the great lie," which is still being taught. What I call "the great lie" is the premise that "if the actor can truly grasp the character's given circumstances, his intimate biography, and his psychological underpinnings, then the physical externals of his performance will take care of themselves."

For me, that misses entirely what the theatre is up to. I don't believe we are in the business, art, or craft of setting a lot of truthful characters loose to interact. We are storytellers. We are at the service of creating "lies like truth," as Diderot put it, in order to interpret and fulfill the author's play with our production. That production must be shown to numerous audiences of paying customers during its life, each of whom deserves to experience precisely how we have decided to do the play.

THE ROLE OF FEELING

I do not believe that "what the actor feels" makes the slightest difference in the actor's playing or the audience's response to that playing, as long as the actor has prepared the role satisfactorily. The actor playing Medea is to me, as she was to Brecht, a reporter. Her job is to tell a story, by means of the most accurate reportage she can muster, about a person "like this" involved in a situation "like that." It has to *look* true, be accepted as true. The comedian

George Burns once said, "The most important thing in acting is honesty. If you can fake that, you've got it made!" For me, that says it all.

Ah, but how do you learn to "fake it"? Whose truth do you use? How much of that truth do you use? Stanislavski would certainly agree that if, as in Ronald Colman's film A *Double Life* about an actor playing Othello, the actor actually believed he was Othello and killed his Desdemona, that would constitute insanity, not acting.

USE OF THE "SELF"

This brings us to another "great lie" about acting—that acting is "pretending to be someone else." The actors who "pretend" are easy to spot. They are tense physically and they make faces. We say they are "indicating," sending signals to the audience that they "feel this" or "are that." We may call that "children's theatre acting," or "college acting," or "musical comedy acting," whichever we happen to dislike most at the moment.

The actor must create from himself. The only emotions he has known are his own. He has only his own body, his own voice, his own memories and life experiences. He can augment them by reading, by seeing plays, by all the devices of imagination. But even in imagining, he must employ his own inner points of reference; he has no other. How then is such a puny being to play a Lear, a Medea, a Hedda Gabler? I like to remind actors, as they approach these parts, that Lear and Medea, Hedda and Macbeth never lived at all, and never see the light of day as figures in drama until an actor gives them life. That actor has lived for twenty-five years—or sixty-five. He has countless fears, rages, ecstasies, victories, bereavements on which to draw. And, as Harold Clurman used to say, "Remember, you're the only Hamlet within three thousand miles tonight."

The actor must find what, in himself, is like the character. What experiences he has lived through have in them ingredients like the experiences of the character? To grasp the nature of Othello's jealousies, explore your own. Similarity—in fact and nature, if not in scale. But, remember, even small events can leave behind reservoirs of feeling. The actor must use his own past—must sift and probe it, and particularly so if the play has not at once reached through to those depths of feeling we call the unconscious. Psychiatrists believe that in artists the unconscious is more conscious, less buried and repressed, than in "civilians." Psychiatrists believe that is why we *are* artists, because as these memories and feelings push through into our conscious lives, we find a constructive way of dealing with them by converting them into the insights of our art. The actor's unconscious affinities with the script will emerge, in the talented, which is why Stanislavski said he was only codifying what good actors have always known. Being aware that we will certainly find Hamlet in ourselves, we must then learn *how* to look for him.

Using Hamlet to *reflect* yourself is, however, an error. "I will find the part in me, therefore the part *is* me"—no. You are bigger and more various than the part, even Hamlet. You will have to leave some of you out. Then, too, parts of Hamlet are *not* like you. Hamlet walks like a prince; you may walk like a basketball player. That part of you will need help. Hamlet speaks in blank verse; you probably don't. You will have to find out what his blank verse sounds and *thinks* like, and bring yourself to *it*. Some other aspects of the character must be *imagined*, because you haven't lived them. Just remember, it is *your* imagination.

The actor's body and voice must be free and open to execute the demands he makes on his physical being through his emotions, memories, mind, and imagination. The channel toward his unconscious, his inner being, may already be open (we call that *talent*), but that will matter only if body and voice can give form to what is waiting to be expressed. Relaxation to help achieve proper body alignment, posture, and control, through such a discipline as the Alexander Method, and relaxation to help achieve proper vocal placement, along with the elimination of constricting and limiting regionalisms of speech— these are the principal effects of good physical and vocal training. Actors cannot all be athletes or become Pavarottis or Hornes, but what they *can* do is take of what they have and make the most of it, so that their bodies and voices become trained channels through which their character choices can be transmitted.

PLAYING THE ROLE

Robert Lewis in his *Method or Madness* reminds us that Stanislavski divides the actor's work into *work on the self* and *work on the part*. Work on the part involves rehearsing and playing. The actor needs techniques for both. Again, I have recourse to the words "technique" and "technical"—bad words to some in our profession. In my view, all of acting is technical. There are the techniques of the internals. The self, that respository of buried treasure—the actor must find those parts of himself which fit and then relate them to the play. Then come into play the techniques of the externals—the use of body and voice and knowledge of the stage to project and convey those inner truths and thus tell the story the actor means to tell, not any other story arising from uncontrolled body, voice, or concentration. All this must be accomplished with "the art that conceals art," so that it appears to be spontaneous, effortless, and "real." George Burns said a lot in his pithy explanation of acting.

The key to *analyzing* the character lies in finding a fruitful super-objective— the thing the character is doing throughout the play that creates the "line" of the part. The director will help the actor find that, so what the actor is doing serves the play properly. Perhaps the director's word-for-word definition of it will work for the actor, but very likely the actor will need to reinterpret the director's statement into words he can personally connect with. So be it. All the director has to do is watch to be sure the actor's "line" through the play is working. The way the super-objective is accomplished is through the intentions—what the character is doing to someone or something, beat by beat.

In analyzing the play's beats, one names the intentions. In early rehearsals, the actor *plays* the intentions, or improvises upon them, being sure the chosen intention informs every look, every experimental gesture or move, and every inflection, until the next intention comes along in the next beat, and so on. The intentions, in the sense of the actor consciously thinking "I want to 'verb' him, and be sure I am doing that through this whole beat," are gradually absorbed, accomplished, and become less conscious. As the individual vocal and physical *adjustments* are selected and refined in rehearsal, the actor begins to play, not the *intention*, which is really a diagnostic tool, but each *moment*, or to play *from moment to moment*. If anyone were to interrupt and say, "What's your intention?" no doubt the actor could approximate what he and the director had agreed on during the second week or so, but the actor's real concentration has gone into listening, looking, responding—into a set of tiny connections, or moments. These are what he will *play*, as the production moves into performance.

REACTING

"Acting is *re*acting." That is an old saw, but when it is examined deeply and applied fully, it has significance for the entire craft of acting. We have been looking at plays for the characters' intentions and dealing with the actor finding his adjustments and making his selections. One might suppose from this that the character in the play and the actor in performance gets himself through by an act of *will*. One has, of course, seen such performances. The actor *commands* himself to execute his line readings, his moves, his business.

Contrast this with what Constance Collier, Katharine Hepburn's acting coach and the *grande dame* in many films, had to say about long speeches. "There is no such thing as a long speech. It is simply that the listener's dialogue is silent." Consider and apply. Further: "The listener writes the long speech for the speaker, in the sense that the speaker says what he thinks will reach the listener and convince him." It seems to me there is a strong logic in that.

Consider, then, that characters in a play are impelled into action by their *response* to something. Higgins, in *Pygmalion*, takes refuge in the church porch because it is raining—in reaction to the rain. He hears (reacts to) sounds that interest him, so he transcribes them—the sounds he hears write his notes for him. Someone challenges him for writing down what people say, and he reacts by answering. And so on. What I get from this idea of "reacting," pressed to its limits, is that one should so construct a role that every physical and vocal impulse in it comes from something outside—something said, a particular word that sets off a particular thought, a sound that produces a reaction, something on the set that the actor answers by word or look or deed. Rehearsing should consist, to an important degree, of a search for those external stimuli from which the energy is drawn for the words and activities of the character the actor is playing. Willing oneself through the life of a part can be enormously draining; drawing energy from a myriad of external promptings can be eternally renewing. The character doesn't know how the play is going to end. He often doesn't even know it is going to begin; Hamlet has no idea that he will encounter his father's ghost. There is, in every play, a wonderful string of surprises in store for every character. If he finds the surprises and the surprising responses to them that create more surprises, the actor will have tapped into a self-replenishing current of playing energy which, if he can relax while reeling from each shock, will send him bouncing off recharged in the new direction.

THE ACTOR'S SCORE

Without an overt discussion of any of this, the director can help the actor react off physical and verbal stimuli throughout the role—can indeed so structure the production that it travels by means of these stimuli, for which the actor must listen and watch.

Within the *directed* framework of an intention for each beat and an adjustment for each section of each speech (where the thought changes, and the actor has to find what produces the change, and what his character is trying to do that leads him to a new adjustment), the *actor* should be trying to construct a score—stimulus, response, which includes everything that *makes* him do something and what he *does* about it. This score is not a set of ideas or feelings; it should consist of sights, sounds, and smells received, and of looks, words, movements sent.

What I am talking about resembles to some extent what some people call the "inner monologue." The inner monologue consists of all the thoughts the character has while other people are speaking, along with all the unspoken thoughts and linkages that bind his spoken thoughts together. I think every actor ought to have a well-constructed inner monologue. What I want him to do, though, is turn it into a *physical* score. Remember, *if the audience can't hear it or see it, it isn't in the play.* If a certain word or phrase sets off a response that five sentences later causes the other character to interrupt and reply, I want the listener to have a physical (and visible) response to that word. It is of no use to have wooden-faced actors standing motionless and thinking wonderful thoughts while somebody else talks. The silent partner has no lines, but *he* is writing the speech of the speaker, and he can't be seen to do that standing still like a polite stick. I am not suggesting that the actor fidget; I am suggesting that the director direct both sides of the scene, not just the speaker.

An actor with a proper score can never forget his lines. One physical moment will lead inevitably to the next, with no moment like any other moment, since each is specific unto itself. The actor's ''cue'' is not the last word of his partner's speech; in real life we always interrupt one another. His ''cue'' is whatever word or phrase or movement makes him ready to answer with his next speech. That word or phrase has to set him off, so that he can hardly wait to speak. Once the actor has clearly defined what in each instance gives him the impulse to speak, he will always know, not ''Oh, God, it's my line!'' but that there is only one possible thing to say, and then he'll say it. No moment in any play should be exactly like any other moment in that play. If that definition really takes place, the actors will always know where they are.

SPONTANEITY

''Not a machine,'' my French fencing master used to say, emphasizing that, although the correct parries, feints, and attacks in fencing must be executed precisely, they must always depend on, and spring from, the response of the opponent. Spontaneity and ''the illusion of the first time'' in acting depend on the actor living in the moment, actually seeing and hearing that to which he must respond. He must never respond automatically (''be on automatic pilot,'' as some actors put it) but must always be aware that every moment on stage contains danger, suspense, and the possibility of many responses, one of which he chooses. Oh, yes, we've rehearsed, so it's always the prepared response, but for the audience, it really *is* the first time, so the actor must always walk the tightrope of other possibilities. Something dangerous, unexpected, the possibility of surprise, must always be in the air.

PREPARATION FOR THE PERFORMANCE

Where does the actor's score begin? How does he start the performance? Playing a long part is rather like walking into a one-way tunnel. Once you enter, you have to keep going. You will, indeed, come out, and into an inevitable, but unexperienced future. ''After the show'' will come, and one can even make plans where to go and with whom, but if it's Hamlet you're starting, there's a long time ahead of you in that tunnel before ordinary living takes hold again.

Beginnings are so important. Acting is, first of all, physical. Body and voice must be warmed up—and not ''warmed out.'' Simple stretches and back rolls are good to do; one hundred pushups will invade the energy the actor needs for the performance. For the voice, there should be some relaxation exercises, some breathing and resonance work, and some articulation ''waker-uppers.'' Fifteen minutes of this before going on will probably suffice, if there has been an additional hour earlier in the day. I am not personally enthusiastic about group warm-ups, feeling that better results are achieved if each actor finds his own personal and private focus in his own way. I believe the actor should review his lines, too, each day, though not immediately before the performance, for fear that in the middle of the show he might suddenly think, "My God, I've already said that!" The best reason for reviewing the lines is to review the previous rehearsal or performance, going over the rough patches and correcting them. There are always some fluffs and mistimings. If there is no review, the actor may well only remember last night's gaffe as he approaches it in tonight's performance. The danger is that either he will again make the same mistake, or in remembering it, fail in concentration someplace else.

Now comes the time just before going onstage. Some people think preparation means "working oneself up" into a mood, a state. "Shaking the ladder" was an old term for it, from the custom, if one had to enter out of breath, of going over the the backstage "A" ladder, grabbing it, and giving it a good hard shake in the name of realism. The entering actor wants, not emotion, but concentration. He must do whatever will narrow his focus, shut out the world, and clarify his mind and senses. He must be ready, in all ways, to "live in the moment," like a tennis champion, a race driver, a basketball star on the court. As his cue approaches, I think he should create one physical sensation, sense memory, smell, distant sound that leads from the last moment offstage to the first moment onstage. Another way to say it is, "The moment before an en-

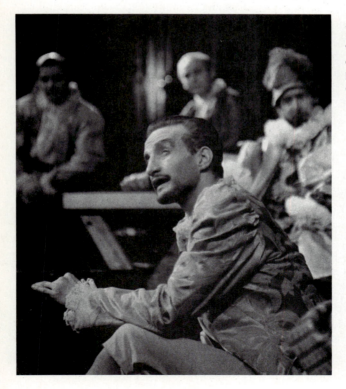

As You Like It
New York Shakespeare Festival, 1958
The young George C. Scott, as Jaques, "still enraptured by a distant melody." This production immediately followed his *Richard* III, and was also directed by Stuart Vaughan.

trance should be a piece of physical action, just offstage." For Henry Higgins it could be pulling his coat collar closer around his neck to keep the rain out. For Dr. Stockman it could be catching the smell of food as he enters the hallway to discard his hat and coat. For Mark Antony after Caesar's murder it could be seeing from offstage the bloody-handed murderers and bracing himself to make the proper entrance into their midst. Jaques, in *As you Like It*, for "A fool, a fool; I met a fool in the forest!" might enter still enraptured by the sound of a distant melody. These are highly personal matters, but the stronger the sense memory is in that offstage moment just before the entrance, the more strongly the actor will enter centered upon the chain of physical moments that will carry him successfully through the play.

E X E R C I S E S

1. Page 222—Does *Godot* require more "organic" or more "technical" skill of the actor? How does your answer reflect your bias as a director? How do you wish actors to respond to you as a director?

2. Page 222—What can you do as a director to promote the idea of ensemble playing? Does this idea prove consonant with your own concept of the director/actor relationship?

CHAPTER 11

MODERN ACTORS/ CLASSIC PLAYS

In the preceding chapter we dealt with acting in a broad spectrum of plays, because the questions of identity, emotion, physical action, and the exact placement of the actor's concentration are matters every actor and director must deal with in every play.

Period plays, however, and especially verse plays, call for specific skills in the handling of text that deserve special attention.

WHY CHARACTERS SPEAK

Just as the director must ask himself, for every scene, "Why do they come in here—why don't they just stay out there where they are?" so for every long speech he must ask, "Why doesn't he just shut up?" In other words, what is the purpose for all these "words, words, words"?

One hears, from the middle distance, someone saying, "The words serve to express the emotion of the character." The emotions? What are they—anger, fear, dread, hatred, sexual desire, anguish, love, satisfaction, relief, triumph, loss, etc.? One doesn't need *words* to express emotion. See if there isn't a word-less sound (roar, grunt, sigh, gasp, scream, purr) by means of which you can express quite clearly each of the emotions listed above. Well, then!

Another voice offers, "Words convey the character's intentions." Yes, of course, and give that person a "B" for knowing about intentions. But ask if most recognizable intentions, expressed as physically and colorfully as possible, really *need* all those *words*. Try using gibberish—meaningless sounds—paralleling some Shaw or Shakespeare speech, and see if you can't express all the intentions by means of inflection and vocal color, using the voice alone to woo, to batter, or soothe . . . you can; I can.

We seem to be approaching the conclusion that (surprise, surprise) the words have an *intellectual* function, that they express *content* and *ideas*.

In order to channel one's energies into ideas, one must *control* the emotions. I suggest that the role of the character's emotion, when it comes to acting long speeches, is usually to function as *obstacle*, something the character must control and keep down so that feeling doesn't get in the way of thinking. Emotions must be held at bay, in order to convey to the partner the *ideas* contained in the speech.

There is plenty of emotion charging around in *Macbeth*, Act II, scene 2, when Macbeth comes down from the murder of Duncan, but Macbeth and Lady Macbeth must hold their emotion in check, to the extent that they need to speak—so that they *can* speak.

Macbeth: I have done the deed. Didst thou not hear a noise?

Lady Macbeth: I heard the owl scream and the crickets cry.
        Did not you speak?

Macbeth: When?

THE FAMILY REUNION
Stadttheater Münster, 1965
Modern verse plays, such as this drama by T. S.
Eliot, demand the same skills of the actor as
playing in Shakespeare does. Left to right:
Elizabeth Flickenschild as Agatha,
Tillie Darieux as Amy.
Photo courtesy German Information Center

Lady Macbeth: Now.

Macbeth: As I descended?

Lady Macbeth: Ay.

Macbeth: Hark!
     Who lies i' th' second chamber?

Lady Macbeth: Donalbain.

Macbeth: This is a sorry sight.
                          (Looking on his hands.)

Lady Macbeth: A foolish thought, to say a sorry sight.

Macbeth: There's one did laugh in 's sleep, and one cried, "Murder!"
     That they did wake each other. I stood and heard them;
     But they did say their prayers, and address'd them
     Again to sleep.

Lady Macbeth: There are two lodg'd together.

Macbeth: One cried, "God bless us!" and "Amen" the other,
     As they had seen me with these hangman's hands.
     List'ning their fear, I could not say "Amen"
     When they did say "God bless us!"

Lady Macbeth: Consider it not so deeply.

Macbeth: But wherefore could not I pronounce "Amen"?
     I had most need of blessing, and "Amen"
     Stuck in my throat.

Even when a character is alone onstage, speech is a way of defining, to himself, what he feels. Raw emotion must be held at bay, so he can clarify his thoughts. Further along, in the same scene:

Macbeth: Whence is that knocking?
     How is't with me, when every noise appalls me?
     What hands are here? Ha! they pluck out mine eyes.
     Will all great Neptune's ocean wash this blood
     Clean from my hand? No, this my hand will rather
     The multitudinous seas incarnadine,
     Making the green one red.

This use of strong emotional forces as the obstacle to the expression of strong ideas lends poetic power to many scenes, but the actor must understand what the relationship is between words and emotion for the speaker. He must remember that the character is inventing the words because she *needs* them.

PLAYING ARTICULATE CHARACTERS

There is a wonderful Elizabethan word that we should keep in mind as we approach all plays of language. The word is "wit." Of course, the word "wit" is in use today, usually in association with the idea of "humor," but the expanded meaning that Elizabethans gave it is what makes it interesting for actors.

Onions, in his *Shakespeare Glossary*, cites the following usages of the word "wit" in Shakespeare's plays. (I omit his citation of specific plays and lines as not relevant to this discussion.)

Wit sb. (the foll. senses are characteristic of the Eliz. period)

1. the mental powers or faculties, the mind; common sense, imagination, fancy, estimation, memory . . .

2. power of imagination or invention; contrivance, stratagem, power of expedients . . .

3. sound sense or judgement, understanding, intelligence . . .

4. wisdom, wise or prudent knowledge . . .*

I see "wit" as the adroit mind finding surprising and revealing relationships between things apparently unconnected and the same mind probing for ramifications of meaning in an objective, distanced, and emotionally controlled way. Relentless curiosity propels "wit," and we see that curiosity in action throughout dramatic literature.

In plays written before, say, 1930 (with some notable exceptions, like plays by Chekhov), most characters were articulate. When they knew what they wanted to say, they had little trouble saying it. The actors who performed in plays by Shaw, Wilde, Pinero, Shakespeare, O'Neill, Barrie, Barry, and Coward were used to playing characters who spoke easily. Film, television, and our later theatre have given us characters who don't have words, by reason of class limitations or lack of education. Where an earlier playwright's hero could express his passions in a lyrical outpouring, some modern playwrights' characters can only squeeze out lines like:

"I love yuh. You know? I just—love yuh, that's all. Like,

it's—you. You're the—I just love yuh!"

Well, having to act that kind of material, actors get out of the habit of speaking. To many modern actors, the loquacity of characters in period plays

---

*C. T. Onions, A *Shakespeare Glossary* (Oxford: At the Clarendon Press, 2nd rev. ed., 1966), p. 251.

seems false and literary. They don't know in their own lives the facile flow of ideas, so they cannot invest characters who talk fluently with reality. The director of the period play must be ready to help modern actors deal with the truth of the act of speaking.

SOME TECHNIQUES FOR LONG SPEECHES

William Poel (1852–1934), a British stage director and guiding spirit of the Elizabethan Stage Society, created productions (1894–1905) that led to the extinction of the old elocutionary, singing style of reading Shakespeare. He pointed out that the chief fault of most actors handling complex language is the tendency to "use" too many words. In an effort to be sure the audience understands what he wants to convey, the actor tries to express everything, investing the text with too much word color, too many inflections, and too much underscoring. Poel was, of course, particularly concerned with verse speaking but his advice serves for prose as well.

What happens when actors use too many words is that while the members of the audience may well understand all the *words* (if the actors speak clearly and loudly enough) they are likely not to understand the *lines*. Emphasis and subordination are suppressed as all words become of equal value in the actor's effort to squeeze out every drop of meaning and color.

THE TELEGRAM

I suggest using the device of the "telegram" to conquer this problem. Real telegrams have gone out of general use, so the image is not as familiar as it once was. The sender of a telegram was charged by the word, so, in order to avoid extra expense, senders usually stripped telegram messages to their essence.

Such a telegram can be extracted from a long speech. First, find the essential words, the words the audience must hear to make sense of the whole speech—the *key words*. Key words are apt to be: (1) the subject of the sentence or clause; (2) the verb; and (3) the object of the verb. Nouns and verbs are apt to be frequent key words, adjectives and adverbs less so, and prepositions and conjunctions even less so. Pronouns are apt to be essential only when they are used as subject or object, or when distinctions are being made: "*You* go, not *me!*"

Here is a verse speech with its key words boldfaced: (Shakespeare's *Richard* III, Act I, scene 1).

Gloucester: **Now** is the **winter** of our **discontent**
Made glorious **summer** by this **sun** of **York;**

And all the **clouds** that **lour'd** upon our **house**
In the deep **bosom** of the **ocean buried.**
Now are our **brows bound** with victorious **wreaths,**
Our bruised **arms hung up** for **monuments;**
Our stern **alarums chang'd** to merry **meetings,**
Our dreadful **marches** to delightful **measures.**

Here is the telegram derived from just the key words:

"Now winter discontent made summer sun York; clouds
lour'd house, bosom ocean buried. Now brows bound
wreaths, arms hung up monuments, alarums changed
meetings, marches measures."

Read it aloud with sense and you will see that it contains the basic message.
Here is the speech again, with an indication of how, by putting dependent phrases in parenthesis, the speech can be correctly phrased. The subordinate, less-important, and modifying words must be thrown in rapidly in connection with the words they modify, leaving the "acting" and color for the key words.

Gloucester: Now (is the) winter (of our) discontent
Made (glorious) summer (by this) sun (of) York;
(And all the) clouds (that) lour'd (upon our) house
(In the deep) bosom (of the) ocean buried.

And so on.
Here is the same exercise using a prose speech.

(*Tanner to Ann, Shaw's* Man and Superman, *Act II*)

Tanner: Is **that** any **reason why** you are **not** to **call** your **soul** your
own? Oh, I **protest** against this vile **abjection**
of **youth** to **age! Look** at **fashionable society** as you
know it. **What** does it **pretend** to be? An **exquisite
dance** of **nymphs. What is** it? A **horrible procession** of
wretched girls, each in the **claws** of a cynical, cunning,
avaricious, disillusioned, ignorantly experienced, foul-
minded **old woman** whom she **calls mother,** and
whose **duty** it is to **corrupt** her **mind** and **sell** her to the
highest bidder.

Here is the telegram:

"That reason why not call soul own? Protest abjection

youth age! Look fashionable society. What pretend? Exquisite dance nymphs. What is? Horrible procession
wretched girls, each claws old woman calls mother, duty
is corrupt mind, sell highest bidder.''

Please note that one cannot *leave out* the non-telegram words and have the speech "work." Look, in the Shaw speech, at the splendid series of adjectives between "claws" and "old woman." Of course the mounting momentum of that series is essential for the laugh that comes after "whom she calls mother," but the laugh itself depends upon the actor being certain that the correct words, and not too many words, are stressed. Understand, though, that the choice of key words is not fixed and immutable. Tastes may differ, but the principle remains the same: it's a matter of getting the greatest amount of meaning out of the most efficient amount of effort.

Each speech in each play is unique in shape, and finding that unique shape and pointing up its key words has the additional advantage of breaking up actors' habitual speech patterns, monotonous stress, and/or repeated inflec-tional devices.

I urge that every actor in every play of complex language find the key words and make telegrams for every speech in every part. Just knowing that it should be done and then relying on instinct is not enough; it is an intellectual task, and its results will often surprise. After all, one is hunting for the *author's* structures, not simply repeating one's own. The resulting clarity will be re-warding.

LADDERS

Pitch ladders or *stairsteps* are an important aspect of the inflectional shape of the English language, and the use of that knowledge matters in the theatre, where, along with being clear and sounding "real," we need to carry the audience along with us through the thoughts of speeches, scenes, acts, and whole plays. Everything must *progress*, build, point forward, and if you drop the audience's attention along the way, there's no getting it back.

Having made your telegram, notice how it gains in meaning and clarity if, when you read it aloud, you raise the pitch slightly as you move through the sentence. That is the ladder in question—a slight climbing upward in pitch, a going up the stairs, ending or dropping the voice only at the end of the thought, to start another ladder with the new thought. One does not drop all the way down, of course, but tension and a build in pitch is maintained through-out a sequence of connected thoughts. It is the key words that benefit from the "stairsteps" approach—the other words simply attach appropriately to the key words from which they depend. In a long speech, one must be careful to start low enough in pitch not to run out of the top range of the voice at the end, and great care must be taken to make the pitch gradations between key words sufficiently subtle and narrow that one can indeed get through the speech. Remember that, as a thought ends, the voice drops, and at the new thought, a change of pitch comes, starting a new ladder carrying the thought forward by means of rising pitch on key words.

One must listen to skilled British speakers to get the best sense of this. The actor Denholm Elliott does a particularly skillful job of it. American speech is less inflected than British speech and most other languages, because of the melting-pot influence of so many accents and tunes and rhythms impinging on our basic speech. There is little pressure in our schools toward an "educated speech" that can reflect, in its melodies, the subtleties of the written language. American speakers tend to rely on length of pause to indicate change of thought, with pitch patterns that are quite monotonous. In the theatre, this is boring, and in the play of complex thought and meaning, the pitch gradations that are needed to carry the audience along with the author are often missing. The audience needs to be helped by the actor's changing pitch when he changes thought. Awareness of "the ladders" makes the tool of pitch available to the American actor for use with our best American playwrights. With writers like O'Neill and Odets, we must in the theatre project, along with the illusion of reality, the truth of the author's ideas. We have to come to terms with the essential artificiality of standing at one end of a room and speaking loudly to the other actors while hundreds of people sit and listen and pretend to believe that the actors are in a living room.

COMPARISON AND CONTRAST

The actor's awareness of the devices of *comparison* and *contrast* and his ability to point them up vocally will help him achieve clarity.

The *comparison*, emphasizing the equality of two elements, will be clear to the hearer if the things to be compared are given equal pitch and a balanced stress. An example:

(*Shaw again, Tanner in* Man and Superman, Act II; *actually a pair of comparisons*)

Tanner: "... the voice of nature proclaims for the **daughter** a **father's** care and for the **son** a **mother's.**"

The *contrast*, emphasizing difference, will be clear if stress points up the contrasting words or phrases, with a little more stress on the second element than on the first, and if, in addition, pitch is raised or lowered for the second element. For example:

(Man and Superman *again*, Act II, Ann *this time*)

Ann: "... Yesterday I was a **boa constrictor:** today I am
an **elephant.**"

It can be argued that we use these devices in real life and therefore know how to execute them instinctively. Yes, but we don't speak with Shaw's complexity, and in daily life we are not communicating to what Shakespeare calls "a whole theatre of others."

INTENSITY AND ENERGY

One other general point needs to be made about plays of long speeches and vigorous ideas. That is, they require intensity in the playing. The speaking must be precise and energetic, and the actors' intellectual intensity must be maintained at a high level. The cast must make the mental duel of ideas exciting by their own excitement. "Laid-back" Shaw just does not work.

Since the question of energy has come up in connection with the play of heightened language, let me address it in a general way here, as it is a subject often misunderstood. Acting energy is not the same as force or loudness. It is more a matter of concentration, of intensity of focus. The axiom to remember here is: *The actor's playing energy is always maintained at a high level—his desire to play, to be watched and listened to. What changes is the way in which the play directs that energy.* There are soft places and slow places and places where the character is silent or asleep. Less *force* will be expended here, but the actor's *inner* energy must not flag. Having missed the performance, I once asked a friend how a certain well-known film star had done in his new stage role. My friend replied, "He was a moving black hole." My friend was describing the absence of what I call "playing energy."

SHAKESPEARE FOR ACTORS

Fashions change, and the changing attitudes toward verse speaking are well documented on disc, film, and videotape.

There was prevalent, in living memory, a "singing style" of speaking Shakespeare's verse. The recordings of Maurice Evans, most notably a *Macbeth* with Judith Anderson, give us a notion of what the old "grand manner" was like. Vowels and voiced consonants were prolonged, "s's" were hissed, an over-resonated, "augmented," "voicey" voice was used, and enrichment by a hearty vibrato was not omitted. All this went with a long stride (what the critic

Stark Young called "the tragic goose step"), florid gestures, and some absurd stage conventions such as "always point at something with *two* fingers, old boy, not one—one can't be seen."

All this was a holdover from the pre-motion picture days of touring actor-managers, huge theatres with several balconies, and primitive lighting conditions that forced the actors to fight their way out of the gloom. The old costumes, with their satins and sparkling glass jewels, give testimony as to how hard actors had to work just to be seen. And, "If you can't see, you can't hear!"

VERSE AND PROSE

There was also a sense that verse demanded a more elevated elocution than prose. This may be due to some influence from the French theatre, where a formalized dramatic declamation for the neoclassic plays of Racine and Corneille has its place to this day. Yuri Zavadsky, director of the city theatre of Moscow, saw his first English-language Shakespeare at New York's Phoenix Theatre in 1959. The play was my production of *Henry* IV, *Part* I. He went with Norris Houghton, co-founder of the Phoenix, a Russian speaker and an American authority on the Russian theatre. According to Houghton, Zavadsky liked the production but had one question: "Why was there no difference between how the actor spoke when the text was verse and when it was prose?" Such a question, of course, would never occur to those of us from an English or American tradition and could only have come from someone trained in a French-influenced theatre such as the Russian.

There *is* a difference between verse and prose, but not in terms of "prose spoken, verse declaimed." Shakespeare uses verse for lyrical, tragic, significant, or otherwise "elevated" parts of the plays; prose is used for lower-class characters and for comedic or "homely" material. Where there is a switch from prose to verse, or vice versa, look for the characters' emotional changes. In *As You Like* It, Rosalind speaks prose when she is teasing Orlando, even though her language is quite elaborate, but she speaks verse on less jocular occasions, such as when Duke Frederick banishes her. The only change the audience should notice, when the actor goes from prose to verse, is this change in the emotional climate of the scene. The actor will, of course, speak the verse with correct stress and meter, and this subtle shift to a more ordered style is precisely what the author wanted. The actor must still sound like a human being spontaneously speaking his thoughts.

Actors must be helped to understand that verse is not just a fancy way of speaking. How often have I heard an actor say, after working out a paraphrase of a complex verse line, "Well, if that is all he meant, why didn't he just *say* it?" Verse is not a matter of grace notes and ornamentation. It is the mathematics, if you will, of language. Verse offers the author the most precise, accurate, and concrete way of saying exactly what he wants to say. Its form and disciplines ensure that he must be economical in his expression and exact in his thought. The actor must come at the verse problem knowing that the verse embodies precisely what *his character* wants to say, because *his character* is writing the speeches, not some blameworthy blabbermouth of an author.

WORD COLOR

Another idea actors of Shakespeare need to hear is that "there is no such thing as word color." Elocution teachers used to ask us to express the emotional content of the words themselves. When you say, "Black night," there really is no way to say "black" to make it blacker. So with the blue of the sky, the patter of the raindrops, the roar of the thunder and the flash of the lightning—oh, you can roar and patter and flash away, but all you sound is phony. Language, in verse drama, derives its full variety and truthful emotional tone from the *intentions of the character*. The characters are using words they have chosen as weapons to win what they want in the scene. The words take on qualities, not from their own abstract musicality (which will be there anyway), but from the nature of the character's intention. Remembering this keeps the actors truthful.

METRICAL AND OTHER TECHNICAL ASPECTS OF VERSE

There are some technical aspects of Shakespeare's verse that actors need to understand. He wrote for actors, and if they accept the built-in help the verse provides, they will find he has pointed them in the right direction.

First is the value of *scansion*. Scanning the verse means finding where the stresses occur in the line. Shakespeare's plays are written in *iambic pentameter*, a line with ten beats and five major stresses, a *foot* (unit of meter) usually consisting of an unstressed syllable followed by a stressed syllable.

Hŏw swéet / tħe móon / lĭght sléeps / ŭpón / thĭs bánk. /

Each foot in this "regular" line is an *iamb*.

Sometimes the *trochee*, a metrical foot consisting of two syllables, is mixed in—an easy matter, in that instead of having one light syllable followed by a stressed one, the trochee has one stressed syllable followed by a light one:

Nów ĭs / tħe wín/tĕr óf / oŭr dís/cŏntént /

Sometimes Shakespeare uses the *spondee*, a metrical foot consisting of two stressed syllables:

Crý há/vŏc ańd / lĕt slíp / tħe dógs / ŏf wár /

There is more to be learned about all this which really has no place in this book. The point I want to emphasize here is that *the actor must scan the verse in order to find which words the author wanted stressed*, and a very important point it is.

Meter, as iambic pentameter, is a way of describing *rhythm*, and is quite separate from *tempo*, which has to do with rate of speed. Within any *meter*, one can, while correctly speaking verse, go fast or slow, accelerate or slow down, according to one's feeling about the passage. In fact, one *must* vary the tempo, in accord with thought and feeling, if one is not to seem a metronomic robot.

The verse keeps going—the *meter*, spoken rapidly or slowly, keeps marching on, without *pauses*. Such pauses as Shakespeare wants he generally accounts for by leaving out beats in a line. A line with only four or three major stresses instead of five means to the actor, "Look for a pause—why do I pause?" On the other hand, a line of verse is frequently split between two speakers, which accounts for the printing of the line in the following fashion:

Ros.   I have more cause.

Cel.   Thou hast not, cousin;

This means that no pause is intended between the characters' speeches and that the meter marches on. The Germans have two phrases for the kind of playing Shakespeare's text requires: "Text on text," meaning no pause between speeches, and "Spoken as if by one voice," meaning the same thing.

Even in verse, the actor has to sound like a human being making the words up on the spot. This doesn't mean "hunting for the right word," but rather maintaining a spontaneity of impulse rather than a reciting sound.

BEHAVIOR IN PERIOD COSTUMES

There is no obligatory "style" in which to play Shakespeare, except that the actor should know how to behave realistically in the costumes and the manners of the period in which the production is placed.

One overall point needs to be made at the outset: in all plays of complex language, the actors will be well advised to stand, as much of the time as possible, three-quarters front or as close to full front as they can reasonably be. The imagery of verse or elaborate prose requires that the actor look up and out front a great deal. (See the section "Acting and Movement," pp. 133–134.) A lot of moving of feet will be saved (even in the modern-dress plays of T. S. Eliot) by "playing front." In period costume, the silhouette of the clothing will show to more advantage viewed front rather than profile.

Various newer books make an effort to describe "period style" for the actor, but the most successful work I have seen on the subject is a slim pamphlet published by Samuel French and in print since the thirties, called *Manners and Movements in Costume Plays*, by Isabel Chisman and Hester R. Raven-Hart. I urge all directors to secure and prize a copy. It covers the basics very well. As for some general advice:

Each separate period has bows and handshakes peculiar to itself. Research and incorporate them.

Behavior of and toward royalty is carefully prescribed; research it.

Behavior of and toward the clergy, likewise.

Shoes differ, period to period, as to heel height, etc. Rehearse in the correct shoes or an approximation.

Skirts differ, too. Rehearse in the best approximation available.

Wigs and collars affect how actors turn their heads. Rehearse with this in mind, to avoid last-minute panic.

The actor must never touch or handle his wig or costume unless absolutely necessary.

Ladies must *never* cling to the sides of their skirts or even lift them except when going *up*stairs, or kneeling, or rising from a kneel. It may be necessary to deal with a skirt or train when sitting or when turning.

Gentlemen must *never* clutch their sword hilt with a fist. They must no more draw a sword unless the character means to use it than in modern life one would flourish a loaded pistol.

FOR SHAKESPEARE:
Men in tights—a broad, open stance is preferred. Remember, no pockets.

Men and women's cloaks—these may be worn in a variety of ways, not just slung from the back of the neck like a laundry bag.

Both sexes—an erect posture, with chest high, neck straight, shoulders back and down, helps speaking.

FOR RESTORATION, MOLIÉRE, EIGHTEENTH CENTURY:
Men were not effeminate, merely mannered.

Men standing—see paintings and sketches. Ballet positions for feet.

Men sitting—violin player posture, one foot forward, one back.

Women's arms—wrists and hands rarely drop below waist because of lace on sleeves.

Women sitting—don't lean back in chairs or cross legs above the ankle.

Male props—quizzing glass, kerchief, pomander ball, muff, sword, walking stick.

Female props—fan, kerchief, reticule, pomander ball, parasol.

FOR NINETEENTH CENTURY:
Men—stood with feet closer together than in previous periods. Hands in pockets not considered well-bred. Neither was pointing with the finger or frequent gestures. Walking stick, hat, and gloves *de rigueur*. Research differences between European and American postures, degree of physical contact, and how close people stood to one another.

Ladies—no leg-crossing except at ankles. When sitting, keep back from touching chair. Fans and reticules still in use. Research things like tea-pouring, ladies kissing, etc.

The research librarian at your local library or college can help you find appropriate sources for historical periods.

THE TWO GENTLEMEN OF VERONA
New York Shakespeare Festival, 1987
Elizabeth McGovern (Julia) vibrant, yet comfortable and correct, in her seventeenth-century dress.
Photo: George E. Joseph

THE TWO GENTLEMEN OF VERONA
New York Shakespeare Festival, 1987
Elizabeth McGovern (Julia), equally vibrant, comfortable,
and correct, in her boy's disguise.
Photo: George E. Joseph

EXERCISE

1. Page 241—In what ways is *Godot* a poetic play? Based upon your definitions, locate passages in the text that verify your understanding. How do you apply the techniques for working on classical texts in verse to a modern prose play? Are the techniques the same? Give a demonstration of the practical application of this.

CHAPTER 12

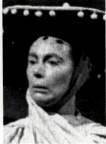

COMEDY

PLAYING COMEDY CAN BE LEARNED

The true comic or humorist has a special gift—the gift of perceiving familiar things in new and previously unexpected relationships. This is a creative act, akin to inventing something or grasping a new scientific principle. Some great humorists have performed their own material in public, as Mark Twain did. To that extent they participate in the actor's task, but their true talent is their idiosyncratic way of perceiving the world. This cannot be learned.

The craft of playing comedy *can* be learned, and almost any actor can learn it. The business of tapping the emotions for acting can be developed, but something approaching psychotherapy is required for the more repressed among us. Comedy, though, is an intellectual affair, a matter of the mind, and it is susceptible to the application of definitions and rules.

THE SOURCES OF HUMOR

The first step in playing comedy is to find out what is funny. In Chapter 2 I discussed types of comedy, from the dramaturgical point of view. The four sources of humor I outlined, and I repeat them here for easy reference, are:

1. *Exaggeration*—the humor of things larger than life, or smaller than life, funny simply because of their surprisingly outsize condition. A rather primitive level of humor, often involving ''sight gags.''

2. *Incongruity*—the humor of things not in themselves funny, but funny

ROMEO AND JULIET
New York Shakespeare Festival, 1957
Peter (Jerry Stiller) has stoutly declared that he has seen no man use the Nurse (Patricia Falkenhain) at his pleasure, and that if he had, his weapon would have been out. The Nurse looks askance at his double meaning. Note how both actors participate in the joke.
Director: Stuart Vaughan.
Photo: George E. Joseph

THE TWO GENTLEMEN OF VERONA
New York Shakespeare Festival, 1987
The humor combines incongruity and recognition. Launce (Dylan Baker) speaks to the dog as if he were human and could respond. The dog, of course, doesn't respond appropriately. Director: Stuart Vaughan.
Photo: George E. Joseph

when we find them unexpectedly combined. Also rather primitive, involving sight gags like slipping on banana peels.

3. *Wit*—the humor of surprising ideas, of language, of verbal jokes. The surprisingly incongruous juxtaposition of ideas produces a goodly portion of this humor, which is not at all primitive.

4. *Recognition*—"Isn't it so?" "Isn't that just like life?" The surprise of the simple, everyday truth aptly shown produces the laugh.

251

SEARCHING FOR "WHAT'S FUNNY"

The jokes the actor must execute and the comic situations in which he will participate in the course of his role will stem from one or another or a combination of these types of humor. The actor and director have to look here first for "what's funny."

Two examples of the search for "what's funny":

Touchstone in *As You Like It* is designated "clown," a professional jester. Perhaps he should be costumed in a jester's motley. Will that be funny? Not today. And if he were to be dressed like Bozo the Clown, it would certainly say "clown," but it wouldn't be funny. The clown's costume is based on exaggeration (red nose, big feet, red fright wig), but it is only a label, not in itself a joke. Well, maybe as a professional "fool" Touchstone has a "funny voice" or a "funny walk." These, too, are based on exaggeration and might even be good for an initial chuckle or two. That sort of thing won't get an actor through a part.

Touchstone is a character in a play, not just a "clown." He doesn't even function as a "clown" until his bravura Act V performance of the "Seventh Cause" routine. Let us look at the real Touchstone. He is introduced as a manservant going into the woods with the two ladies. If he is not a sexual threat or a love object (and he is not), then why does the author have him going into the woods with the girls? For protection, it would seem. Does he do his job well? Hardly. Rosalind herself has to take on the task of getting information from the first countryman they meet. As a man he might be able to carry things and make the tasks easier. Does he? He seems to be quick only at complaining. Gradually we see, if we listen carefully to the play, that Touchstone, a professional court jester, is hopelessly out of his *métier* in the country—a fish out of water. He tries with his court manners to "come it over" the shepherd Corin but makes little headway in proving his superiority. Audry, simple though she is, is shrewd enough to hold him at bay and keep him to his promise of marriage. "Incongruity," then is the key, but it is not in his position of clown but as the city dweller incapable of coping in the country that we find him funny. It is Touchstone the human being who gives rise to the genuine comedy of the role.

What is "funny" about Jack Tanner, the ebullient hero of Shaw's *Man and Superman*? Is it his egotism? Hardly. His ideas? Well, sometimes, and he does have "wit." Once again, though, we find our humor in incongruity, but this time it is the disparity between the know-it-all, idea-spouting, intellectual and revolutionary thinker that Tanner sees himself as, and the "little boy," knowing so much and yet lacking *self-knowledge*, whom Ann inexorably claims as her own. There is a hint of recognition working here as well, for women in the audience will respond to the "little boy" in Jack whom Ann finds she can love.

Once actor and director have decided "what is funny," the real work begins. What there is for the actor to learn about playing comedy can be *stated* quite simply. There are, I hasten to mention, only thirteen notes on a piano, arranged in various octaves. That is simply stated, too; but I sometimes think that learning to play comedy is harder than learning to play the piano. But comedy *can* be *learned*.

THE JOKES

The building blocks of comedy are the "jokes"—what the audience laughs at. In the preface to this book I refer to my meeting, as a graduate student, with the veteran actor Walter Young. Among other subjects I picked his brains about, I remember saying, "I don't know how to play comedy. I can't make anybody laugh." He answered, "Don't you even know about the five parts of a joke?" I confessed my abject ignorance. So he told me what they were, and I have used the formulation ever since. I have passed it on many times, as I shall do here, but I have never come across "the five parts of a joke" since, in any book or discussion. Every good comedian, from Jackie Gleason to Rex Harrison to Jackie Mason, has put these principles to good use, no matter what he has called them. Still, Walter Young's remains the only statement of the structure of a joke I have ever come across.

THE FIVE PARTS OF A JOKE

A joke is like an equation. The audience is given almost everything it needs to know to find the answer to the question posed by the joke. They get everything they really need *before* the "equals" sign in order to register what comes after it. Before the audience can figure out the answer, a surprising and correct answer is given, and the audience laughs. This transaction has five parts:

1. *The Plant*. The plant gives the audience the clues needed to solve the riddle and get the joke. One character may deliver the plant all by himself, or it can be shared, as in:

   A: Who was that lady I saw you with last night?

   B: That was no lady—

2. *The Pause*. In every joke there must be a pause, however short or long, during which the audience is invited to supply the answer. The pause creates suspense. Everything stops. What *is* the answer? "Not a lady—?" Then . . .

3. *The Point*.

B: That was my *wife*.

The unexpected but apt solution, also called "punch line," or "gag line," or "tag line," or simply "the joke," stops us for a moment in surprise, as it sinks in.

4. *The Amplifier*. This is a physical punctuation that follows The Point. Its function is to drive home what the audience has heard, to clinch it, to give the people time to realize what they've heard. In the example above, it could be a "take" from A, as he registers the news (and as the audience registers the news). It could be a triumphant gesture of "Gottcha!" from B. It could be the snare drummer's rim shot from the orchestra in the burlesque house pit. It could be Jack Benny's folded arms and the slyness of his sidelong glance. It could be simply an innocent shrug and "walk away" by the speaker, as if saying, "Sorry, that's how it is." The slow burn, the take, the tag, the stinger, the button— these are all names for kinds of amplifiers. I have heard the amplifier discussed this way: "A joke won't work unless someone reacts to it onstage." The above discussion of the amplifier explains why such a reaction is necessary.

5. *The Bridge*. This is, strictly speaking, not part of the joke, but one must identify it in order not to mistake it for part of the last joke or part of the next joke. I am discussing it here on the basis of "knowing what's funny." The bridge isn't funny, ever. The bridge is simply material needed after one joke is over to get on toward the next one. It is transitional material. In a comedy with a plot, the bridge may actually be material that advances the story. For our hoary old chestnut above, the bridge that leads to the next joke might go like this:

A: Your *wife*? I thought it was your mother-in-law.

B: My mother-in-law? Hey, you should see my mother-in-law. Why, she . . .

And we're off again, headed for a mother-in-law joke.

The actor has to know which part of the joke he is executing in order to be sure how to get his laugh. .One can amuse the audience along the way with winks and funny faces, but every chuckle earned in this way detracts from the big scripted laughs. Better to get three big ones than six little ripples.

MOVEMENT AND JOKES

The question of movement and focus during the parts of the joke must be addressed.

No *movement* (gesture, cross, crossing of legs—anything) on *key words of plant*. (Remember, movements cancel words. The audience has to retain those key words.) Move before or after, on transition words. Key words—no movement.

No *shift of focus during pause*. It is better to hold still during the pause. Even turning the head during the pause loses suspense and makes the audience think the thought has changed.

No *movement on key words of point*. (See *key words of plant, above*).

The amplifier probably *is* a movement. After that, one will probably want to move, in transition.

The matter of *timing* must also be addressed.

Spreading or excessively lengthening the sound of words in plant or point is to be avoided. The plant words must be clearly and crisply spoken, and the words or phrase of the point must be deftly packaged so the audience hears it as a word group, not as a meaningless series of individual words.

The pause must be long enough to create suspense and not so long that the audience "beats" the actor to the "punch line," or point. The audience must not be allowed to get ahead of the joke.

OTHER ASPECTS OF PLAYING COMEDY

The pace of comedy playing needs to be brisk and relatively quick. The audience must be kept alert, ready for anything. Playing *too* fast can prove wearing to the audience; they may give up trying to listen. Too slow a pace makes them sluggish of mind and slow to respond. Plays that depend on lots of sight laughs can go faster than plays that depend on the audience listening carefully, like the plays of Shaw or Wilde.

The tone, or pitch, of comedy playing must be "up" in the voice. Everyone should be encouraged to use a middle register and a lighter, rather than heavy, voice quality. Think "head voice" rather than "chest voice." Avoid, except in peculiar instances where the character demands it, casting deep, bass voices in comedy. The bright tone and pitch keep the audience cheerful.

When it is a play of wit and funny ideas, keep the movement simple. For a physical farce, condition the audience toward movement and sight laughs.

One wants the audience to laugh, in comedy. When the audience does laugh, the actors must wait until they can be heard before speaking the next line. If, by accident, an actor "walks into" a laugh, he should stop—and only start speaking again *when he is sure he can be heard*. No one will have noticed his false start. Very often, if his line is drowned by laughter, his partner's reply will make no sense and the next joke may well be lost. If he thinks he may not have been heard, he must *say the line again*. If he doesn't, the partner in question should simply say "What?" and *make* him say the line again.

In plays of heightened language, it is best, while the audience laughs, for the actor to stand quite still—not a "freeze," just realistically still—and then move slightly as the audience gets quiet and it is time to speak again. In plays of much physical action, the reverse works; the actor can move, or "fill," during the laughter and stop moving when ready to speak. These are not *rules*; they are merely time-tested devices for getting and holding attention of which actor and director should be aware.

Comedy sequences seem to work best in odd numbers. A series of props, sounds, entrances, gestures, all involving something repeated is the kind of sequence I mean. The laughs in such a series will come on the odd-numbered items in the series—one, three, five, etc. In that classic film about the Macy Santa Claus, *Miracle on 34th Street*, there is a trial scene in which a series of exhibits is brought into the courtroom by officers. In a full house, such as I was in when I first saw the film, the principle was completely illustrated and confirmed. Exhibit one got a nice laugh; we recovered our breath on exhibit two; three got a bigger laugh that lasted through four; and five got the best laugh of all.

The director should be aware of the dynamics of rehearsal laughter. There are directors who make the actors work in rehearsal to make the director laugh. This is bad on several counts, one of them being that the game becomes "to please the director," and another being that we tend to laugh out loud mainly at what is new to us, thus leading the actors to invent something different each time instead of perfecting what is right for the scene and moment. "Coterie" laughs are useless, too. These come in rehearsal from little packets of watching friends—fellow actors or staff—who go into hysterical giggles each time their buddy in the show, usually playing a "cameo" role, does one of his "shticks." I have seen leading men and women totally unnerved by this, losing all confidence in their own work and the director's until the first audience comes along, when they find that the real audience laughs, not at "in jokes," but at story values—all of which lie in the leading players' hands. Actors and directors must trust that, if they work at the craft of comedy, knowing what is funny and what treatment each part of each joke should receive, the audience will respond as wanted.

How certain can you be of audience laughter? If the actors and director know their craft, "as certain as death and taxes." Luck has nothing to do with it. What does vary is the size and makeup of the audience. The larger and better-attended the theatre, the better the chance of playing to a cross-section of the population and the more likelihood there is of a uniform response from performance to performance. There is a variation in the quality of laughter depending on what night of the week it is. People seem less ready to laugh on a mid-week night when they have to go to work the next day. Matinee audiences are less vociferous, being made up largely of women and senior citizens. Friday night is often the best night for laughter; Saturday may be less good because people tend to eat and drink more on Saturday before coming to the theatre, creating loud but slow houses. Within these limitations, well-constructed jokes should always work, the difference being a matter of the size of the laugh, rather than the presence or absence of response.

TWO STORIES AND THEIR MORALS

Two perhaps apocryphal tales and the morals to be drawn from them:

My director and teacher F. Cowles Strickland was director of the famed Berkshire Playhouse in Stockbridge, Massachusetts, during its early years, when many stars and film personalities appeared there in the summer. He recalled working with Walter Catlett, a character actor in many pre–World War II films, who had accepted a small part in a play starring his wife. He had nine lines, as the story goes. Each night, offstage, he would predict, before his entrance, "what he was going to get." "Tonight, I think, three chuckles, two laughs, and an exit hand." He'd get it. "Tonight, I'll go for four laughs, one chuckle, and no exit hand." He'd get it. Now, perhaps this story belongs among "tall tales," and I certainly cannot personally vouch for its accuracy. Still, I admire the precision it describes and which we should all aspire to, even if I don't approve of varying the performance in such a fashion.

The other story demonstrates a major principle of comedy acting. Alfred Lunt, so the story usually goes, came off after a scene and said to his wife, Lynn Fontanne, who had played the scene with him, "I used to get a laugh when I asked you, 'Can I have another drink?' I seem to have lost it. Do you know why?" She is supposed to have replied, "You used to ask for another drink. Now you're asking for the laugh."

TWO SIMULTANEOUS STRUCTURES

In comedy, there are two structures operating simultaneously. One structure is made up of beats, intentions, adjustments, moments—all those stage events that advance the story. The other structure is the joke structure, comprised of plant, pause, point, amplifier, bridge, and all the associated devices by which laughter is provoked. On television's broadest sitcoms, one can see how the actors neglect story, neglect character development, neglect moment-to-moment truth and just play the joke structure. This superficial work may be sufficient to sustain audience interest for a half-hour show. In the longer span of the theatre, however, one must take care, if the performance is to maintain a high level of humor throughout an evening, that the truth and humanity of the characters and the strength of the story line are the elements that remain at the forefront—the elements into which the jokes are melded. "Time out for the joke; then back to the play," is not good enough. One must rehearse so that "playing the play" is funny enough.

The great satisfaction of playing comedy comes from having one's finger on the pulse of the audience. In comedy, the audience lets you know, moment by moment, "how you're doing." I remember Howard Lindsay, author and star of the long-running play *Life with Father*, saying, "If you can't amuse them, convince them." He meant that if, when you start the evening, they just aren't laughing as fully as usual, don't try to be funnier—don't push. Just play as truthfully as you can, and you will gradually draw them in, converting the smiles into chuckles and the chuckles into laughs by Act Two. That can be almost as much of a triumph as the evening that starts with a laugh as the curtain goes up and then just keeps bowling along.

EXERCISE

1. Page 255—Identify three joke structures in *Godot* and break them down according to the five parts. How does Beckett's play make use of vaudeville structure? What does the play accomplish as a result? Present your "jokes" to the class. Are they funny outside of their proper context? How does this technical breakdown relate to the earlier analysis of beats? Which structure is more useful to you?

CHAPTER 13

MORE REHEARSALS: WEEKS TWO, THREE, AND FOUR

THE SECOND WEEK

After the first "day off," the new week starts back at the beginning of the play. For the first time, scenes are called individually, so that for much of the time smaller numbers of people are involved. This is a relief. Now one can talk to individuals, not always to the group. The actors begin to sense their partnership with the director in creating their roles. The director becomes coach and trainer, not just chair of the meeting.

Hand props, or substitute hand props, must now be on hand. Rehearsals now begin to create and connect the moments of the play, so the actors need to have things to pick up and handle as the script requires. Often, real props don't yet exist or are too fragile or expensive to bring into the rehearsal atmosphere, where each day they must be unpacked by the stage management and then put away at the end of the day. The stage managers must, at the beginning of each scene, identify the rehearsal props for the actors. "This paper cup is your jeweled goblet." "That ruler is your dagger."

GETTING THE ACTORS OFF BOOK

Remember that, from now on, as each scene is scheduled, the actors have been asked to be off book.

I like to begin each scene this week with, "Let's walk the scene, for the words." This reviews the blocking and also allows time for proper attention to be given to that important moment when the actors are saying their lines without a script in their hands for the first time.

Here, the prompter's role and function become of critical importance. In most productions, there are two stage managers present at every rehearsal. I prefer that the assistant stage manager be selected for skill in prompting, and that prompting be left to that one person in so far as possible. First, this gives the actors only one voice to get used to. Second, this one person becomes attuned to each actor's rhythms and preferences. It annoys the actor to be interrupted during a silent moment by a prompt. "I'm *acting*," is often his aggrieved response. On the other hand, it annoys the actor if, when he needs the prompt, it isn't there. Some stage managers, much given to pedantic precision, attempt to get the entire company to ask for prompts in a uniform way, insisting that everyone say, "Line, please," or some such formula. These well-intentioned efforts to promote uniformity just won't work. Actors whose habit it is will go right on saying, "What?" or just looking expectantly out toward the prompter, or even snapping their fingers (a truly bad habit, since it has been known to creep inadvertently into performance). It is the prompter who must adjust. After all, the actors outnumber him. Happily, his adjustment is not difficult. The prompter should use a pencil with an eraser to follow the lines, with the eraser moving lightly from word to word as the actor speaks. The prompter should look up at the actor and down at the page in rapid alternation, so that the moment the actor "goes up," or "dries," as the English say, the prompter can provide the missing word or phrase. Just saying "The . . . ," in case the line begins with "The" is not enough, but "The door was . . ." probably would be. The prompt must be given in a loud, clear voice. There is no audience from which to hide. The prompter's tone must never reprove or admonish. His role is to provide objective help.

The actor probably needs to learn some things about being prompted that will make everyone's life easier. Actors should remember that directors hear actors forget lines as often as plumbers see leaky faucets, so there's no need for the actor to say, "Oh, damn—what is it? What? No, don't tell me—damn, damn, damn . . . line, please!" He must stay relaxed, remain in character, not even look out at the prompter if he can possibly manage such composure, and, in the simplest manner possible, get the prompt and get on with rehearsal.

One of the surprising things about rehearsals in the German-language theatre, to someone from the United States or England, is the activity of the prompter. Once the play is on its feet, even during blocking and before lines are learned, the actors work without scripts. The prompter, usually a clear-voiced woman seated close to center front, says each phrase just before the actor says it, and the actor repeats the short phrase after her. This leaves the actors' hands free to use props from the earliest rehearsals. In addition, the production is free from the tension caused by the fear of forgetting that haunts so many actors. As the actors absorb the lines, the prompter will say less and less, but will mouth the lines along with the actors, and on into performance there she is, inhabiting her little prompter's box at the front of the stage, ready to toss in a word or phrase in case of need.

In the first go-through without book, the actors should be encouraged to ask for the lines as often as they need them. The problem, of course, is not the learning of lines—a nine-year-old can probably do that splendidly. The task is to begin associating the words with the environment, the partner, and the physical tasks the scene requires. However well or badly actors remember the words, the director should not yield to their desire to carry the book. The director's task is blithely to reassure. After working on a few scenes this way, their confidence and their glibness will increase remarkably.

THE FIRST "DETAIL" REHEARSAL

This first "for the words" go-through may take ten or fifteen minutes. Then ask the actors to go back and start the first beat, with the object of working through only to the end of that beat. The first task is to define their intentions and to link them with speaking and moving. The director's question must be, "What are you doing to . . . (object)?" The actor should remember from the reading rehearsal. If not, remind him. Now, begin to make certain, just within this first beat, that everything the actors are doing vocally and physically carries out those stated intentions. When that work has been roughed in, go back and run the beat. Then go on to the next beat, and so on through the scene. You should have allowed time, after working through each beat, to run the entire scene, to "print" the progress, so to speak. You should then proceed to the next scene, going through it in the same way, first for lines, then through each beat for intentions, and then running the whole thing. So, on to the next day, and the days following, until the company has worked through to its end-of-the-week run-through.

During this week of line-learning and intention-defining, the ten or fifteen minutes while the actors struggle through for the first time off book give you a chance to review your promptbook and to refresh yourself as to your objectives for the scene. You can make notes as the actors go through the scene, so that when the time comes to proceed, your comments and questions will be based on what you see the actors doing. Then, as you move slowly from beat to beat, you can work always in terms of where the actors are in their understanding of the scene.

PHYSICAL DECISIONS

During this process of defining and clarifying intentions, the physical side of the actors' work will become more specific. The question of "words first" or "move first" will keep coming up. "What are you looking at as you enter?" "What makes you stop—something you see or something you hear?'' ''On that phrase, should you be looking at her?'' ''Should your cross start on this word or that word?'' These decisions will begin to emerge, less specifically this week than next week, as the blocking becomes, not a mechanical thing any longer, but something that is increasingly connected truthfully to the text.

THE VALUE OF QUESTIONS

I phrase many of my comments as questions. After all, it is the actor who will play the role, and who must be stimulated to understand the choices available and their respective effects. Questions are no more time-consuming than commands like ''Do this,'' or ''Do that,'' but when the actor participates in the decision making, he maintains a more creative relationship to the production. The director is fleshing out, during these rehearsals, what he discovered about the play in his study. The director's preparation, however thorough, can at best be only an outline. Thought by thought, connection by connection, the actor must develop the director's outline into a rich and detailed characterization. The director's perceptive questions may well bring to light areas the actor had been taking for granted or had been unaware of.

A useful question-asking technique is the device of dividing things into opposites. For example:

Director: Do you think he should:

stand ....or sit?

Actor: Stand.

Director: All right. Should he be:

standing still .... or moving?

Actor: Moving.

Director: All right. Toward:

the window .... or the desk?

Actor: Toward the window.

Director: Ah. In order to:

look out .... or to escape her eyes?

Actor: To escape her eyes.

Director: OK. Is the next line:

to himself ....or to her?

Actor: To himself.

Director: Yes. Then:

eyes closed...or eyes open?

Actor: Eyes open.

Director: Looking

at floor...or at ceiling?

Actor: At floor.

This questioning by opposites can slice large or vague questions right down to detailed and surprising choices in a remarkably short time. The degree of detail sought will depend on the phase of rehearsal one has reached, but the device can be employed throughout the rehearsal period.

WORKING SO ACTORS CAN REPEAT THEIR DISCOVERIES

One cannot direct the whole play, moment by moment, in the course of the second week, even though you may begin to see exactly what you want in detail. After all, the actor must be able to do it and repeat it. That means the director must work in layers, content to accomplish this much now, leaving some things for later and others for later still.

During rehearsals of the Broadway production of Enid Bagnold's *The Chalk Garden*, I was present at a late afternoon rehearsal of a scene involving Gladys Cooper, our vastly skilled, elderly British star; Siobhan McKenna, just over from Ireland for her New York debut; and a young English girl who shall be nameless here because she was later fired. George Cukor, the famed film director, was doing his first play in thirty years. The scene they worked on was delicate, subtle, elusive. Cukor wove a tapestry of words, evocative and mesmerizing, spinning a web of mood. The actresses responded, and, with his interspersed suggestions and promptings, they built a breathtakingly touching edifice of spun-glass, or "the moonlight's watery beams." There were tears in everyone's eyes by the end of the scene when Cukor said, "That was very good. We can stop for today."

Next morning when we came in, he said, "Let's do that scene from last night again. Start at the top, please." And they did. And there was nothing there. He had "talked them through," the night before, and they had followed, but they had no idea how to do it again; *he* had done it all. Had it been filmed on the spot, the result would have been magnificent. But he didn't know what he'd done, either, and they never found it again. The great lesson for me: nothing can be accomplished durable enough for the theatre unless the actors know how they achieved their result and can repeat it.

GOALS FOR WEEK TWO

What you can accomplish in Week Two, so the actors *own* it, is:

1. Getting the lines learned sufficiently well that, when lines are dropped, everyone will know it is a symptom of something wrong with *connections*, not merely lack of study.

2. Creating, through the entire play, a road map of intentions that guide actors and audience through the emotional and intellectual line of the play.

THE THIRD WEEK

The play was discussed and blocked in the first week. In the second week, lines were learned, and the beats, intentions, and adjustments were established. This two-week period could be called ''finding the what's''—establishing what the production's goals are and what the characters are doing. The third week, or those weeks before the run-throughs should the production have five or six weeks of rehearsal, is the period of ''finding the how's''—establishing exactly how each acting task and moment should be accomplished.

The same hour-by-hour, scene-by-scene schedule that took the production through the second week can be used. Happily, though, one hour given to five pages at this stage is a more spacious hour than one in which lines must be digested and blocking corrected, along with starting to define intentions.

The first thing to do with each scene is to give some notes on it from the end-of-the-second-week run-through—those notes that need discussion: comments on general tone, elements of characterization, and so forth. Then I start the scene, and, beat by beat, work it through. The working (as opposed to discussion) notes from the last run-through will suggest needed changes in business and moves. Those can be incorporated as you come to them. This is the time, too, to encourage more input from the actors. ''Does this move serve you?'' ''You seem a little uncomfortable here. Is there anything else you'd like to try?'' ''Early on you thought this speech should be done standing. Do you still feel that way? Would you like to do something else?''

The third week provides a chance to test every look, gesture, and move for truth, story value, and psychological detail. Exactly how each character's mind and senses are working must be scored. ''I'll work on that and bring it in next time,'' should be discouraged. Tell the actor, ''Here we are. Let's rehearse it now.'' Go into everything. Dig. You may not get all the answers at once, but this is the time to ask all the questions.

PROBLEM SOLVING

A much-honored axiom when I was beginning to direct was, ''Don't stop the actors until you know exactly how to fix the thing that bothers you.'' I no longer believe this is the best way to solve problems. Oh, sometimes you *do* know exactly what's wrong and how to fix it. If so, say so at once, do your fixing, and get on. When all you know is that *something* is wrong, get help; every actor in the show is your collaborator. ''Something isn't right here. What is it?'' You may well discover that one of them does know and was only waiting for a tactful moment. You may find somebody is trying to do what you've asked for and is succeeding in doing the opposite. You may find that everyone is aware of discomfort but no one has an answer.

So, to solve those problems for which no one has an easy answer:

1. Taking a fresh look at "who is standing or sitting next to whom" is often productive. Sometimes a simple thing like putting the speaker between people instead of facing them can make all the difference.

2. Taking a fresh look at "who is upstage and who is downstage" may help. Try reversing positions.

3. Look again at who is moving and who is standing still, who is seated and who is standing. Try reversing current choices. These alterations in the physical relationships can make more difference than you might think in whether a scene "works."

4. Trying "opposites" can be productive. Let the loud be soft for a change; let the slow be fast; let the nasty be sweet. "I love you" can be said tenderly; it can also be said pugnaciously.

5. There is an interesting technique involving "colors" that can reveal hidden treasures. Let's say the scene in question is the one from *Richard* III, between Richard and Lady Anne, in which Richard must win her from loathing him to an acceptance of his courtship. Suppose Richard is having trouble finding a variety of intentions towards her. Together let director and actor assign a palette of, say, five ways Richard can try to convince her of his love. Perhaps he can (1) challenge her, (2) tempt her, (3) plead with her, (4) reason with her, (5) throw himself on her mercy. Let Richard play through the whole scene five times, each time using only one intention, giving the whole scene, regardless of what is appropriate, just one color each time. Some moments will be wrong. Others, though, will be illuminated by what becomes a surprisingly interesting choice. Finally, out of the exercise, he can weave all the strands together, using the strongest and most exciting choices he has found.

6. If the staging is getting in the way, sit the actors down and just let them say the lines, to remind everyone of the "bare bones" of the text.

7. If the voice patterns are getting in the way, have the actors whisper—not a stage whisper or *sotto voce*, but a real, voiceless whisper. An actor can become so accustomed to his own voice roaring along in its usual way that a speech can lose all immediacy for him, and feel "canned." By removing the voice, the whisper exercise frees the thoughts and emotions to come through spontaneously. Then the voice can be added, to make use of the new discoveries. A variation on this exercise is to have one

actor play fully, the other whisper, especially if the whisperer has been the one carrying the scene vocally.

8. See if the actors can do the scene without words, just walking the moves. Don't let them mouth or whisper, but get them to do everything in the scene in total silence. See if each can tell where the other is in the scene. See if you can tell what is going on in the scene without hearing the words.

AVOIDING UNPRODUCTIVE DISCUSSION

The director must not allow these rehearsals to get bogged down in discussion. The actor says, "I think I ought to walk around the room here, instead of sit, because I feel that. . . ." Stop him as soon as possible, before "because I feel. . . ." Don't let him justify it or explain it. Say "Fine, do it for me." The director should accept, for trial, but without discussion, every suggestion the actor makes. If he is allowed to do it, to show it, he won't mind relinquishing it if it's wrong. In fact, *he'll* probably know it's wrong *first*. But if the director doesn't let him try it, it will rankle.

If the actor is allowed to go into "because I feel . . ." the director may be tempted to join in the discussion by saying, "I don't think that's right, because . . ." and then they're off on an hour of discussion when one quick experiment would have settled the matter.

Beware of always accepting one actor's suggestions, or trying them, and never accepting or trying some other actor's ideas. Actors are all too quick to seek approval from the director, and the opposite of approval is rejection, which they are equally quick to sense or to imagine. On the other hand, a misplaced egalitarianism can lead the director to allow the servant who says, "The carriage waits," to monopolize twenty minutes of rehearsal time talking about his motivation, while the leading actors are left high and dry, with much, much more to do.

Indeed, these before-the-run-through working rehearsals are often rehearsals to which non-speakers need not be called. Intimate questions of character relationships and the shaping of performances take place best without many watchers. People who sit around waiting to say, "The carriage waits," can get tired too. Some time away from rehearsals at this point will help to ensure that they are not burnt out by the time run-throughs and dress rehearsals demand their constant attendance.

RELATIONSHIPS AMONG ACTORS

A recurring problem is the leading actor who takes it upon himself to evaluate his fellow performers and comes to the director pointing out their faults. This happens in the upper reaches of the professional theatre more frequently than elsewhere, but it has been known in community theatres and university theatres as well. The leading actor, in such an instance, feels that "it is his show and he is carrying it." He wants "support" from the other actors. He also wants to be seen as the director's chief collaborator, one who is himself a guardian of standards.

This attitude may actually be justified in the case of a Broadway star whose name sells tickets at the box office and on the strength of whose name production money has been raised. The star's status as a salable commodity depends upon, not simply merit, but success.

I remember an incident from my early days on Broadway. The distinguished aging female star was announced as "called away from rehearsal" one day, and I, as assistant stage manager, had to stand in all day for her, walking her part and reading her lines. At one point, when "I" was offstage, I had to deliver a message to the producers who were watching out front in the totally darkened theatre. Feeling my way up the aisle to the "command post," I almost stumbled over our lady star, swathed in mink, secretly ensconced among the producers, scathingly denouncing the work of the distinguished male star, who was at that moment doing a scene with the play's young man. She was trying to get rid of her co-star and using all her pull to do it. She didn't succeed, and he did open—contributing fully as much to the production's success (it ran a full season) as she did.

Competitiveness and paranoia have no small part in the tendency of leading actors to criticize their co-workers, but the leading actor is not without theatrical judgment and his carping is often to the point. My advice to the director would be, don't let the actor's "note-giving" become apparent to the rest of the company. Discourage the actor from coming to sit beside you, when the play gives him a chance, to share his views. Try not to be vulnerable during rehearsal breaks—go quickly to the rest room or plunge into conversation with the stage manager. Suggest that the actor telephone you at home with his comments or have a private lunch with him. Accept the suggestions, make use of the ones that are applicable, and bury the ones that aren't. Above all, the director must never be seen to be carrying out the actor's instructions.

MEMORIZATION PROBLEMS

The older actor who simply cannot learn lines on schedule presents a more serious problem. Sometimes he just cannot bring himself to learn lines on your schedule, out of lifetime habit. If this failure amounts to a genuine act of defiance, take the matter up with him tactfully but frankly, and if the condition persists, the best course is to dismiss him and get someone else, even if it is late in the day. If it is a genuine inability to keep up, then a judgment must be made. Is the actor's skill and value in the role worth the time he devours, and is the time spent leading him along that slows the directing process, impedes other actors in their work, and damages morale really being well spent for the good of the whole play? Can you find anyone good enough to replace him?

Sometimes the problem will prove to be getting him to buckle down to actual study. Here, an intern or apprentice, or an actor with a small part and lots of compassion, can be brought in to assist. Every time the older actor leaves the stage, the helper must be there with the book, ready to cue him. As far as possible, all waking hours of helper and helpee should be absorbed in cueing. This usually works. Sometimes, in rehearsal, panic sets in, and I have, on several occasions, taken up the promptbook and prompted such an actor myself. An even tone and a sure, strong prompt does much to help them know you are on their side. Too, when the director prompts, it gives the line-learning a certain amount of emphasis. Still, it is one of the most serious intrusions on proper rehearsing to be prevented from directing the play, and from directing a role, by an actor's lateness in learning her part.

FIRING AN ACTOR

Dismissing an actor is always a sad business. Failure to learn lines, drunkenness, incessant absence or lateness—these are the usual reasons. Bad morale and general unpleasantness can also be reasons. And just plain "not good enough," which means the director has made a mistake in casting the part, can also be a reason. If finally you decide that replacement is the only recourse, you must not hold back from doing it. No one would bring in a new Hamlet on twenty-four hours' notice, unless the new actor had recently played the part, but once you know in your heart of hearts that replacement is the only answer, and if replacement is physically possible, then it is always better to replace than to continue in a bad situation while all options disappear as time passes.

For *The Power and the Glory* at New York's Phoenix Theatre, I had engaged a fortyish, heavy-set character actor, whose work I had always admired, for a part of moderate size. We rehearsed in the theatre, where I could work from the first row and so had little reason to go up on stage. After two weeks I could see that this actor was not making progress, but I didn't know why. Technical rehearsals approached. During the load-in of sets and lights we rehearsed across the street in a hall with a restaurant and bar on the ground floor. An evening run-through was scheduled, and during his first scene this actor fell from his chair to the floor, dead drunk. Someone had seen him line up nine double scotches and drink them off in a series just before rehearsal. I then learned that alcohol had been heavily on his breath every day at morning rehearsals, that everyone in the cast knew he came in drunk in the mornings, and that the only reason I didn't know was because I had done all my work from the first row. With two days to go, we replaced that actor, and the new man was immediately more satisfactory than the first had ever been.

INTERRUPTING THE ACTORS

Directing the play during this third week means continuing to interrupt the actors. Those actors who are used to just running scenes and getting notes afterwards may resist these interruptions. They want to "feel" the scene, "work themselves into it," without the director stopping the flow. I interrupt chiefly to make decisions about moments of connection and transition and set them. The actor may not remember a verbal note, but he will remember a change if there is an interruption and a rehearsal of the thing to be changed.

I believe a production benefits from frequent interruption because the stops force the actors to "cool down." In order to start again with emotional accuracy after the "mood is broken," the actor must know exactly where he is emotionally at every point in the scene. He should be able to pick up, with precision and truth, at exactly the right level, after any stop whatever. With sufficient careful work, this degree of emotional understanding and clarity can be achieved. And, after working through the scene with as many stops as it needs, the director should always run it without interruption once or even twice before moving on to the next scene of the day.

Some directors, after blocking, do nothing but *run* scenes and acts, and then give notes. This isn't directing; it's note-giving.

I was once witness to a classic example of the consequences of note-giving. The Schiller Theater was West Berlin's principal theatre when I visited it in 1961. It employed over a hundred actors, had both performance and rehearsal stage crews, and supported elaborate scene, prop, costume, and wig shops. Rehearsals used sets and costumes very early on, and several productions played in rotating repertory in the course of any given week. I saw von Kleist's *Amphitryon* in rehearsal. The auditorium was totally black, and when we guests entered, we were able to slip in a few rows behind the director and his assistant without being seen by anyone. An urbane leading man and an attractive leading lady were in the scene in progress, plus an actor and an actress playing their servants. The dialogue was proceeding confidently in mouthy German verse—but all was singsong, hollow, and "classic." The director, in the dark beside his assistant, became increasingly agitated. Visible to us against the stage lights, he was clawing the air, beating his hands against his forehead, shaking the seat in front of him in rage and despair, and tearing his hair. The scene ended. The director, all smiles, bounded from his seat up onto the stage. "Now look," he chirped, and oh, so cheerfully, began to explain, persuade, and cajole. The actors seemed perplexed, though the leading lady kept nodding vigorously. The leading man looked increasingly dubious. "All right, again!" said the director, and he leapt back to his seat. The actors began again, now less confident and somewhat uncertain, casting sidelong glances out into the dark to see how they were doing. Once again, we were privy to the silent tantrum in the stalls, the beaten forehead, the torn hair, the silent scream straight out of *Mother Courage*. The scene ended. Again the smiling director-cheerleader bounded to the stage. Again, but with patience strained, he gave his as-if-to-erring-children lecture, to the accompaniment of earnest nods of assent from the now floor-squatting leading lady and an air of cold disdain from the leading man. Suddenly from the side of the auditorium came the clang of a bucket and a shaft of light as a door was opened accidentally by a cleaning lady and hastily and loudly closed again.

"Silence!" shrieked the director. "I say, silence," he screamed again, as he hurled himself from the stage to rush to the offending door, where he flung it open and sprayed the lobby with a torrent of abuse. Banging the door closed, he lurched back to the apron of the stage, sank against it in despair, and moaned, "How can I be expected to create in an atmosphere like this?" The leading lady and the actress playing the servant gathered around, clucking and soothing, saying "Poor Walter," while stroking his fevered brow. Unseen except from our vantage in front, the leading man and the other actor backstepped into the wings, and as the women crooned sympathy, the leading man put a cigarette into his holder, lit up, and turned to his buddy, saying something we couldn't hear, which simply had to be, "Look at the little sonofabitch." That director didn't direct; he lectured. The scene couldn't get better, because he didn't work on it; he just talked about it. Oh, he knew what was wrong, and that made him more tense and frustrated. The cleaning lady incident let him vent his feelings and lost him further respect in the eyes of his cast. The upshot of the story is that when we went back after the production had opened, there the actors were, confident again, singing and yammering their way through the verse as if "poor Walter" had never given a lecture or had a conniption.

OTHER ASPECTS OF THE THIRD WEEK

The production's third week, although its rehearsals are broken by the director's frequent interruptions, is a time of relative calm and pulling together. Unless the cast is hampered by some actors who are slow of study, the lines are under control. The basics of interpretation have been agreed upon. The staging is by and large settled.

Connections.   All the tiny but important connections can now be made in an atmosphere of creative collaboration. Connections between thoughts, connections between actors, precise defining of looks and touches—all the hinges on which the play turns and moves forward can be made precise and secure.

Moments that haven't worked can be refined, clarified, or taken back to the drawing board. Actors can be allowed latitude in which to experiment or challenge. As important aspects of the play settle into shape, opportunities to improve less-crucial sections will become apparent.

"Dead Air."   Now is the time to take out the "dead air"—those noxious little pauses between speeches that drain the energy out of a scene and prevent its building. Of course, one can say, "Pick up the cues"; "Move and talk at the same time—don't take time out for business." But in these third-week rehearsals, one should take time to ask, "Why do you want to pause there?" Sometimes there is a valid reason, but if there isn't, the director has a chance to establish organically why the actor must speak "on cue."

Jokes.   These are the rehearsals, too, in which to fix the jokes. Everyone now knows the play well enough to be told, "Your line is the plant. Give him a good feed so his joke will work." Or, "*This* word is funny because she's just said *that* word." Fusing the movement properly to the words can be done in increasingly careful detail as the tensions and anxieties about line learning depart.

Pace.   Attention can be given to the proper pacing of scenes at this time. If the actors are playing the right values and the characters are in proper relationship to each other, it should be readily apparent which scenes should be fast and which should be slow. Exhaustion, trouble learning the lines, awkwardnesses of staging, preoccupation with props and costumes that aren't right—these are some of the outside elements that can keep the actor from finding the appropriate speed for a scene. Everything going too fast is as bad as everything dragging; each scene should achieve its own separate tempo, and an interesting production provides a variety of tempos as it proceeds from one scene to another.

THE MOVE INTO THE THEATRE

One important step that ought to be part of the third week is the move into the theatre. The fourth week almost always involves a move *out* of the theatre for loading in scenery and lights. If one has been rehearsing *in* the theatre the whole time, moving out for a couple of days for load-in is no problem, but if one has *not* been in the theatre, one really needs to get used to it in a quiet and calm rehearsal atmosphere. If rehearsals have begun, as I prefer, in a rehearsal hall, then the third week is the ideal time for adjustment to the place of actual performance.

With scenes blocked, lines learned, and the emotional outline established in weeks one and two, the third week's time of relaxed concentration on detail ought to include fitting the action and the voices into the real playing space. You will now be able to move back from the actors when you need to, in order to ensure that you share the audience's perspective. The theatre's wing space, worklight, and darkened auditorium will provide the assistance to the actor's concentration that he needs at this stage of the work, both when you are out in the house and when you are onstage refining details.

Those scenes that by their nature require robust speaking can now be given their head; those scenes that in the rehearsal room have become too "precious" for the larger spaces of the theatre can be pumped up; and working in the actual performing space will convey that sense of "playing for keeps" that gives importance to each moment of the work.

The run-through that caps the third week should show a production almost fully formed and already strong in its detail, its connections, its logic, and its clarity.

THE FOURTH WEEK

Now, the gears shift indeed. Each day now has its run-through.

The rhythm I prefer devotes the first half of the rehearsal day to scene work and the second half to the run-through.

The scene work chosen for each day should be those scenes from the previous run-through that need most work. One or two hours might be spent on scenes using smaller groups of actors working on mood, builds, size, tone, and so on. The entire company will probably be needed for an hour or two before the run-through to work on choreographic problems, the pacing and building of climactic scenes, or the bits-and-pieces work that requires saying a few little things to several different combinations of people, such as fixing up scene ends and beginnings in a Shakespeare play. Fights, songs, and dances should receive attention during these working half-days, and sometimes those rehearsals can go on simultaneously with work on smaller scenes.

But the daily run-through should resemble a performance as much as is possible without scenic elements and lighting, though swords, skirts, shoes, and the real hand props and set props should be used as available.

NOTE-GIVING

At these run-throughs, I introduce the use of the production secretary (or assistant to the director, or note-taker—whichever title one chooses for the function). Prior to the final run-through period my notes always are notes to me—working notes, things to be rehearsed. I may scribble them on a pad myself or, if I can be far enough from the actors, whisper them to a helper. The presence of the assistant means I don't have to take my eyes from the scene.

At the start of the final run-through phase, and from then through technical and dress rehearsals and previews, the assistant becomes essential. I ask the assistant to prepare a tabbed clipboard or a tabbed loose-leaf notebook. There must be a tab for me, for each actor, for the stage manager, and for each production department (set, lights, costumes, sound, props, and so on). At each run-through this clipboard or notebook must be slip-sheeted with clean paper, so that at the end of rehearsal each person or department head can be handed his notes, on his own separate sheet of paper. This procedure accomplishes several useful things:

1. It saves time. People don't have to sit around afterward listening to other people's notes.

2. It provides a written reminder, which the actor or staff person can hang onto.

3. The director can say things privately on paper which he wouldn't say in public.

My most recent assistant has also kept carbon copies of every note, so we have a complete record of the notes given. I have also learned recently to pass all technical notes through the stage manager, so he can be abreast of what's going on before handing notes out to the staff people.

A few cautions about this note-giving procedure:

1. Get an assistant who can write legibly!

2. Be sure the assistant writes precisely what you say and only what you say. No translating, paraphrasing, or original contributions allowed.

3. The director must therefore be brief and clear.

4. If the note is complicated, ask the actor to: "*Ask me about* holding the dagger during 'To be or not to be.'"

5. Don't use irony or sarcasm or even humor in these notes. Too easily misunderstood.

6. Most actor notes become: "At (quote the line from the play):
   a. Remember to . . ."
   b. Don't do . . ."
   c. Pick up the cue"
   d. Why did you . . . ?"
   e. Ask me about . . ."

7. Give every note affecting more than one person, or every note that requires rehearsal, to yourself. "Note to me . . ."

8. Tell the actors in advance about the note-giving process and why you use it. Emphasize its importance. Make it their responsibility to find the assistant and get their notes.

9. The assistant must never give out the notes until the director has fin-

ished speaking and all announcements have been made. Otherwise the actors will read their notes instead of listening.

10. Don't let the notes become an excuse for avoiding personal contact with the actors. The notes are a helpful device, not a hiding place.

11. Never let your assistant give a note in his own right. He is not the "assistant director"; he is "assistant *to* the director." You must take care that the only guidance the production gets is from *you*.

You will find that the actors *like* getting notes; they feel looked after—and if they *don't* get any, they will come to you asking for some. Occasionally your assistant may put a note on the wrong piece of paper, but all that happens is that an actor comes up saying, "This note must not be for me."

WHAT RUN-THROUGHS MUST ACCOMPLISH

More important than the note-taking process is what the notes are going to be about. During the fourth week the director has at least six run-throughs coming up. What are they meant to accomplish?

1. They give the actors a chance to develop stamina, energy, and concentration enough to sustain the whole play.

2. They give the actors a chance to experience the play cumulatively, not just as a series of single scenes, but with a growing sense of how each scene affects and builds toward every other scene.

3. The director can watch for story values: the first times names are said, the way characters are introduced, the clarity of the exposition, the sharpness of reversals, the stages of the rising action. After all, one becomes inured to the story after weeks of rehearsal. These run-throughs are the place to examine things you may have been taking for granted.

4. The director can watch for weak spots, dull spots, slow spots, unclear sections.

5. The director can check for emphasis: Are the important things important and the lesser elements subordinate, or does it all seem to be of equal importance (or dullness, or sameness)?

6. The director can check for stylistic consistency: Are all the elements combining to tell the right, or the same, story? Are the performances in key and tone with each other? Are they speaking in the same style, acting in the same style? Does anyone seem to have walked in from another play?

7. Is the stage used with sufficient variety, or are pictorial effects repeated or duplicated?

8. Does the staging tell the story pictorially, or would you have to understand the words to know sometimes what was going on?

9. Would your dog understand the actors' intentions?

10. Will the audience like the people they are supposed to like? If not, why not, and how can you fix it?

11. Is it funny where it's supposed to be?

12. Is it emotionally moving, or do you just sit there and watch it go by?

DISTANCING

As you watch the run-throughs, you must allow yourself to experience a distancing. You must forget the creative paths by means of which effects were achieved; you must gradually withdraw from asking yourself how well people are doing what you and they have set out to do, and instead you must try to focus on what is actually present on the stage—what the audience will truly see and hear. You must become neutral. Instead of being an enthusiast and participant, you must become a passive receptor—but actively aware.

"Every time you watch the play, sit in a different seat," is the advice Howard Lindsay (author, actor, director of many plays, among them *Life with Father*) once gave me. This helps, not just for checking sight lines, but chiefly because the somewhat different angle of sight makes you perceive things in a somewhat new way. Be sure, too, that you sit at different distances. Up close, details of acting values can be seen and assessed. At a greater distance, questions of focus and composition will be more apparent, and too, one can check as to whether the actors are audible and understandable. We hear because of vowels; we understand because of consonants. Watch for ends of sentences that trail out of hearing, key words that disappear. Watch too for actors who constantly look down at the floor (anything you can play looking down can be played looking up) and actors who constantly upstage themselves.

Try to ensure that those acting values that seemed so splendid up close in the rehearsal hall are sufficiently physicalized throughout the actor's body that they exist for customers sitting at a distance. The entire production should not be aimed at the back row—or at the front row, for that matter, although I have known New York directors who directed their shows for the critics' seats. An effective compromise must be found that is true in the front rows and also complete at the back of the house. Remember, this is not so much a matter of bigness of gesture but of the use of the whole body—gesture, posture, position. For film or television, everything has to show in the eyes and face, because the rest of the actor may be out of the shot. On the stage, the whole person is visible and all of him must contribute. Vocally, too, projection is not just a matter of size or loudness. Clarity and focus of tone are more important. Women's voices, though not as loud as men's, can reach the remote corners of the theatre as effectively. The hero's "I love you," though audible at the back, must not deafen the first row or the actress to whom the line is spoken.

TIMINGS

The stage manager's timings now become of interest. Naturally, the director will have been concerned with the total playing time of acts and of the play itself. Much can be learned, as well, from establishing timings on the smaller units. If Act One suddenly adds five minutes, one wants to know if this is the result of an overall spread or of a self-indulgent change in a particular scene by one or more actors. Such timing changes are symptoms. Only by starting to get accurate timings of the various units of the play as run-throughs begin can an estimate of desirable average timings be arrived at, as the play settles down. It was supposed to have been George Abbott, years ago, who would take the train from New York out to Chicago, when the stage manager wired him that the play had run two minutes longer the previous night. Abbott would come out to rehearse, the story goes, to "take out the improvements."

GETTING READY FOR THE AUDIENCE

Remember that the play still lacks an important human element during these run-throughs—the audience. In comedy, especially, the audience becomes a vociferous member of the cast, participating actively by laughter and applause. The play, during these fourth-week run-throughs, is incomplete in its intended music without the audience's sounds, and only when they are there, in performance, will the play's rhythms be complete and its score fully heard. To incorporate the audience, the actors must be as deft as possible before the public turns up.

Designers and staff will want to see some of these run-throughs. Occasionally, friends and relatives of the cast will be allowed in. The actors are very aware of these new presences and immediately direct their playing energy and their antennae towards them. This is a good thing, as long as the actors don't expect laughs and chuckles from these special guests, who may be too well-behaved to respond normally. It sharpens the actor's concentration to have people in at this stage of rehearsal. Remember, though, that the work is unfinished, and that strangers tend to notice only that which seems unfinished. Until the sets and costumes and lights and audience are there, and the work is finished that must be done before those elements are incorporated, your guests are looking at something with gaps, without the help of those aids to belief and attention that must still be added. Don't pay too much attention to outside comments at this time or even invite comment. Somebody watching is what you need from guests, and that they have provided by attending.

EXERCISE

1. Page 273—Go into the theatre and sit in the auditorium. Ask for a technician to operate the light board and for several actors to stand on stage. Call "Blackout!" In the dark, make a note of everything that you can *see* on stage. Is there such a thing as a blackout? What physical details have you overlooked or failed to consider in your production plan?

CHAPTER 14

TECHNICAL REHEARSALS, DRESS REHEARSALS, AND PERFORMANCE

TECHNICAL REHEARSALS

The "tech rehearsal" is the rehearsal that combines the acting with the physical elements that complete the production.

Success in this process depends on proper planning. Earlier on, as the director prepared the production, he has made decisions, later more fully defined by the designers and technical department heads, about the nature of the physical production. He has prepared and distributed detailed light, music, sound, costume, and property plots. The stage manager has kept the technical staff abreast of developments and changes during rehearsal.

PRODUCTION MEETINGS

Various production meetings will probably have occurred. These may have been presided over by the stage manager or the technical director, or the director, but their function should have been to assess progress and to ensure that all departments have been properly scheduled for and are ready for the load-in, set-up, and hanging of the show.

PROP PARADE

The director should ask for a "prop parade" before the technical rehearsal—probably a week before, to leave time for changes. At the prop parade, every hand prop and piece of furniture to be used should be assembled in one place, for approval by the director. One can, of course, review the props in stages, going to the furniture store to approve of a rental or purchase, inspecting the hand props on another occasion. The chief point here is that no piece of furniture or hand prop should appear at the technical rehearsal that has not been seen in advance and approved by the director. The technical rehearsal is not the time to discover that the sofa is too long, the table is too low, or the coffin won't go through the door.

DRESS PARADE

Visits to the costume shop during the rehearsal period will prevent surprises in this area. Seeing the clothes as they are made will help to resolve any questions the director may have harbored about the difference between sketches and reality. Elements like armor, or breakaway clothes, or elaborate ruffs, farthingales, or bustles, all of which require much actor adjustment, can be monitored. Indispensable to the costume area is the "dress parade." Actor time must be set aside, several days before the technical rehearsal, so the cast can assemble in the dressing rooms, put on the costumes, and appear before the director, designer, and costume staff one by one and then in appropriate groups for a detailed review of look, fit, and practicability. Sleeve length, hems, shoulders, undergarments and padding, the demands of movement in the particular garment, hair style, gloves, purses—every aspect of every costume must receive complete examination and comment, with careful working notes taken by the costume staff. There will be, at this time, certain details unfinished, but at the dress parade the clothes must be complete enough to provide no surprises. The dress parade must be held just early enough that any necessary changes and refittings can be accomplished prior to the "tech."

SOUND—THE REHEARSAL TAPE

If the sound department and the composer can do their work in time, a rehearsal sound and music tape can be provided for use during the last run-throughs before the technical rehearsal. Such a rehearsal cassette tape can be operated by a stage manager from any portable cassette deck equipped with a counter for cueing. The sound quality won't be right, but the timing and nature of the sound and music cues can be related to the acting prior to the "tech," thus saving time.

ADDING OTHER TECHNICAL ELEMENTS

If the floor of the set is much broken up with steps and platforms, most directors and designers will have found a way to get the actors on them before the "tech." Rehearsing in the theatre is desirable whenever a complex floor plan with many levels is involved, if the levels can be constructed before rehearsals begin. Sometimes a mockup can be provided in the rehearsal hall. An early production decision may involve weighing the value of a complex floor plan against the difficulty of having it available for rehearsal. One of the real nightmares of the theatre is meeting a complex floor plan only at the "tech" rehearsal after four weeks of walking around on taped lines, and finding that the entire show needs to be reblocked because the actors, in spite of the director's best efforts, have failed to visualize how their positions have to relate to the set.

Technical elements can be added to a production on a variety of timetables. Whether or not the crew is a union crew may determine how the technical schedule is drawn up, since in the case of union stagehands all departments must usually be called at once. The director must also be quite sure that all members of the production team are quite clear about how complete things must be for the technical rehearsals. Customs and expectations vary, and the guest director or anyone directing in a theatre new to him must take nothing for granted but must be careful that terms are defined. In some theatres, costumes don't appear at the "tech." In others, the painting of scenery and props is not normally complete until the final dress rehearsal. In some theatres makeup isn't worn until the final dress, "to keep the costumes clean." In some so-called educational theatres the light board operator has never met a light board until the technical rehearsal. I once directed at a place where Brick's bar in *Cat On a Hot Tin Roof* wasn't available at the "tech" because it was cheaper to get the truck the following day, nor had I been able to see it in advance. The damned thing turned out to have mirrored doors, reflecting every spotlight! To me "technical rehearsal" means a rehearsal where every element is complete and ready for the public, lacking only the combining of them all to make a show.

In university and some resident theatre situations, where there is a permanent technical staff, it is sometimes possible to start lighting the show during the run-throughs of week four, holding those run-throughs in the theatre. If this is possible, why not? The designer can write the cues as the actors rehearse. The designer can watch the actors, check things out as he goes with the director, and with luck the lighting is entirely finished by the "tech." One must take care only that the director's attention isn't absorbed by the lighting at a time when the first order of business should be finishing the acting. Too, the lighting process must be handled discreetly enough that actors are not left in the dark or distracted from the important task of getting the play right.

THE "DRY TECH"

Conditions usually dictate that scenery, props, lights, sound and music, and costumes all have to come together at the same time. If this is the case, an essential tool for saving actor energy and for achieving technical efficiency is the "dry tech," or "tech without actors." Prior to this, the lighting cues will have been written, and during this process you will do well to take some time at the end of the rehearsal day to watch while the cues are being created to be sure you like the lighting. Your attention to this is both important and will be appreciated. At the beginning of the "dry tech," while the set is being readied and props set up, the director and sound operator can seize twenty minutes to set basic levels. Once scenery and props are set and with running crew in position, with all headsets in place and working, the stage manager takes charge and executes every technical task, every scene change and prop change and light and sound cue, in sequence, jumping from cue to cue. Timing and coordination between lights and music or sound, and between all that and the scene shifts, are rehearsed and set. When mistakes occur, the transition can be taken again. Scene shifts can be smoothed out, and all the goals for smooth running of the show can be established. No actors have been worn out during this process, and by the time they come in, the physical side of the show will be set. During this "tech without actors," you will have been able to devote your entire attention to technical matters without any concern for watching acting tasks. This special time for the technical side is only fair, since after all the actors have had four weeks to rehearse.

Equity contracts allow one or more twelve-hour days (ten hours of work out of twelve hours, including time for breaks). On the technical rehearsal day, I don't use all those actor hours. I prefer a four-hour call for the "dry tech," lunch, and then four-hour afternoon and evening calls for the actors to do a relaxed "tech-dress" of the entire show. Indeed, if it is technically a simple show, the afternoon can be a "tech," with stops, and the evening may prove to be a dress rehearsal, without any stops at all.

THE "TECH-DRESS"

The "tech-dress" of the whole show combines the actors, in costume, with the other and already rehearsed technical elements. I always instruct the actors "not to act," ask them to "take it easy," and to stay aware of the nature of the light, sound, props, scenery, and above all the costumes they are meeting. I warn them I may stop at any time, and that they in turn can stop to ask any question, make an adjustment, or run anything at all over again. This rehearsal is to find and solve all physical problems.

This is the rehearsal in which one deals with questions of actor safety. Is there enough "running light" backstage, so that actors don't have to deal with the hazards of darkness? Are the crossovers clear of scenery, tools, paint buckets, and the detritus of getting the show ready? Are ladders safely stowed? Are there guard rails on escape stairs and platforms? Are there chairs backstage for actors who must wait? Are electric cables safely out of the way or covered with carpet or otherwise secure from tripping people up? Are there quick-change areas, equipped with lights, mirrors, clothes racks? Has glow tape been placed at the appropriate spots to guide actors in blackouts? Of course, the stage managers should have looked to all these things—but the director, before curtain, must tour the backstage area to verify that precautions have been taken. It is, however, during the "tech" that the actors' routines may well reveal safety problems not foreseen. "The show must" *not* "go on" without dealing with these problems as they come up.

Costumes must be worked with in relation to doors, chairs, and stage spaces. Exact placement of onstage and backstage hand props may require review. The matter of when doors are to be open or closed will have to be defined. Quick changes will have to be routined and timed. Remember that a stop at a *scene* change may deceive everyone about the amount of time available for a *costume* change.

All pressure to perform must be removed from this rehearsal. B*ut the whole play must be gone through.* The danger of cutting "from cue to cue" in this technical rehearsal with actors is that some crucial piece of routine or timing may be bypassed. Further, it usually takes as much or more time to start and stop as one jumps "from cue to cue" as it does just to do the whole play straight through.

You won't take many actor notes during this rehearsal. For one thing, stops will come often enough that most notes can be given verbally. More important, though, you will be seeing everything together for the first time, and your sensibilities will be largely engaged by watching the technical side of the production.

EMERGENCIES

This discussion takes for granted a state of affairs that may not, in fact, obtain—namely, that scenery, props, lights, sound, and costumes are actually ready on time. Yes, they *should* be ready. If they are not, it is *wrong*. Yes, someone may be *at fault*. But—lecturing, hectoring, yelling, screaming, and blaming will do no good. You may deserve revenge and your pound of flesh, and you may find a way to exact it later, should you still care. However, the job at the time in the production's life when emergency strikes is to do what is necessary to surmount the difficulty. Holding on to reality and figuring out a way to get the task done is the director's chief responsibility. You must, above all, protect the cast from the consequences of lateness as best you can. Controlling your own rage and frustration is paramount. You must remain able to say, "Very well. We wanted it ready and we can't have it. What *can* we do?" Everything you say and do, in relation to the whole production team, must be *constructive*.

These emergencies are not always the product of low budgets or incompetence. When it rains for days and nights on end in Central Park just as a production is headed for technical and dress rehearsals, even the technical departments of the New York Shakespeare Festival, the nation's best-financed and best-staffed professional theatre, grind to a halt. Elements of the set cannot be completed, lighting is halted, and whole days can be lost.

As director you have to keep the acting company at the correct pitch. In any outdoor production, where the elements may steal your time, or in any marginal situation where bad management, lack of funds, or technical inadequacy may play havoc with your schedule, you must have your actors so securely rehearsed, so well-prepared to meet technical hurdles, and so strong in morale that they will hold together, possessed by the love of the play and their excitement about what they're doing with it no matter what difficulties they encounter. A director of an outdoor production or one in a chancy situation who waits for the dress rehearsal for acting values to jell will lose his show in the abyss created by technical lateness.

"They peaked too early" is nonsense. Get the production as ready as you possibly can, and then hold onto it. If you can't rehearse onstage because the set is late, rehearse in the lobby. If you can't rehearse there, borrow a church's parish house. Keep the actors at it; stay creative! There is always something to refine, to improve. Use the opportunity to go further. If you can't dress rehearse, fix the little things that would have had to wait for notes later on. Above all, stay cheerful, and don't transmit the tensions and anxieties you are feeling to the actors. Meantime, *let the technical people feel that you care about them*. They won't work that twenty-fifth hour if they feel you hate them for "ruining your show." Encourage them—you're *their* leader, too. Bring out their best; don't give them an excuse to let down by indulging yourself in a fit of pique. Pitch in yourself, on the set or the lights or the costumes. You must see that the actors get the right amount of rest, but, energies permitting, encourage them to pitch in and help too, with whatever skills they have.

Hal Holbrook told me that, when they were readying the ANTA Washington Square theatre downtown (the temporary quarters for the Repertory Theatre of Lincoln Center), on the afternoon of the first preview of Arthur Miller's *After the Fall*, he, Jason Robards, and Robert Whitehead, the producer, were all out in the house on their knees screwing down seats.

DRESS REHEARSALS

Every production, after its "tech-dress," needs at least three dress rehearsals. Even with a very short time to put up a show—say three days—one can usually manage three real dress rehearsals. Use one day to dry tech and tech-dress. The second day could have two dresses—afternoon and evening. The third day

THE TWO GENTLEMEN OF VERONA
New York Shakespeare Festival, 1987
After the dress rehearsal, the director (Stuart Vaughan) attends to details: in this instance,
blending Elizabeth McGovern's rouge.
Photo: George E. Joseph

could have a short rehearsal call in the afternoon—or even a dress in the afternoon and another one or a preview that night. But whenever your three dresses occur, three is the minimum number. The first one will feel preoccupied, as the actors, walking on eggs, try to remember the adjustments from the tech. The second dress may well, as some relaxation sets in, be more inaccurate than the first. Only by the third dress rehearsal will the production hit its stride again, playing almost as well as it did in run-throughs a few days ago.

A dress rehearsal, for me, is a rehearsal with all its elements present and sufficiently well rehearsed that it doesn't stop.

WHAT TO WATCH FOR AT DRESS REHEARSALS

What should you watch for at dress rehearsals? Everything. Does the conjunction of light, scenery, and sound cues at scene transitions really do what you had hoped for? Is the light bright enough? How is the masking? Are there light leaks? Does the set shake? How does light affect makeup, costume color, set color? Is there noise backstage—why? Is the stage floor sufficiently padded or covered with rugs? Do the doors stay closed? Do the actors handle their hats well? Are they dealing well with their period clothes—togas, capes, skirts, swords? How are sound levels? How are sight lines?

Does the show look better now that scenery, costumes, and lights are here—or worse? Believe me, I've known shows where the magic departed the moment the physical elements were added.

How does the story come through? Are things as fast as they should be, or too slow? Do the actors seem confident? If not, why not? Can you hear? Is there suspense—do you want to know what will happen next? Are the actors enjoying it, or do they seem to be in pain as they struggle to pass a test?

More than anything else, the director's job now is to help get things out of the actors' way. The show belonged to them only a few days ago. Then the crew and the "things" took it over. Now the director must give the play back to the actors.

NOTES

A short meeting after each dress rehearsal between the stage management, the designers, and the technical department heads usually takes place while actors are getting out of costume and makeup. This meeting is to make sure that the next day's crew calls accomplish the repairs and improvements needed for the next day's rehearsal. The director's help may be needed in setting or accepting priorities. "We can't have that till Wednesday because . . ." "You'll have it tomorrow night, not tomorrow afternoon." One needs to know these things. I was once surprised to learn that a tech-dress had to be canceled because the light board had been flown to California for repairs. I prefer to be involved in these decisions.

In non-union situations, where there are no contractual restrictions on rehearsal hours, a short meeting in the house with actors after they have changed can always be managed, and often in union situations such a meeting can be planned as part of the working day. Such a meeting should be used for general encouragement or announcements only. No *general comments of a negative nature should be made at this time.* The wrong people are always the ones who feel guilty, when guilt is passed around. The conscientious people at whom you are *not* aiming are the ones you will upset, and the targets of your broadside need direct and personal action, not a general and impersonal scolding.

Others may, but I *never* say things like, "Act One was slow," or "You were all a bit down tonight." The director must build the production in rehearsal so Act One *cannot* go too slowly. A constant energy and pace from night to night must be achieved organically by rehearsing properly, so the production will be unaffected by the changes in mood, morale, fatigue, anxiety, and other human chemistry that are sure to come.

Sometimes there simply aren't enough minutes at the end of the dress rehearsal for a gathering in the house. In such an instance, the note-taker takes the notes around to the dressing rooms, I follow around with positive remarks, and I save the proddings and reminders till half-hour next time, when my trip around the dressing rooms lets me give a few notes.

In the dress rehearsal period, big things that are wrong keep you from seeing smaller things that are wrong, and anything wrong keeps you from seeing things that are right. One general reminder to the acting company may indeed be in order: that anything you don't give notes about can be assumed to be all right, because there is never time to single out the good things for comment. Gradually, though, as the actors and the director do their work, the annoyances will decrease, and by the third dress rehearsal you may even find yourself dictating some complimentary notes.

As the final dress rehearsal comes around, the number of notes you give will decrease. There may come a point in rehearsals when so many notes have to be given that the actors will begin to come on the stage to "act the notes" instead of playing the play. You will want to build their confidence by a retreat from constant note-giving. After all, once a note has been given and then re-hearsed, and you then find yourself giving the same note two or three times again as a reminder, you must face the fact that this actor is not going to get this point put in that way. There may be another way to say it or achieve it, but sometimes you just have to give up on a particular issue. In the dress rehearsals, the production becomes what it is going to be.

PERFORMANCES

With even one or two guests at rehearsal, you will find yourself extraordinarily aware. Things you have accepted or learned to ignore become suddenly un-bearable because you see them through a stranger's eyes. Things you have always liked may begin to seem awkward and gauche. And sometimes with the first real audience, and particularly on opening nights, your tension and anxiety can so interfere with your perceptual equipment that normal tempos seem slow because your own inner tempo is so fast.

My point is that the presence of the audience combined with your own inner state can alter how you see things. You may no longer be as object-

KING JOHN
New York Shakespeare Festival, 1988
A battle scene in performance, as choreographed by B. H. Barry.
Photo: © 1991 Martha Swope

ive as you usually are. You must add these factors into your calculations of how well things are going, and, while recognizing the value of your heightened state of awareness, still retain trust in the work you and your cast have done.

THE FIRST AUDIENCE

Previews—invited or paid audiences prior to the official opening and the attendance of reviewers—are vital to a production's success. For the actors, the worst nerves come with the *first* audience. After all, for weeks they have been striving for certain results. Will all their plans and preparations really pay off?

KING JOHN
New York Shakespeare Festival, 1988
Another battle scene in performance, as choreographed by B. H. Barry.
Photo: © 1991 Martha Swope

HENRY VI (WARS OF THE ROSES)
New York Shakespeare Festival, 1970
The Duke of York (Paul Sparer) kills Old Clifford
(Frank Borgman) on the battlefield, in
performance. Director: Stuart Vaughan.
Photo: George E. Joseph

Well, very likely—but not always with the first audience. That tension-filled evening must simply be got through. Tension constricts voices, slows down the pace, makes actors drop props, reduces authority, infects the very air. All this is a matter of degree. Sometimes the tension leaves the air in fifteen minutes; sometimes it haunts the entire evening. Never mind; things *will* get better. Don't worry about the laughs they missed on this first night, just be glad of the ones they got. Look to see if the audience is smiling—those smiles can be turned into chuckles and the chuckles into laughs. If the audience is restless and coughing, you will wonder why, but you won't learn much about that until the second or third audience, as the tensions recede.

This first preview, whether it is a great evening or an awkward one, simply has to be endured and surmounted, like getting over a cold. Then you can go to work again.

WORK DURING PREVIEWS

Rehearse as much as your actors' schedules permit. If you can't rehearse, give notes. Your object—to:

1. Build the laughs.
   a. Examine the plant, for clarity.
   b. Be sure there is a pause.
   c. Check focus.
   d. Be sure the "point" is clear, without excess movement.
   e. Is there an amplifier?
   f. How's the timing?
   g. Keep people from walking into laughs and killing them.

2. Get rid of dead air.
   a. On exits.
   b. During business.
   c. Between speeches.

3. Check the play for audibility from different parts of the house. Theatres change with people in them.

4. Be sure that suspense, builds, and climaxes are working. Heighten curtain lines.

5. Keep all dance and fight choreography tight.

6. Keep light, sound, and curtain cues accurate.

7. Don't let the audience direct the play.
   a. Watch for milking laughs by doing things during laughter. Once they laugh, get on with it.
   b. Watch for added business—doing things twice that should only be done once.

c. Keep the actors from "signaling"—gestures and looks, meant for the audience, that say, "I'm going to talk now," or "This is going to be funny," sometimes accompanied by too-obvious "playing front."

d. Stop any "pushing"—the tendency to play too loudly, rapidly, or violently, which the audience may encourage by laughter or applause.

CUTS AND CHANGES

The audience may teach you that some cuts in the script are necessary. Don't hesitate to make them, provided that:

1. You cut *chunks*—several lines at a time, not single words here and there. A line here, a word there—that kind of "trimming" can be done in weeks two or three, not now.

2. You rehearse each cut so the actors are secure. Don't try to give cuts just by writing notes.

3. The stage manager must receive any cuts, as well as the actors involved.

No change in any business, prop, costume, or line should be made during the dress rehearsals or previews, and certainly not after opening night, without careful rehearsal, and never without the director's permission and involvement. At a major regional theatre, where I was directing my own play and my wife was playing a leading role, the "name" designer, without telling anyone, added some decorative tree branches beside the upstage entrance just before the opening night house was opened. My wife's first appearance, in a nineteenth-century skirt, had been accomplished without incident until opening night, when she tangled her skirt in the unrehearsed and added twigs. Not even a warning to the actors who would use that entrance—how unprofessional and foolish!

GROWTH DURING PREVIEWS

During the previews, the actors will learn about large audiences, small audiences, student audiences, and the like. They will gain in confidence and authority. People will come up to tell you how much the show has improved since dress rehearsal. Do not take offense—they only report on what they see; you know the show is growing into itself. I have come to believe that no production is ever better than its best rehearsal, but as the actors learn to play it for an audience, it will become more pointed, more direct, broader, and will take on added authority, even as it inevitably recedes somewhat from the more subtle values you were hoping to convey.

THE PRESS

Inevitably, the press will come, and reviews will be written and read.

I don't read them anymore.

Someone has to, to learn whether any of them is a "money" or a ticket-selling review, and if so, to extract the quotes. The only value reviews have is to bring in audiences, when they do. They also seem to be of validating use with administrations or when included with grant applications to funding sources. As a source of learning for us about our work, they are useless.

You, as director have set out to do something. You have achieved it, or not, to some degree or other. You know, full well, where the lapses in your own production are and who is responsible for them. You are generally far better informed and trained, theatrically, than any reviewer. Why submit to the bother of reading some sadistic pundit's view of how right or wrong you were to do what you did?

The reviewer serves a function for the public—he tells them whether, in his opinion, they'll get their money's worth if they come. In the light of today's prices, that's a function. But his opinion of the worth of your efforts does not establish their value; it has bearing only on the size of the house.

In my view, the reviewer for the daily newspaper, in serving his public, has no right to an esthetic agenda that he sets out to force on the art he writes about. I think he should try to assess what the artist was trying to do, and the artist has a right to try to do any bloody thing he chooses! The reviewer, as audience, certainly has a right to offer his opinion as to whether the artist succeeded in fulfilling his intentions. "Mr. Ruth was attempting to hit one more home run, right out over second base. He hit a home run, but the ball was barely inside the third-base line." He also has every right to say whether he liked the result. "Mr. Ruth has succeeded in giving the game to the Yankees—but as a Dodger fan, I deeply regret it!" But he has no justification, as a journalist and layman, to set himself up as an authority and tell Mr. Ruth how to do his job better: "I've played a lot of sandlot baseball, and if Mr. Ruth wanted to put the ball over second base he should have held the bat . . ." unless he knows as much about batting as Mr. Ruth, in which case he'd probably be doing it instead of writing about it.

In other words, I accept the reviewer as doing his job properly when he:

1. Describes what the artist was trying to do;
2. Reports on whether the artist succeeded in achieving his goal;
3. Reports on his subjective reaction—"I liked it," or "I didn't like it," or "I hated it, but the audience seemed to be having a good time."

The reviewer forfeits my respect and attention when he presumes to tell an artist of substance how to do his work or what work he should be doing.

I am particularly averse to the reviewing of student work. Student actors need to get response to their work, but from audiences, not from critics; from their teachers, not from the press. And if the student actor is reviewed by a student reviewer, then the depths of absurdity have been reached.

In any case, I deplore the practice of posting reviews backstage on the call-board. Our emphasis should be on the work and the audience's response to it. We should not give the "enemy's" words status by providing access to them ourselves. I also deplore the practice of reading the advance copy of the review aloud at the opening night party after the show. Even the best review has a barb or two for some luckless soul concealed in it. I remember well my chagrin when, having accepted the call to read the triumphant *Times* review of George C. Scot's *Richard* III aloud, I stumbled into the one sentence that chopped down an actor. Many actors read the reviews only after the show closes. Others, and I now do this, let a spouse or the press agent or someone else read them first and say which ones are good. Then one can decide whether to read the good ones or not.

The public can be very strange about reviews. After carefully avoiding reading the mixed notices of one production, I was astounded to get through the mail, from a civilian acquaintance and admirer, what he said was a good notice—"I send you this with my warmest congratulations"—so I read it, and it seemed particularly poisonous. I phoned him, saying, "What the hell do you mean, sending me that?" He was genuinely shocked by my response. I think maybe people think it's just great whenever your name is in the paper.

We can be strange enough about reviews. I've now and then accidentally come upon a review from the past I had read and been hurt by, to find that twenty-five years later, it seemed like a pretty decent notice, after all.

THE DIRECTOR AND THE RUN

So—the play is running.

It may be scheduled to play only three nights—the director should be there every night. Or—it may play two three-night weekends. I would still be there every night, though perhaps in and out one or two of those nights.

If, though, the play is to run several weeks, or months, or for fifty or sixty performances in rotating repertory, then I try to see it about once a week after the opening, without letting the cast know I'm there. I bring a pocket-sized pad, find I must jot two or three things on it, and go backstage after the show.

"Good show, everyone!"

"Stuart! Hey, were you out there tonight?"

"Sure. It went well."

"Oh, well, if you say so. You should have been here *last* night. That was the best show of the run!"

"Yes," I say. "The director always just missed the best performance."

Then I whisper one or two carpings to the people involved and slip away into the night.

TWO DIRECTORIAL MALADIES

There are two more directing phenomena of which I have experience, about which no one ever warned me. They are connected.

The first I call "going blind." I always go backstage the second night, whether the reviews were bad or good. If good, one shares the triumph, passing through the dressing rooms. No one reads the reviews, of course, but everyone "knows." If they have been mixed or bad, I'm there to smile and seem normal as ever—not mentioning the press—and to share whatever the actors are feeling. If the director is there the second night, it helps stave off "second night letdown," a state of dullness which may occur because it's all over but the playing.

But "going blind" starts on the second night, for me. The play begins—and I go into a catatonic state. I'm not asleep—just in a state of annoyed but suspended animation. I don't enjoy it if it's going well and I only notice it at all when the tiniest little thing goes wrong. The only sensation I can compare it with is having to stuff yourself with a $100 gourmet dinner when you've had to have a $50 gourmet lunch the same day, an experience I had once in Paris and intend never to repeat. If I let a week go by, I can really *see* the play again—for one performance. But if I have to watch an understudy play or be there for any reason for a second performance that week, I "go blind."

"Going blind" is connected with the other director's disease: "the postpartum whim-whams." After giving birth to the production, forming bonds of intense feeling with actors, fighting the technical battles, and winning through somehow to the opening—everything stops and the director is left without a function. Tired, strained almost beyond endurance by keeping the whole unwieldy mechanism afloat, the director is left stranded, high and dry. This means a really rotten week of depression ahead for me. I can surmount it by working, if I am forced to go right to work, but no diversion, vacation, fancy dinner, excursion, or god-forbid-other-theatre is reward sufficient to compensate. I sulk.

A week of this usually finds me back among the living. But during that week, it is very hard for me to think positively about the play I have just done or about anything else. The involvement has been so intense that one simply feels stunned when it abruptly ceases.

Be warned. I am of relatively sunny disposition. What darker souls may endure, I know not.

EXERCISE

1. Page 293—There are at least two productions of *Godot*: the one in your head and the one on the stage. Compare these two productions. How similar is the actual production to your conceptual one? Is closing the variance a goal worth striving for?

EPILOGUE: DIRECTING FOR THE THEATRE: CAREER PATHS

Taste can be achieved only through the artist's inquiring exploration of a wide range of artistic modes and experiences. Talent cannot be taught, but channels can be created for its emergence. This book has been about opening those channels and developing techniques for realizing whatever choices talent and taste dictate.

The chief purpose of this book has been to describe, within the chronological framework of bringing a play from its selection to opening night, a method for directing a production that works, and to propel the developing director toward finding an ever-more-concrete technique for both the thorough preparation for his task and an efficient process for accomplishing it.

Theatre, unlike writing or painting, is a collaborative art. Neither the writer's pad of paper nor the painter's colors, brushes, and canvas require large expenditures of funds or institutional spaces in which to do the work. Theatre artists, however, cannot function at even a modest level without quite complicated social and financial mechanisms at their disposal.

The director needs a place in which to rehearse and perform, funds to mount the production, a group of coworkers, a script, and the means to reach a potential audience. Every director of plays must find solutions to these very practical aspects of being a theatre artist.

During the last half of the twentieth century, there have been four main areas in which directors of plays could seek for the means to practice their craft and art:

1. Educational theatre

2. Community theatre

3. Regional professional theatre

4. New York-based professional theatre

The conditions of work, the opportunities available, the qualities required for survival and success, and the advantages and drawbacks of each area differ. It may well be that surviving in the profession will bring a given individual into contact with each of these separate areas at one time or another. On the other hand, a director may work exclusively within only one of them for an entire career. The requirements for success in all four areas are similar, it is true, but with varying emphasis. It is also true that there are only two kinds of theatre, good and bad. Professional productions can be awful, community theatre productions can be exciting, and student productions can be inspiring. Every individual who has the talent and capacity for directing plays will find himself searching for a career path that satisfies his need for his own particular mix of teaching, promoting, competing, experimenting, and so on. The career paths themselves demand their own special mix of directorial talents.

EDUCATIONAL THEATRE

Many readers of this book find themselves, as faculty or students, already within an educational theatre, and the dynamics of such a theatre institution will be apparent to them in varying degrees, depending on their particular perspective. They may elect or seek to stay within that framework, either in higher or in secondary education.

Certainly one requirement for admission into the teaching profession is a degree, and advanced degrees are required for advancement in the teaching ranks. The M.F.A. degree has become the standard basic requirement for entry-level college teachers of theatre, and, of recent years, most graduate schools across the country offer such a degree. Some advertise themselves as "conservatories," professing to train and graduate artists of professional quality.

I am sure it matters where one's degree is from. In two respects, it can matter a great deal. Of most importance is, "How much can you *learn* there?" That depends on who is doing the teaching. Also important is, "How can they help me later?" That also depends on who is doing the teaching. But we can't all get to one of the distinguished graduate programs. Well, it was ever thus. But, partly because of the increased opportunities for employment due to the growth of regional professional theatre throughout the country, there is a great deal of contact and crossover between academic faculties and the professional theatre. Good training is being offered at the college level these days at many institutions, and students with talent and drive have a chance to learn the basics just about wherever they find themselves. After that, it's up to them, isn't it? And it was also ever *thus*.

Degree in hand or in immediate prospect, the candidate must make for the relevant annual academic convention, be it regional or national, doing the needful in terms of submitting placement forms and references, signing up for interviews, and joining in the yearly employment scramble. The candidate will have read ArtSEARCH and *The Chronicle of Higher Education* sedulously, writing letters of application for every likely opening.

Still, in applying for any position in theatre, educational or otherwise, you should remember that word of mouth and personal recommendation are the most reliable connections for future employment. "Who you know" *is* important, not in any sense of undue influence or pull, but because personal connection puts one that much closer to the position in question. When someone tells you about an opening, you can be that much more sure that an opening actually exists, instead of the ad being the obligatory gesture about an opening already destined for a secret shoo-in. Even more to the point, our profession is so dependent on the smooth collaboration of strong personalities that employers are rightly influenced by the comments of those they know and respect.

Indeed, one of my earliest teachers passed on an axiom he had learned from experience: "You will never get a job from a cold application." I may say, in passing, that every position down the years that has proved important to me has come through prior recommendation or nomination. There has always been some personal contact along the way that helped things happen, when they happened. I would augment my teacher's useful warning with this advice: When you hear about an opening for a job you really want, find someone who knows the employer and also knows your work to put in a good word for you.

What are the satisfying and attractive aspects of working in the educational theatre?

Job security is surely one of them. If the new faculty member is hired on tenure track, there is a clear set of rules that gives him a clear shot at making good and a time frame in which to do it. If he is hired on contract, that too spells out the time frame in which checks will arrive and over which benefits will extend. The value of the emotional security fostered by job security must not be underestimated.

Adequate-to-excellent facilities are usually available. Educational institutions have usually been able to spend money on physical plant, and the best theatre facilities in the country are on college campuses. Computer lighting boards came into use in university theatres while banks of resistance dimmers were still being used backstage on Broadway. Clean and up-to-date rehearsal and performance spaces need not be paid for out of the production budget; they come with the territory on college campuses. There are usually well-trained technicians in the department faculty, with a core of students supporting them. Physical productions can therefore be adequate or even excellent.

Generally the director in educational theatre is involved in actor training, and this permits him to prepare actors for his productions who are philosophically and technically in step with his ideas and his personality. Of course, a school is a place that people pass through, and each year actors who have just achieved some competence go away. But they are replaced by talented freshmen who begin their training, and last year's secondary players become this year's leading actors, and the cycle continues. A developed audience usually follows the educational theatre faithfully, since theatre is one of the cultural services offered to the community by the institution. "The town" as well as "the gown" comes to the productions. Aggressive promotion and development practices can increase attendance even for established departments, but empty houses are a rare thing for educational theatre.

The director in educational theatre needs to retain perspective about his work. He must remember that he is the teacher of an art, who practices his art in order to enable students to practice theirs. His work is with and for these student—not mature—actors, who are limited by their youth and inexperience, if not by their talent. His work is performed for the public, but even the act of meeting the public with the production occurs for primarily educational purposes. The audience is served as part of the process of training students.

Does it compromise the director's work to direct student actors? Only to the extent that all directing involves compromise. When I am asked, "Do you direct professional actors differently from the way you direct students?" my answer always is, "No—I just take whoever they are *from* wherever they are to doing the best production of the play we possibly can."

The increase in regional theatre around the country has diminished the *hubris* one used to encounter occasionally in educational theatre people—that sense that "we are as good as Broadway, so who are *you*?" I would hope that, as the director in educational theatre does his best to create exciting and valid productions and to grow in his own art, he will remember that his purpose for being where he is is not to prove his own genius but to teach, teach, teach. Good directing and good teaching are not, I hasten to add, contradictory.

Securing a foothold in educational theatre will begin a progress toward other goals. What opportunities exist for a future within the academy? Tenure track can lead to a tenured full professorship, still teaching and directing, within the same institution or in bigger and more important departments. One could aspire to head an acting or directing program at the graduate level. Perhaps, if administrative chores are not repugnant to him, a director/teacher may come to chairing a department, and such positions have been known to develop into the deanship of a school of theatre. Another career step could be the establishing of a conservatory within the department, even leading to the creation of a professional theatre associated with the university. Models for this exist at Florida State, with its School of Theatre in Tallahassee and its Asolo Conservatory and Asolo State Theatre at Sarasota, and, of course, the Yale School of Drama with its Yale Repertory Theatre. University theatres have spawned summer theatres, as with Indiana University's Brown County Playhouse, and Shakespeare festivals, as in Colorado and Utah.

Empire building is no doubt still possible in the educational theatre, where there will always be access to funds. Models as yet unrealized will no doubt arise from the dreams and energies of new wheeler-dealers who choose to plough the academic furrow.

COMMUNITY THEATRE

The collapse of the local stock companies in the late twenties and early thirties, brought about by the almost simultaneous arrival of the "talkies" and the Great Depression, contributed to the birth of community theatres. With casts of amateurs and former professionals, these organizations attracted audiences, created memberships and subscriptions, built buildings, and eventually hired full-time directors (who functioned as producers and business managers as well) and even developed paid technical and office staffs. Some, like The Cleveland Playhouse (which actually had an earlier beginning) and the Pasadena Playhouse, developed schools and their own professional companies. Others (Kalamazoo, Theatre Memphis, Shreveport, New Orleans) stopped short of full professionalism but continue to offer employment to directors, technical staff, and business staff.

These organizations vary greatly as to the functions and powers they assign to their professional director. In some, the director is a czar, making all the decisions, doing all the directing, and holding a virtually lifetime tenure. In others, the director's power is circumscribed by a play selection committee, a casting committee, a management committee, and other forms of membership input and control.

Most community theatres are governed by a board of trustees, drawn from the membership, that controls the building, policy making, and hiring. Others function through city recreation departments, with the director a city employee and performances taking place in city-owned facilities. The community theatre takes on many organizational shapes.

Artistically, community theatres' standards vary considerably. Casting is an area in which excellence is possible. Roles can be filled with performers of appropriate age levels. Former professionals, teachers of theatre, local radio and television personalities, lawyers and bankers with a flair for acting and years of amateur experience, homemakers who have given up decent acting or musical careers while the children are growing up—a wide range of responsible and able people may well be available.

The facilities, while seldom as opulent as those that universities can provide, can certainly be satisfactory, and tend to be free of the strictures that can come with using public property in state institutions. The technical staff can be as efficient and talented as in the educational theatre, and, without the need for degrees, can be recruited from a level of craftspeople not always qualified for college teaching.

The limitations likely to be placed on play selection seem to me to offer the least acceptable artistic compromises one is apt to encounter in the community theatre field. Very often the community theatre sees its function as providing its audience with the latest releases from Broadway and Off-Broadway. There seems to be a bias, too, in favor of giving patrons and performing members a goodly share of musical theatre offerings of the *Annie Get Your Gun* and *Guys and Dolls* ilk. To paraphrase Abe Lincoln, for the directors who like that sort of thing, that's the sort of thing they'll like. For those whose tastes run to classics and/or new plays, or toward more experimental work, the community theatre seems a less likely place to seek employment.

Another aspect of the community theatre career deserves comment. In my view, in no other area of the theatre does one's success and professional longevity as a director depend so much on one's social and political skills. In the academic situation one must, of course, get on with one's colleagues, and achieving tenure depends on proving your worth to your peers. In the regional theatre, there are boards of trustees to reckon with, and in the commercial theatre, getting on with the producer and getting good reviews make for success. But the community theatre, with its members who perform, with its board of trustees who really *are* the theatre, with its plethora of committees, calls for the director to be a deft and shrewd handler of people. One's job is a political balancing act. Some community theatre directors are hail-fellow-well-met glad-handers. Some are slick operators. A few are "artistes," pampered in their eccentricities by adult theatre "groupies" on their boards. Some are fellows in suits and ties who seem more like accountants than theatre people. Every one of them I've ever met has to spend much more time keeping his fingers on the pulse of his board than he does on questions of theatre.

Now, some theatre people come to this task with a special delight and talent. Some of those people can even direct plays. For them, community theatre offers autonomy, security, self-expression, and professional status. Fine, for them.

Working with boards can be learned. The first theatre board I ever worked with, when I was twenty-three, was just like every board I have met since. The first job many young directors get after college *is* with a tiny community theatre in some not-very-urban town where they are put in charge of the whole works—scenery, lights, tickets, directing, and janitorial services. The training they get there in dealing with boards and committees will be valid wherever they go. It just needs saying that politics, in that kind of job, turns out to *be* the job, and the beginner needs to know that going in—before he finds himself going out.

The director who chooses to stay in the community theatre field appears, at the present time, to have fewer options for advancement than his educational theatre counterpart. One choice is to stay as long as he can in one place and, by hard work, expand the operation—building its audience, improving its facilities, developing a children's theatre, offering classes, and so on. Another choice is moving on to a more developed community theatre in a larger place, where some of the expansions mentioned earlier have already taken place. The transformation of a community theatre into a professional theatre, which might be someone's dream, has rarely occurred in recent years. The one instance I have personal experience of happened because all the members of the theatre group who wanted to act died off or left town, but the board still owned the building and there was an audience to fill it. This community theatre hired a director who then was able to hire actors. Community theatre directors have been known to start their own commercial summer theatres, but the day of successful summer-stock companies seems to be over. It would appear that there are a few substantial community theatres where a director and a core of support staff can still make a living and have a satisfactory artistic life. There are more marginal groups, barely able to hire a recent directing graduate for a pittance. The community theatre field doesn't seem to offer much between these two extremes.

REGIONAL THEATRE

There has been a momentous revolution in the American theatre during my lifetime, but not an artistic one. The face of our theatre has been changed by the emergence of the not-for-profit professional company.

In the recent past, "professional" and "commercial" were synonymous in the American theatre. Somebody put up money, or found investors who would, and found a play to put on or a building to run a season of plays in, with the hope of making a profit. Only since the mid-fifties has the idea taken hold that theatre is an art form deserving of public support and charitable contribution, the function of which is to preserve the art of the past and foster the art of the present for the good of the community, just as museums and symphony orchestras and schools function for the public good. Theatres have spread across the land, and though the arts are having a harder time finding funds in the nineties than they did in the sixties, the not-for-profit theatre seems to be here to stay.

Employment opportunities for actors, directors, designers, technicians, and management people have greatly increased as a result. Theatre departments, instead of just "teaching people to teach people to teach people," get to train artists who have some chance of actually working at their art.

Still, there will always be fewer openings for directors than for other participants in the collaborative business of play-making. Though "a cast of thousands" happens only in films, there are still more acting than directing jobs around, because there's only one director per play.

How does a director fresh out of graduate school with a hard-won M.F.A. in hand find a place in a regional theatre? As a director—he doesn't, not at first.

I am reminded here, for reasons that shall become apparent later, of Herman. Herman Palmer. But his name wasn't really Herman. He was an elderly union stagehand in Terre Haute, Indiana, where I grew up. He made a living sitting backstage at the Grand Opera House, which was by this time a movie theatre, pushing the button to open and close the electric front curtain between showings. He also painted scenery for Terre Haute's community theatre. Backstage at the Grand, he had spent all day for years reading novels, in lousy light, for the rental library for Root's Department Store, to tell them which books to stock for their customers to borrow, and his sight had begun to go.

When I was in college, the community theatre paid me a time or two to help Herman paint scenery, doing the straight lines he couldn't see anymore.

"How did you get into the theatre, Herman?" I asked one day.

"In the first place," he replied, "my name isn't really Herman. You see, when I was about twelve or so, we lived down the block from this stock company's theatre, and I got to hanging around out in the alley with the stagehands. Now and then they'd send me down the block to the saloon to bring back a bucket of beer, and I'd make a dime or two. Well, one day after I'd brought back the beer and was sitting around the open loading door with the men, the stage manager began yelling, 'Herman! Herman?' inside on the stage.

"Then he came out, saying, 'Where's that damned boy, anyhow?'

"It seems that Herman, the prop boy, was no place to be found, and the prop dishes had to be washed for the show that night and furniture had to be set out and all kinds of stuff got together.

"'I could do it, sir,' I said. 'What's the pay?'

"'Five dollars a week,' says he, 'and I guess you can.'

"'Yes, sir! Thank you, sir,' says I.

"Says he, 'Well, all right, Herman—get a move on!' So, that's how I got into the theatre, and I've been Herman ever since."

The moral of this story is: One way to get into a theatre is to find a theatre you like and hang around! Become a "groupie." Be a "gopher." Make yourself useful. If you do, in time you'll find yourself on the payroll. Of course, there are theatres where they know they need someone like you, and for those jobs you can actually apply.

The job a young director is likely to get, and without having to change his name, is an internship, paying barely a living wage, with duties as a production assistant. A production assistant does the job of an assistant stage manager, but he is called production assistant because assistant stage manager is a union title. The number of union positions a theatre must fill is obligatory, based on the nature of their union contract, but once they've met that quota, they can hire production assistants in any number they like to do those jobs, at less than union wages.

What, an M.F.A. in such a lowly job? If he wants the professional theatre, she should jump at it. Being around can be everything. There is a goodly amount of turnover in any theatre, and someone who has been there and knows the ropes will be the one asked to step in. Assistant to the director, assistant stage manger, stage manager, assistant director—all these steps up are not only possible but probable. Then the chance may come to propose directing a reading or some other "dark night" project, or working with some small-part actors on an evening of scenes. Attracting attention within the organization and arousing some interest in what he might want to do is something an enterprising candidate for directing plays should be well able to do.

Some few regional theatres have internships that at the outset involve working as an assistant to the director. These are designed to bring talented young directors along who may in time be given a chance within the organization schedule to direct a small-scale project. This may indeed lead to a full production someplace down the pike.

After the fledgling director has found a niche within the world of the regional theatre, what career aspirations can he satisfy there?

There are three tiers of directors in regional theatres as they currently exist.

The artistic director is the artistic leader of the company. He or she selects the plays and hires the actors and the artistic staff. He or she will probably direct a significant proportion of the season's plays. He or she will have been hired as a result of a considerable number of successful productions along the way, combined with demonstrated leadership ability and the kind of prestige that attracts funding. If he or she is the head of the entire theatre, to whom the business management reports, the job's title may be producing director. An artistic or producing director will be paid a salary comparable to that of a full professor in a theatre department of national standing similar to that of the theatre in question.

One or more associate or staff directors may be attached to the theatre under the artistic director. Certain plays will be assigned to them, and their other duties may include the reading of scripts, experimental programming, supervising a second theatre, teaching classes, or heading other spin-offs from the theatre's main production schedule. These directors may have come up from within the organization, or have been hired as staff from among guest directors of past seasons; they may even be senior people who no longer want the chore of artistic leadership but who are valuable as consultants and advisors as well as for their directing contributions. Again, compensation is apt to be comparable with relevant academic salaries.

Guest directing in regional theatre is a way of life for some directors. These are people, generally in their thirties or forties, young enough to handle moving about from town to town. Their year may be made up of directing four or five shows in different theatres around the country. Suppose an artistic director elects to do only three of his theatre's five productions, in order to make time for his other duties, and that the theatre can afford no other directors on its staff. Guest directors will be brought in. Once a guest director has done one or two shows at a given theatre and proved his compatibility with company, staff, and audience, he may be asked back every season. Four or five such relationships with theatres, and the guest director's schedule will be filled.

The drawback here is that the number of shows one can do in a season is limited by the number of weeks available for rehearsal, casting, and preparation. The pay rarely amounts to more than seven or eight thousand dollars per production, often less, and four or five shows a year is one person's limit. Even this can mean leaving by plane the day after the opening to start rehearsal next day for the next show in the next town. All this amounts to financially is about what the average assistant professor makes in one academic year.

A director's work in the regional theatre can be artistically rewarding in the highest degree. One has the chance to work with professional actors, all of whom are apt to be competent and some of whom may be brilliant. Sometimes distinguished actors come for a particular play and role, and the chance to work with them can be rewarding, both in the present and for the future. The chance may come to develop an important new script, and its future can be bright for all those involved with its production. Classic and experimental work is there to do in the regional theatre as well. All in all, the experience of being part of a full-time, professional producing unit is precisely what being in theatre ought to be.

Career advancement can certainly be achieved within the regional theatre. The ladder from assistant to director to guest director to associate director to artistic director exists. The artistic director can "trade up" to a larger or more prestigious theatre, or, by staying in place, can expand his organization to second and third theatres, touring, creating new play programs, developing a conservatory, associating with university programs, building new facilities, taking productions to Broadway or Europe—even forming a film unit.

Two negative considerations should be raised. The first is the matter of financial compensation. When we pioneers of the regional theatre movement started all this, we envisaged resident theatre companies much like the German *stadttheaters*, with permanent companies of actors, paid decent salaries, in which an artistic and a humane life could be lived simultaneously. This is yet to come about. Sending the kids to college is something few regional theatre actors get to do. Even having kids is something few can afford. As for directors—there is one artistic director per theatre. He usually is paid an adequate salary. The position of staff director or associate director exists only infrequently, and anyone in that job could generally be paid more in teaching. As for the guest director—"Good luck." Now, being an artist implies accepting certain hardships, and I am not suggesting that the benefits of the American business class are essential to happiness. But even artists must live in the society, shop in supermarkets, and, outside of New York, sustain an automobile. In the regional theatre, it isn't easy.

The second negative: burnout. Budget strictures make it inevitable that the artistic staffing of regional theatres is usually at the minimum number to get the job done. This means that those lucky enough to have the jobs are working very, very hard. The pressure to turn out the work is severe, and what was once a consuming pleasure too easily becomes a consuming duty and burden.

Actors and directors who "settle" for the regional theatre life are in danger of becoming worn-out hacks. Starting the next show, beginning yet another season—the excitement can drain away, leaving people just going through the motions. "Running as fast as you can just to stay in place" loses its charm. This is what causes the lackluster performances and productions one so often encounters in the regional theatres in middle-sized cities. Enormous energy, vitality, physical health, and love of theatre are essential tools in the survival kit of the regional theatre artist.

NEW YORK–BASED DIRECTING

Despite the growth of what in the thirties *Theatre Arts Monthly* called "the tributary theatre" into what we call "regional theatre," which is currently the largest employer of members of Actors' Equity Association, New York remains the nation's theatrical center. Broadway, the "fabulous invalid," still staggers on, and the concentration in New York of producers, agents, casting directors, TV and film people, to say nothing of the showcase potential of the various Off-

Broadway theatres, serves as a magnet to draw people of the theatre to live there.

Those who job regularly into regional theatre usually maintain a New York residence; those who come to New York directly from school or regional theatre to create a New York base for the first time must seek housing, along with a means of maintaining themselves between theatre jobs.

New York used to be a more hospitable place for those seeking a foothold in the arts than it is now. Prior to the 1970s one could find less expensive housing in New York than almost anyplace else in the country. It was the ability to exist cheaply on the edge of the cultural riches of the metropolis that induced so many of the country's brightest talents to try their wings there.

Now, housing costs have mounted catastrophically. Low- and middle-income families are being forced out of Manhattan, and living space has become crushingly expensive. When the beginner comes to New York to find a place to live, one thing he has to do is be sure he can pay for it, and that may mean sharing an overcrowded apartment. The most serious dilemma the aspiring artist finds himself in is that often the job that pays him enough to pay his rent (temporary office work and waiting tables being among the most frequent sources of employment) takes so much time and energy that rounds can't be made or contacts pursued that might lead to doing what he came to the city to do. This side of "coming to New York" is much more discouraging and difficult than it was when "the Village," instead of providing luxury housing for "yuppies," was aswarm with young writers, actors, and painters living in cold water flats.

On the other hand, ways to make contact with the working theatre have proliferated. Off-Broadway, Off-Off-Broadway, small nonprofit theatres, classes, "groups"—all this activity offers many opportunities for getting in touch with what is going on.

My advice to the recent theatre graduate who decides to try New York is:

1. Find a place to live before you come, through friends or relatives or friends of friends.

2. Have funds or have a truly marketable skill (word processing, restaurant skills, secretarial or accounting skills, selling experience) so you can support yourself while creating the theatre opportunities you have come to seek.

3. Through friends or through the "trade papers"—*Show Business* and *Backstage*—make contact with whatever theatre groups you can. Establish a no-pay association with an Off-Off-Broadway company as soon as you can. Take classes. Do what you can to get where you can listen and learn and meet people. Networking will produce results.

Breaking into directing in New York is harder than breaking into acting, which is hard enough.

The best path is through access to the new script. The director who has the scripts of one or two writer friends in his pocket has something to talk to people about, something to sell. With the writer's permission he can make contact with various producing groups around the city, knocking on doors that just might open to a good new play. He can get together a play reading and invite people. He can seek funds herself for producing the play. In Chapter 1, the path of the new play toward New York production was discussed. The new director, attached to the new play, can move from obscurity into some visibility.

While searching for an angle from which to attack New York, you would do well to remember that wide range of skills you have acquired to become the best director you can be—a knowledge of acting, of stage management, of design and writing, and even of the business side of the theatre. Any of these skills that are sufficiently developed to be salable can become the source of that essential survival income one needs. It is always better to work inside the theatre than outside it, and contacts made while acting or stage managing can lead toward chances to direct.

The name of the game is *sustaining* oneself first, then finding some *visibility* as a director, next attaining some *recognition* as an *able* director, and then making one's living *as* a director.

Luck, persistence, resilience, and energy play a large part in this. Having the ability to *do* the work is even more important, but this comes into play only after you have created the *means* to do the work.

MAKING YOUR OWN THEATRE

Within each of the four areas of theatre dealt with in the previous discussion (educational, community, regional, and New York-based), another option exists. Instead of looking for a "big daddy" to employ or discover him, the director can create his own theatre.

All our college and university theatres came about because somebody who was teaching English or rhetoric or something decided there should be some plays produced and then agitated to get some classes offered to help make the plays better. There still must be schools out there where such evangelism can bear fruit.

The community theatres all started with a group of people who wanted to put on plays in their town or neighborhood or church. There are still communities where a director could get some like-minded people together, and, without benefit of theatrical unions or public institutions, put on plays for audiences. This kind of theatre can be created by people who work at other jobs in the daytime, and it can be made to happen in New Harmony as well as New York.

Look at the history of our regional theatres. Oh, some few, like Seattle, began with a lot of money and city-wide sponsorship. Most, however, are the products of determined individuals who decided they could make a living, as professionals, by creating a theatre in their own locale, rather than going to look for work in existing institutions. Zelda Fichandler in Washington and Nina Vance in Houston created important regional theatres that survive as examples.

Even in New York, the examples of Gene Feist in the creation of the Roundabout Theatre, Joseph Papp with the New York Shakespeare Festival, and Ted Mann with the Circle in the Square prove that determined individuals, with the support of the theatrically talented people they can gather around them, can build theatres that endure.

Creating a theatre requires drive, dedication, and making a series of intelligent choices along the way. It is beyond the scope of this book to trace how these and other successful people have made their theatres work, but out of my direct involvement in theatre founding I can offer some perhaps obvious but still serious questions to consider as one sets about to start a theatre:

1. Can the community in question provide a potential audience of the size and quality necessary to support the projected theatre?

2. Is that audience sufficient to allow the theatre to grow beyond its modest beginnings?

3. Does the community offer sufficient fund-raising potential (foundations, corporations, wealthy individuals) to justify the effort made to reach them?

4. Are there well-placed and significant members of the local community committed to the project's success?

5. Will the artistic policy of the proposed theatre fulfill a need and fill a gap in the community's cultural life?

6. Are the communications media (press, radio, television) sufficiently centralized that the theatre's message can reach its potential public?

7. Is there an existing building appropriate for the theatre's use, in terms of audience capacity, production facilities, location, parking, local access, public recognition? Or do the means exist to build a theatre?

8. Can the organization be capitalized sufficiently from the outset to get it past the growing pains of the first few seasons?

9. Can a core of talented individuals in both the artistic and manage-

ment areas be assembled, possessed of enough skill, loyalty, and energy to bring the project off successfully?

10. Can the creator of the project sustain himself financially and emotionally long enough to get the project off the ground?

Positive answers to each of these questions *must* be achieved if a project is to come to successful fruition. Of course, because we live in a less than ideal world, they will not be achieved all at once, or even on schedule.

FINAL WORDS

Choosing to make a career in the theatre is an act of faith.

Perhaps, for most of us, making that choice is also hurling a challenge. "I don't want to do it if it's too easy." "Why climb the mountain? Because it's there!"

But an artistic act—painting a picture, writing a book, doing a play—expresses faith in other people, faith that there really is someone out there who can see, who can read, who can hear.

The arts reinterpret human experience so people can see where they've been, where they are, and where they are going, so that they can learn to live better lives.

The arts deserve the attention of our first-rate minds. And directing is a demanding art. It demands of its practitioners leadership, human insight, the ability to read and interpret, the craft of organization, and vision both ocular and spiritual.

Laws have been made, philosophies propounded, governments instituted, religions enunciated. The world muddles on.

But if the proper study of mankind really is man, perhaps it is through the arts that this study can best be made, that understanding can best be achieved, that peace and healing can be most fully embraced.

The art of putting on plays is not a trivial business. It has room for the best that is within us.

APPENDIX A

REHEARSAL SCHEDULE FOR
TEMPEST

A University Production Covering A Six-Week Rehearsal Period

Note: This schedule for a university production of a Shakespeare play allows one day off per week, until the final week, for study and personal chores. It covers approximately the same number of hours and employs a similar use of time as the professional four-week schedule discussed in Chapter VIII.

WEEK 1 (REHEARSAL ROOM)

Monday, January 13
    7–10 Read play; "Show and Tell"

Tuesday, January 14
    7–10 Slow read-through, Act I

Wednesday, January 15
    7–10 Slow read-through, Act II

Thursday, January 16
    7–10 Slow read-through, Act III

Friday, January 17
    7–10 Slow read-through, Acts IV and V

Sunday, January 19
    7–10 Read through whole play

WEEK 2 (ON STAGE WITH BASIC SET)

Monday, January 20
7–10 Block and run Act I

Tuesday, January 21
7–10 Block and run Act II

Wednesday, January 22
7–10 Block and run Act III

Thursday, January 23
7–10 Block and run Act IV

Friday, January 24
7–10 Block and run Act V

Sunday, January 26
7–10 Run-through of whole play, still on book

WEEK 3

Monday, January 27 (without books from here on)
7–8   I-1, Shipwreck only: Master, Bos'n, Gonzalo, Alonso, Ferdinand, Trinculo, Stephano
8–9   I-2, Prospero, Miranda
9–10 I-2, Prospero, Ariel, Mark, Will, Miranda, Caliban

Tuesday, January 28
7–8   I-2, Ferdinand, Miranda, Ariel, Prospero
8–10 II-1, Alonso, Sebastian, Adrian, Antonio, Gonzalo, Ariel

Wednesday, January 29
7–8   II-2, Caliban, Trinculo, Stephano
8–9   III-1, Prospero, Miranda, Ferdinand
9–10 III-2, Caliban, Stephano, Trinculo, Ariel

Thursday, January 30
7–8   A. Music rehearsal—all helpers, Caliban, Trinculo, Stephano, room to be announced
        B. III-3, Gonzalo, Alonso, Sebastian, Antonio, Adrian, Prospero
8:00 IV, All called (except Caliban, Trinculo, Stephano) including helpers
9:00   Add Caliban, Trinculo, Stephano

Friday, January 31

    7–10 V, Prospero, Miranda, Ferdinand, Alonso, Sebastian, Antonio,
        Adrian, Gonzalo (no Ariel)

    8:00   Add Caliban, Trinculo, Stephano, Master, Bos'n

Sunday, February 2

    7–10 Run show (All)

WEEK 4

Monday, February 3

    7–8 I-1, All

    8–10 I-2, (including "Dumb Show") All who are in scene

Tuesday, February 4

    7–8:30 II-1, Alonso, Sebastian, Gonzalo, Antonio, Adrian, Ariel,
        Will, Mark

    8:30–10 II-2, Caliban, Stephano, Trinculo

Wednesday, February 5

    7–8 III-1, Prospero, Ferdinand, Miranda

    8–9 III-2, Caliban, Stephano, Trinculo, Ariel, Mark, Will

    9–10 III-3, Alonso, Sebastian, Antonio, Gonzalo, Adrian, Ariel, Prospero,
        all helpers

Thursday, February 6

    6:30–8:00 Dress parade, All (in costume shop to get costumes 6:30;
        on stage 7:00)

    8–10   IV, All

Friday, February 7

    7–8:30 V, Prospero, Miranda, Ferdinand, Ariel, Alonso, Sebastian,
        Antonio, Gonzalo, Adrian, Caliban, Trinculo, Stephano

    8:30–10 V, Add all others

Sunday, February 9

    7–10 Run play (All); work notes after

WEEK 5

Monday, February 10

    7–8 I-1, All

    8–10 I-2, All in scene plus "dumb show"

Tuesday, February 11
    7–8 II-1, All in scene plus Will, Mark
    8–9 II-2
    9–10 III-1

Wednesday, February 12
    7–8 III-2
    8–9 III-3, All
    9–10 IV, All

Thursday, February 13
    7–8 V, All
    8–10 Run Part One (I-1, I-2, II-1, II-2), All

Friday, February 14
    7–8 Run Part Two—All
    8–10 Run show—All

Sunday, February 16
    7–10 Run show, work notes—All

WEEK 6

Monday, February 17
    7–10 Run show

Tuesday, February 18
    7–10 Run show, adding technical elements (incl. sound)

Wednesday, February 19
    7–10 Run show, adding technical elements

Thursday, February 20
    7–10 Run show, adding technical elements

Friday, February 21
    6:30 Half-hour
    7–10 Tech dress

Saturday, February 22
    1:30   Half-hour
    2–5   Tech dress

7:00   Half-hour

7:30–10 Tech (without costumes?)

Sunday, February 23

Dress rehearsal—time to be announced

1ST PLAYING WEEK

*Monday, February 24

Morning school performance—time 10 a.m. (9:30 $\frac{1}{2}$ hr.)

7–10 Dress rehearsal

*Note: Since there will be no front curtain and the house must be opened at half-hour, you must check your on-stage props *prior* to half-hour for each performance.

APPENDIX B

PROMPTBOOK PAGES
FROM *KING JOHN*

LF-to confirm what all have long suspected	LF(1)w/ sigh of relief, confirms w/apology (2)remembers w/amaze-ment her exhaustion (3)pleading hopefully (4)warm and loving (5)pleading with him to understand	LF B seated
B-to con-gratulate her	B(1)exultantly (2)urging her warmly to forgive herself (3)reasoning with her as if persuading a child (4)warmly reminds her (5)joshing her (6)suddenly deeply sincere (7)w/ fierce pride	②GET HER UP ③LIFT UP, EMBRACE ⑤ PUT HER DOWN
B-to show her off LF-to surrender	(8)happy idea (9)persuasively (10)cavalierly (11)pertly	LF ⟵B TAKE HER HAND RUN UP ⑪ PICK HER UP, CARRY HER OFF,

		THROUGH TOWER AS SET TURNS #1 TOWER TURNS #2 SET TURNS PL ENTER DL. ① AU U.R w/ BANNER, ALSO SOLDIERS, BANNERS UL +L. #3 C+AR ENTER D.R. ② P. GREETS AU ③ C AR ↓ P
P-to bind Au to Ar publicly	P(1)hailing Au w/relief (2)man to man, reminds Ar of his proud lineage (3)admits (4)demonstrating his power over Au to Ar (5)promising Ar vengeance (6)prompting	

322

LADY FAULCONBRIDGE

①King Richard Cordelion was thy father:
②By long and vehement suit I was seduced
  To make room for him in my husband's bed.
③Heaven lay not my transgression to my charge!
④Thou art the issue of my dear offense,
  Which was so strongly urg'd past my defence.

BASTARD

①Now, by this light, were I to get again,
  Madam, I would not wish a better father.
②Some sins do bear their privilege on earth,
  And so doth yours; your fault was not your folly.
③Needs must you lay your heart at his dispose,
  Against whose fury and unmatched force
  The aweless lion could not wage the fight,
④Nor keep his princely heart from Richard's hand.
⑤He that perforce robs lions of their hearts
  May easily win a woman's.⑥Ay, my mother,
  With all my heart I thank thee for my father!
⑦Who lives and dares but say thou didst not well
  When I was got, I'll send his soul to hell.
⑧Come, lady, I'll show thee to my kin;✗✗
⑨And they shall say, when Richard me begot,
  If thou hadst said him nay, it had been sin;
⑩Who says it was, he lies;⑪I say 'twas not!✗✗

(Exeunt.)

ACT SECOND

Scene One

(France. Before the walls of Angiers. Enter
PHILIP, KING OF FRANCE; LEWIS, THE DAUPHIN;
AUSTRIA; CONSTANCE; ARTHUR; and their forces
and attendants.)

KING PHILIP

①Before Angiers well met, brave Austria.
②Arthur, that great forerunner of thy blood,
  Richard, that robb'd the lion of his heart
  And fought the holy wars of Palestine,
③By this brave duke came early to his grave;
④And, for amends to his posterity,
  At our importance hither he is come,
  To spread his colours, boy, in thy behalf,
⑤And to rebuke the usurpation
  Of thy unnatural uncle, English John.
⑥Embrace him, love him, give him welcome hither.

Ar-to play his part	Ar(1)formally absolves
	   (2)genteely warning
	
	   (3)gracefully
	
	   (4)gracious but formal
		③ AR EXTENDS HAND, AU KNEELS

	P-approving Ar's effort	
Au-to shine in C's eyes	(1)making a fatherly show (2)vows on sword, building ends catching C's eye (3)more human, easy, pleased with self	AU RISES, SWORD LIKE CROSS ③ AU KNEEL AGAIN
C-to size him up	(1)gushing (2)modestly (3)warmly (4)very genteel Au-stoutly, glaring about, daring anybody to take issue	C →AR AU P L AU RISES

P-to get going	P(1)covering a smile
	   (2)briskly
	   (3)a public announcement
		AR C AU P
		              L

C-to give wise advice	C(1)confidentially
	
	   (2)reminds him hopefully
		AR AU
		C L
		          P

ARTHUR

①God shall forgive you Cordelion's death
②The rather that you give his offspring life,
 Shadowing their right under your wings of war.
③I give you welcome with a powerless hand,
 But with a heart full of unstained love.
④Welcome before the gates of Angiers, duke.

KING PHILIP

 A noble boy! Who would not do thee right?

AUSTRIA (wears Lion skin)

①Upon thy cheek lay I this zealous kiss,
 As seal to this indenture of my love,
②That to my home I will no more return R
mf Till Angiers, and the right thou hast in France,
 Ev'n till that England, hedg'd in with the sea,
 And confident from foreign purposes,
 Ev'n till that utmost corner of the west
ff Salute thee for her king;③till then, fair boy,
 Will I not think of home, but follow arms.

CONSTANCE

①O, take his mother's thanks,x②a widow's thanks,
③Till your strong hand shall help to give him strength
④To make a more requital to your love.

AUSTRIA

 The peace of heaven is theirs that ᴿlift their swords
 In such a just a charitable war.

KING PHILIP

①Well, then,②to work our cannon shall be bent
 Against the brows of this resisting town.
③We'll lay before Angiers our royal bones,X
 Wade to the marketplace in Frenchmen's blood.
 But we will make it subject to this boy. (Trumpet.)
                                            MCY

CONSTANCE

①Stay for an answer to your embassy,
 xLest unadvis'd you stain your swords with blood.
②The Lord of Melun may from England bring
 That right in peace which here we urge in war;
 And then we shall repent each drop of blood
 That hot haste so indirectly shed.

 (LORD MELUN enters.)

325

P-to show her he has been right	P(1) briskly requests (2) doing this for C (3) prompts him	

M-to rouse P to action	M(1) alerting and
	    challenging
	
	(2) proclaiming the
	    bad news
	(3) urgently explains
	(4) facts, a roster
	
	(5) with contempt
	(6) incredulous
	
	(7) "Imagine that!"	

M-to prove his point	(8) points out (9) severely warning (10) urgently!	
P-to get his ` bearings Au-to shine in C's eyes	P-taken aback Au(1) bucking P up (2) cheerfully declares (3) with a swagger	
J-to test the water	OFF STAGE ORDER: J(1) a friendly greeting (2) dryly inquires (3) crisply confident	J + BANNER ENTER ALONE
P-to put burden on J	(4) piously (5) coldly spells out P's punishment P(1) tit for tat (2) ironically (3) proudly asserts (4) Q.E.D.	ALL FOLLOW: FRENCH BANNERS CLUSTER

KING PHILIP

A wonder, lady! Lo, upon thy wish,
Our messenger, Lord Melun, is arrived! MX
①What England says, say briefly, gentle lord;
④We coldly pause for thee;③Lord Melun, speak.

LORD MELUN

①Then turn your forces from this paltry siege
  And stir them up against a mightier task.
②England, impatient of your just demands,
  Hath put himself in arms;③the adverse winds,
  Whose leisure I have stay'd, have given him time
  To land his legions all as soon as I.
④With him along is come the mother queen;
  With her her niece, the Lady Blanch of Spain;
  With them a bastard of the king's deceas'd;
⑤And all th' unsettled humours of the land,
⑥Rash, inconsiderate, fiery voluntaries,
  Having sold their fortunes at their native homes,
  Rearing their birthrights proudly on their backs,
⑦To make a hazard of new fortunes here.

     (Drum is heard.) MC9 ⟶

⑧The interruption of their churlish drums
  Cuts off more circumstance;⑨they are at hand,
  To parley or to fight;⑩therefore prepare!

KING PHILIP

How much unlook'd for is this expedition!

AUSTRIA

①By how much unexpected, by so much
  We must awake endeavor for defence,
②For courage mounteth with occasion.
③Let them be welcome then; we are prepar'd.

     (Enter KING JOHN, BASTARD, ELINOR, BLANCH,
      SALISBURY, PEMBROKE, and their train.)

KING JOHN (ALL ALONE)

①Peace be to France,②if France in peace permit
  Our just and lineal entrance to our own; (GENERAL ENT.)
③If not, bleed France!⎦and④peace ascend to heaven,
⑤Whiles we, God's wrathful agent, do <u>correct</u>
  Their proud contempt that beats his peace to heaven.

KING PHILIP

①Peace be to England,②if that war return
  From France to England, there to live in peace.
③England we love;④and, for that England's sake
  With burden of our armour here we sweat.   (MORE)

327

P-to rebuke J	P(5)severely reproaches (6)points out tartly (7)shaming him, piling it on (8)stoutly asserts (9)daring him to find an answer	⑦ P HOLDS OUT HAND ↳C AV J P⟵___AR
J-to challenge P's credentials	J-cooly inquires P(1)righteously tops him (2)proclaims (3)truculently defying him J-unimpressed, dryly P-hotly ripostes	J P AR⤴ Bi ⟨P ↑ ⌒E J P AR ⟵P AR
E-to beard him	E-leaping in--best defense is offense	E ⟩ P AR
C-to seize the chance to measure swords with E E-to load her with contempt	C-light of battle, joyously taking her on E(1)quashing her (2)"I'm onto you" C(1)stung, indignant (2)getting idea how to needle her (3)gust of rage (4)stingingly E-"sweetly"--complimenting Ar on his mother	J ↓E P AR COUNTER↴ AR⟵C J E AR C P

328

⑤This toil of ours should be a work of thine;
⑥But thou from loving England art so far,
That thou hast under-wrought his lawful king.
⑦Look here✗upon thy brother Geoffrey's face;
These eyes, these brows, were moulded out of his;
That Geoffrey was thy elder brother born,
And this his son;⑧England was Geoffrey's right
And this is Geoffrey's in the name of God.
⑨How comes it then that thou art call'd a king,
When living blood doth in these temples beat,
Which owe the crown that thou o'ermasterest?

                    KING JOHN
From whom hast thou this great commission, France,
To draw my answer from thy articles?

                    KING PHILIP
①From that supernal judge, that stirs good thoughts
To look into the blots and stains of right.
②That judge✗hath made me guardian to this boy,
③Under whose warrant I impeach thy wrong
And by whose help I mean to chastise it.

                    KING JOHN
Alack! Thou dost usurp authority.✗

          "d," not "z"
                    KING PHILIP
✗Excuse it is to beat usurping down.

                    ELINOR
✗Who is it thou dost call usurper, France?

               CONSTANCE (JUMPS IN)
✗Let me make answer; thy usurping son. ¹ºx
                                      ʲx

                    ELINOR
①Out, insolent! ②Thy bastard shall be king,
That thou mayst be a queen, and check the world!

                    CONSTANCE
①My bed was ever to thy son as true
As thine was to thy husband②and this boy
Liker in feature to his father Geoffrey
Than thou and John in manners; being as like
As rain as water, or devil to his dam.
③My boy a bastard! ④By my soul I think
His father never was so true begot:
It cannot be and if thou wert his mother.

                    ELINOR(TO AR.)
There's a good mother, boy, that blots thy father.

329

	C-a savage rebuttal	*(handwritten diagram: C LEAD AR DL / E ARC, L AU, P, arrows)*
Au-to keep women in line	Au-shocked	
B-to give Au fair warning	B-"get him!"	*(handwritten: B, Bl ← B)*
Au-to stand up to them	Au-annoyed	*(handwritten: ← E AU)*
	B(1)takes him up	*(handwritten: Bl B → AU)*
	(2)ironic discovery	
	(3)a happy promise	"MORTUO LEONI ET
	(4)"now, I warned you"	LEPORES INSULTANT"- A DEAD LION EVEN HARES INSULT.
Bl-to support B	Bl(1)scornfully	*(handwritten: Bi S P, E, Bl ← B AU, P ARC)*
	(2)to B, stoutly avers	
	B(1)sharing his contempt with her	
	(2)to Au bluntly	
	(3)vowing earnestly	
	Au(1)inquires "blandly"	*(handwritten: AU →, Bl B ←)*
	(2)warns boastfully	
P-to cut them off	P(1)impatiently	*(handwritten: ← P, AR C)*
	(2)a scornful label	
P-to lay out his terms	(3)brisk, back to biz.	*(handwritten: Bi S P, Bi B AU, E → P, C AR)*
	(4)spells out clearly	
	(5)severely requests	
J-to counter with his demands	J(1)dryly (2)cheerful	*(handwritten: J, E, C AR)*
	(3)a pleasant offer	
	(4)contemptuously	
	(5)pleasantly	
E-to woo Ar	E-kind, coaxing	*(handwritten: E, J P → C AR)*

CONSTANCE
There's a good grandam, boy, that would blot thee. ✗

AUSTRIA

Peace! C + A ✗

BASTARD (TO BLANCH)

✗Hear the crier.

AUSTRIA

✗What the devil art thou?

BASTARD
①One that will <u>play</u> the devil, sir, with <u>you</u>,
✗And 'a may catch your hide and you alone.
②You are the hare of whom the proverb goes,
"Whose <u>valour</u> plucks <u>dead</u> <u>lions</u> by the beard!"
③I'll smoke your skin-coat, and I catch you right.
④Sirrah, look to't; i'faith, I will, i'faith.

BLANCH
⓪Ah, Cordelion, how thy glory's wrong'd!
④Oh, <u>well</u> did he become that lion's robe,
That did dis<u>robe</u> the lion of that robe!

BASTARD
①It lies as sightly ✗on the back of <u>him</u>
As great Alcides' shoes upon an <u>ass</u>.
②But, <u>ass</u>,③I'll take that burden from your back,
Or lay on that shall make your shoulders crack.

(ASK L. + P.)   AUSTRIA
①What cracker is this same that deafs our ears
With this abundance of superfluous breath?
②Methinks✗that Richard's pride and Richard's fall
Should be a precedent to affright you all!

KING PHILIP
①Women and fools, break off your②"conference."
③King John,✗this is the very sum of all:
④England and Ireland, Anjou, Touraine, Maine, (ANGLICIZE)
In right of Arthur do I claim of thee.
⑤Wilt thou resign them and lay down thy arms?

KING JOHN
①My life as soon! ②I do defy thee, France. ✗
③Arthur of Britaine, yield thee to my hand;
And out of my dear love I'll give thee more
④Than e'er the coward hand of France can win.
⑤Submit thee, boy.

ELINOR
✗Come to thy grandam, child. (KNEEL)

331

C-to protect Ar from E's wiles	C(1)inviting, "baby-talk" (2)ironically building mocking picture	
Ar-to die of shame	Ar(1)implores (2)miserably (3)insistently	
	E-sadly clucking, to J	P J ← E C_AR
C-to finish E off	C(1)blazing (2)asserts fiercely	B.S.P J → E → P → L J+P "GIVE UP" AS C STARTS
	(3)seeing holy picture	
	(4)fiercely	E C TOE TO TOE
E-to stone-wall	E-in shocked loathing	
	C(1)flings back (2)contradicts (3)spells out accusation (4)incredulously (5)with disgust	
	E(1)w/ scornful pity (2)witheringly	
	C(1)scornfully (2)astonished (3)throws in her face (4)mockingly	B.S.P J
P-to bottle them up	P(1)"patiently" (2)confidentially	E C ↗ L AR
P-to setttle things	(3)briskly commands (4)"I'll show you"	B.S.P J → E C → P AR

CONSTANCE

①Do, child,"go it grandam, child;
②Give grandam kingdom, and it grandam will
  Give it a plum, a cherry, and a fig;
  There's a good grandam."

ARTHUR

①Good my mother, peace!
②I would that I were low laid in my grave;
③I am not worth this coil that's made for me.

ELINOR

ˣHis mother shames him so, poor boy, he weeps.

_____

CONSTANCE

①Now shame upon you, whe'r she does or no! ♩ P C Xˣ Xˣ
②His grandam's wrongs, and not his mother's shames,
  Draws these heaven-moving pearls from his poor eyes,
③Which heaven shall take in nature of a fee;
  Ay, with these crystal beads heaven shall be brib'd
  To do him justice④and revenge on you.

ELINOR

Thou monstrous slanderer of heaven and earth!

CONSTANCE

①Thou monstrous injurer of heaven and earth!
②Call me not slanderer;③thou and thine usurp
  The dominations, royalties, and rights
  Of this oppressèd boy,④This is thy eldest son's son,
⑤Infortunate in nothing but in thee!

ELINOR

①Thou unadvisèd scold,②I can produce
  A will|that bars the title of thy son.

CONSTANCE

①Ay, who doubts that?②A will?③A wicked will:
④A woman's will; a canker'd grandam's will!

KING PHILIP
         ˣ
①Peace, lady! Pause,|or be more temperate.
②It ill beseems this presence to cry aim
  To these ill-tuned repetitions.
③Some trumpet summon hither to the walls
  These men of Angiers; let us hear them speak
  Whose title they admit, ʌor John's. ♩ E P C Xˣ Xˣ
      (MC 10)   ④↓Arthur's,   Av X
  (Trumpet sounds. CITIZEN appears on wall.)

APPENDIX C

COSTUME LIST AND PLOT,
   KING JOHN
MUSIC AND SOUND PLOT,
   KING JOHN
LIGHTING, AREAS AND GROUND
   PLAN, ***TEMPEST***
LIGHTING, CUE PLOT, ***TEMPEST***
PROP LIST, ***TEMPEST***

KING JOHN COSTUME LIST

KING JOHN — KINGLY ROBES, ARMOR W/ CLOAK, CORONATION
MANTLE, GOWN FOR DEATH SCENE

BASTARD — TUNIC, ARMOR, CLOAK

KING PHILIP — ARMOR, CLOAK

LEWIS (DAUPHIN) — ARMOR, WEDDING CLOAK

HUBERT — ARMOR, TUNIC

SALISBURY — TUNIC, ARMOR

PEMBROKE — TUNIC, ARMOR

GURNEY, 1ST MONK, SOLDIER — TUNIC, SOLDIER, M's ROBE

FAULCOMBRIDGE, BIGOT — TUNIC (F); (B) TUNIC, ARMOR

AUSTRIA — ARMOR, W/ LION SKIN OVER

PANDULPH — RED CARDINAL's ROBES

MELUN — TUNIC, ARMOR

FR HERALD — ALSO SOLDIER, MONK — TABARD OVER SOLDIER,
MONK's ROBE

ENG. HERALD, SOLDIER, MONK — TABARD OVER SOLDIER,
MONK's ROBE

CITIZEN, 1ST. EX., COURTIER, ABBOT — TUNIC, LEATHER
TUNIC, COURT TUNIC, ABBOT's ROBE

ELINOR — DRESS W/ MANTEL, CHAIN. MAIL COIF TO
ADD

CONSTANCE — COURT DRESS, SIMPLE DRESS

BLANCH — COURT DRESS, WEDDING CLOAK

LADY FAULCOMBRIDGE — RIDING DRESS

PRINCE HENRY — TUNIC

ARTHUR — COURT TUNIC, SIMPLE TUNIC, SHIPBOY's GARB

+ SOLDIERS
   COURT LADIES   } NUMBERS LATER
   2ND EXECUTIONER
   OTHER MONKS

KING JOHN COSTUME PLOT

	I	II	III_1	III_2	III_3	III_4	IV_1	IV_2	IV_3	V_1	V_2	V_3	V_4	V_5	V_6	V_7
KING JOHN COSTUME PLOT	COURT	ANGIERS	AFTER WEDDING	BATTLE	BATTLE	AFTER BATTLE	CELL	CORO-NATION	ARTHURS DEATH	COURT	FRENCH CAMP	BATTLE	BATTLE	ABBEY	NIGHT	DEATH
K. JOHN	ROBES	ARM.	ARM.	ARM.	ARM.			ROBES		ROBES		ARM		GOWN		GOWN
BASTARD	TUNIC	ARM.	ARM.	ARM.	ARM.			TUNIC	TUNIC		ARM.	ARM.		ARM.	W/CL.	ARM
K. PHILIP		ARM.	ARM.	ARM.	ARM.	ARM.										
DAU. (L.)		ARM.	ARM. W/ WED. C.	ARM.	ARM.	ARM.					ARM.				MON.	
HUBERT	TUNIC	ARM.	ARM.	ARM.	ARM.		TUNIC	TUNIC	TUNIC		ARM.	ARM.		ARM.	MON.	TUNIC
SALISBURY	TUNIC	ARM.	ARM.	ARM.	ARM.			TUNIC	TUNIC		ARM.	ARM.	ARM.			TUNIC
PEMBROKE	TUNIC	ARM.	ARM.	ARM.	ARM.			TUNIC	TUNIC		ARM.	ARM.	ARM.			TUNIC
GUR/M/S	TUNIC	S.	S.	S.	S.			S.	S.	S.		S.		MONK		
FAU/BIGOT	F.TUN.	ARM.	ARM.	ARM.	ARM.			B.TUN.	B.TUN.		ARM.	ARM.	ARM.			B.TUN.
AUSTRIA		ARM.	ARM.	ARM.												
PANDULPH			ROBE			ROBE				ROBE	ROSE					
MELUN	TUNIC	ARM.	ARM.	ARM.	ARM.						ARM.	ARM.	ARM.			
F. HERALD	S	TABARD	S	S	S	S						S	S			S
E. HERALD	S	TABARD	S	S	S			S		S		S	S			S
C/E/Ci/A	COURT	C.T.					EX.	COURT		COURT				ABBOT		
ELINOR	DRESS	DRESS W. COIF	DRESS W/COIF		DRESS W/COIF											
CONSTANCE		COURT DRESS	COURT DRESS		COURT TUNIC	SIMPLE DRESS										
ARTHUR	COURT TUNIC	COURT TUNIC	COURT TUNIC	COURT TUNIC			SIMPLE TUNIC		SHIP-BOY T.							

337

MUSIC/SOUND PLOT, KING JOHN

Q No.	Page No.	Act & Scene No.	Line	Description (KING JOHN MUSIC & SOUND PLOT) ①	Time
1	1	I,	Overture, Beg. of Play	A. Big, attention-getting fanfare; full, stately, ominous	8 sec.
				B. (Body of overture: use anthem for last speech as basic theme — here, a darker version, under speech at end more patriotic and uplifting ending in:	40 sec.
				C. Fanfare for entrance of procession, more thrilling and higher in pitch	6 sec.
LIVE	1	I,	Entrance: Bishop, King, Elinor, Monks, etc.	Plainsong chant sung by all entering, solemn & reverent, at moderate walking tempo till all are in place.	25 sec.
2	1	I,	Bishop Raises Crown	Solemn, Noble Fanfare	5 sec.
3	1	I,	"I crown thee John, of England... King! (Flourish) A. Vivat! (Flourish B.) Vivat! (Flourish C.) Vivat! (Longer Fl. D.)	A. Short jubilant flourish. B. Repeat. C. Repeat. D. Longer version, to cover Bishop stepping back. (Note: Trumpets for English, horns for French? They need to be identifiable. I'll just note French trumpet or English trumpet) (Leader between play as one cue.)	3 sec. 3 sec. 3 sec. 6 sec.

338

MUSIC/SOUND PLOT, KING JOHN CONT.

Q No.	Page No.	Act & Scene No.	Line	Description (King John Music + Sound Plot) ②	Time
4	1	I_1	EL." ... IN HIS EMPERY."	SHORT TRIUMPHAL FLOURISH	3 SEC.
5	1	I_1	J." ... HANG UPON A CROWN."	LONGER FANFARE / FLOURISH, COVERING EXIT OF BISHOPS.	5 SEC.
6	6	I_1	J." ... FOR IT IS MORE THAN NEED."	FANFARE, EXIT OF KING + COURT. PLEASANT BUT KINGLY.	7 SEC.
7	9	$I_1 - II$	B." ... I SAY, 'TWAS NOT." SET TURNS.	A. PLEASANT, CHEERFUL BUTTON TO COVER EXIT. B. FRENCH FANFARE + DRUMS FOR THEIR ENTRANCE C. AUSTRIA'S FANFARE (CHANGE DIRECTION, TOO - FROM U.R.)	4 SEC. 7 SEC. 5 SEC.
8	10	II	C." ... HASTE SO INDIRECTLY SHED."	SINGLE FRENCH TRUMPET CALL.	3 SEC.
9	11	II	M." ... NEW FORTUNES HERE." 2ND DECK ? →	A. DRUM APPROACHES, UNDER SPEECH, AND ARRIVES, TO HALT ! B. SHORT ENGLISH FLOURISH, FOR JOHNS SOLO ENTRANCE	18 SEC. 3 SEC.
10	14	II	P." ... ARTHUR'S OR JOHN'S."	BUGLE CALL FROM CITY (NEITHER FRENCH NOR ENGLISH.)	4 SEC.

339

MUSIC/SOUND PLOT, KING JOHN CONT.

Q No.	Page No.	Act & Scene No.	Line	Description (KING JOHN MUSIC & SOUND PLOT) ③	Time
11	17	II	ALL (SHOUTING) "GOD AND OUR RIGHT!" FUNNY GROTESQUE (	A. FRENCH AND ENGLISH TRUMPETS BRAY DEFIANTLY AT EACH OTHER ON EXIT. B. BATTLE CACAPHONY WITH BARE STAGE (YELLING, SWORDS CLASHING, STABBING BRITISH & FRENCH TRUMPETS THROUGHOUT.) ABRUPT END — SILENCE.	5 SEC. 10 SEC.
12	17	II	AFTER SILENCE, ON 2ND DECK.	SINGLE SAUCY FRENCH TRUMPET CALL	5 SEC.
13	17	II	F.H. "... ENGLAND'S KING AND YOURS."	SINGLE SCREING & CONFIDENT ENGLISH TRUMPET.	5 SEC.
14	18	II	CIT. "... YET FOR BOTH."	FRENCH AND ENGLISH TRUMPETS AND DRUMS, ANGRY, AS KINGS ENTER. BRING TO HARSH ENDING.	6 SEC.
15	23	II	KJ "... UNPREPARED POMP."	HAPPY FRENCH AND ENGLISH TRUMPETS AS THEY ENTER ANGIERS. (PEALING BELLS COME IN UNDER THIS ON 2ND DECK)	8 SEC.
16	23	II-III	B. "I WILL WORSHIP THEE." SET TURNS →	A. 2ND DECK: PEALING BELLS SOUND EFFECT B. ORGAN UP FOR WEDDING TABLEAU ON UPPER LEVEL (1ST DECK) +OUT (C. BELLS TO NATURAL DECAY AS CONSTANCE ENTERS BELOW)	A { 5 SEC. + 10 SEC. } B 8 SEC. (C. BELLS FADE)

①

AREAS

CENTER:

    D.S. - AREAS 1, 2, 3 WARM/COOL

    C. - AREAS 4, 5, 6 WARM/COOL

    UNDER BRIDGE C, POS. #2 - A. 7, WARM/COOL

    UPSTAGE OF BRIDGE

        BETWEEN POS. 2 + 3: A: 8, 9, 10 WARM/COOL

    WARM WASH ⎰ COVERING ALL OF

    COOL WASH ⎱ AREAS 1 2 3 4 5 6 7

             MORE SATURATED IN COLOR THAN

             AREA WARM + COOL.

      DOWNLIGHT - A WHITE/NO COLOR DOWNLIGHT

         IN EACH AREA (ESP. 1 2 3 4 5 6) WHICH

         CAN EACH WORK INDEPENDENTLY, IF NEC.

S.R. SIDE

    CELL (LOWER LEVEL, INC. FRONT STEPS) - WARM/COOL

    STUDY (FRONT OF 6' PL., W/ CURVING STAIRS) -

                         WARM/COOL

    UPSTAGE 8' - WARM/COOL

S.L. SIDE

    LOWER LEVEL - WARM/COOL

    FRONT 4' - WARM/COOL

    UPSTAGE - WARM/COOL

BRIDGE IN #2 POSITION, TOP - AREAS 11, 12, 13

                      WARM/COOL

BRIDGE IN #3 POSITION - AREAS 14, 15, FLANKING

                           7

                  WARM/COOL

②

SPECIALS:

Sp. 1. — SR LOWER LEVEL

Sp. 2. — SR 6' LEVEL, AT LECTERN

Sp. 3. — SR 8' LEVEL, CENTERED

Sp. 4 — DC, FLOOR LEVEL

Sp. 5 — CENTER, TOP OF BRIDGE, POS. #2

Sp. 6 — SHIP SCENE (2 INSTRUMENTS, PLUS DOWNLIGHT)

Sp. 7 — SL UPSTAGE 4' LEVEL

Sp. 8 — CENTER, TOP OF BRIDGE, POS. #1 (D.S.)

Sp. 9, 10, 11, 12   DOWNLIGHTS FOR "ISLANDERS"

Sp. 13 — "CHESS GAME" UPSTAGE OF BRIDGE, POS. #2
BEHIND SCRIM.

Sp. 14 — SCRIM CIRCUIT (IF POSSIBLE)

EFFECTS:

"NET" GOBO III_3 (IN AREAS 1 2 3 4 5 6 ON FLOOR
"SPIDER" PROJECTION ON CYC III_3
"BOREALIS" PROJECTION ON CYC IV (MASQUE)

CYC: NEED ABILITY TO COLOR IT FROM PALE BLUE TO
YELLOW, TO RED, TO GREEN. NOTE: USE BLACK
SCRIM SO BLACK IS POSSIBLE.

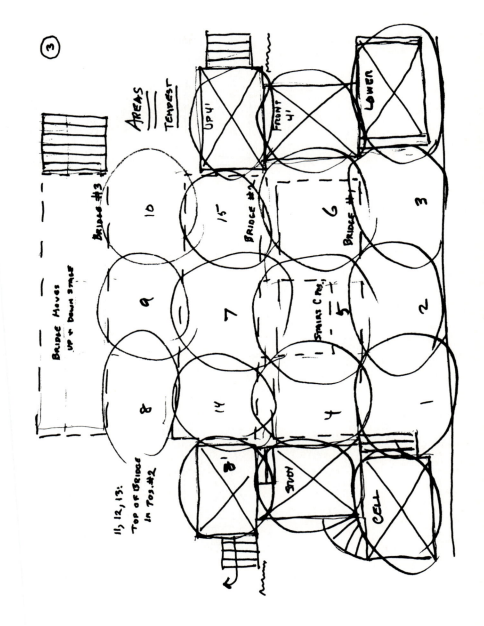

LIGHTING AREAS, TEMPEST

③

AREAS
TEMPEST

BRIDGE MOVES
UP & DOWN STAGE

11, 12, 13:
TOP OF BRIDGE
IN POS.#2

UP 4'
FRONT 4'
LOWER

BRIDGE #3
BRIDGE #2
BRIDGE #1

STRAIGHT C PROJ.

SPECIAL
CELL

10   9   8
15   7   14
6   5   (1)
3   2   1
4

LIGHTING SPECIALS, *TEMPEST*

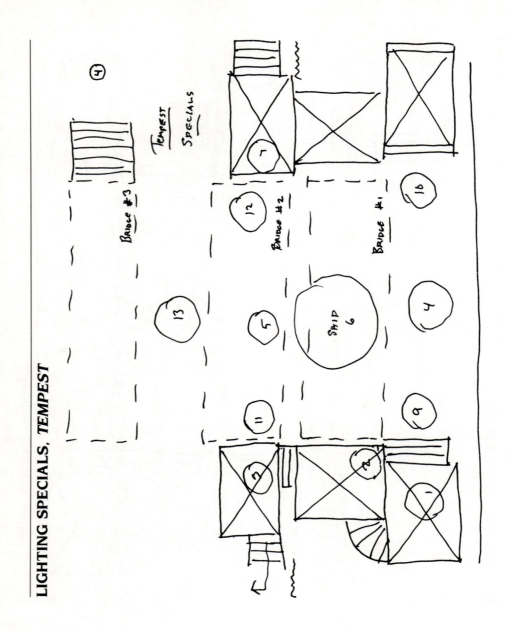

LIGHT CUE PLOT, TEMPEST

PAGE/ ACT/ SCENE	Q NO.	LINE or BUSINESS	DESCRIPTION (TEMPEST LIGHT Q PLOT)	SUGGESTED OPERATION P.1
I₁ P.1	PRE-SET	HOUSE OPEN	BLEAK PALE OVER-ALL "WORK LIGHT"	AREAS 1 THRU 10 ↑ TO READING (NO SKY TILL Q14)
I₁ R.1	1	HOUSE OUT, ACTORS ENTER	ADD INTENSITY TO LIGHT ACTORS AS HOUSE GOES OUT	HOUSE ↓ X ↑ AREAS 1 2 3 4 5 6 7 8 9 10 (STILL NO LIGHT R+L SIDES)
I₁ P.1	2	MUSIC BEGINS. LINE OF ACTORS BREAKS, "CLOAK" IS DRAWN OUT OF PIT + ATTACHED TO PROSCEAD	REDUCE INTENSITY UPSPACE OF "CLOAK" SO SCRIM EFFECT IS NOT GIVEN AWAY	↓ ADJUST 45 67 89 AREAS
I₁ P.1	3	PROS. + MIR. X UP STAIRS TO BRIDGE, NOW IN POSITION #2. "CLOAK" DRAWN UP AS "SAIL"	REDUCE INTENSITY DOWNSTAGE, ADD LIGHT TO TOP OF BRIDGE, CENTER	AREA 12 ↑ X ↓ AREAS 1 2 3 TO READING, ALSO 4 5 6 7 8 9 10 EVEN LOWER
I₁ P.1	4	THUNDER, WHEN "SAIL" IS AT HEIGHT.	LIGHT GOES FROM PROSPERO EMPHASIS TO "SHIP", DURING WHICH "RATLINES" COME DOWN AND ARE ATTACHED TO "SHIP" PLATFORM.	AREAS 123 456 789 10,12 ↓ X ↑ SHIP St.
I₁ P.4 L.66	5	"FAREWELL, MY WIFE AND CHILDREN," AD.LIB., + THUNDER.	"SHIP" LIGHTS OUT AS "SAIL" DROPS. IMMEDIATE FOLLOW W. St. 5, TOP OF BRIDGE	A. SHIP St. ↓ B. St. 5 ↑
I₂ P.4 L.6	6	"OH, I HAVE SUFFERED..."	BRING UP BRIDGE TOP AS MIRANDA X'S	AREAS 11, 12, 13 ↑

345

LIGHT CUE PLOT, TEMPEST CONT.

Page Act Scene	Q No.	Line or Business	Description (Tempest Light Q Plot)	Suggested Operation P.2
I₂ p.5 L.31	7	"The direful spectacle" M+P X	P + M X off bridge and down to "cell". Light follows them.	Areas 11, 12, 13 ↓ X ↑SR 8' SP 6' cell. 6' + 8' can stay up till he X's back to them
I₂ p.6 L.55	8	"'Tis far off."	3 women behind "cloak-scrim" (draped from bridge) are picked up. Running through light.	Areas 8 9 10 ↑
I₂ p.6 L.59	9	"Thou hadst."	Light behind scrim out.	Areas 8 9 10 ↓
I₂ p.6 L.65	10	"Twelve year since…"	Light behind scrim up to show P. double in place.	Areas 8 9 10 ↑
I₂ p.9 L.157	11	"Thy crying self"	Light behind scrim out as soldiers hurry "P" away.	Areas 8 9 10 ↓
I₂ p.11 L.193	12	"Noble Neapolitan"	Scrim light up, reveals Gonzalo	Areas 8 9 10 ↑
I₂ p.11 L.201	13	"Might greet that man".	Scrim light on Gon. out.	Areas 8 9 10 ↓
I₂ p.12 L.216	14	"Enemies brought to these shores"	P. X's onto bridge; lights follow him.	Areas 11, 12, 13 ↑ X ↓SR 8' SR 6') adjust cell

LIGHT CUE PLOT, *TEMPEST* CONT.

Page Act Scene	Q No.	Line or Business	Description (TEMPEST LIGHT Q PLOT)	Suggested Operation P.S
I₂ P.12 L.224	15	"Approach, my Ariel, Come!"	Ariel runs into spot upstage of bridge	Sp. 13 ↑
I₂ P.12 L.232	16	"To every article."	Ariel x's D.S. on bridge	Area 5 ↑
I₂ P.14 L.300	17	"Bate me a full year"	Ariel tries to escape D.S.	Area 2 ↑
I₂ P.16 L.269	18	"Hence, with diligence."	A. Ariel leaves B. Pros. x's down to cell C. P. arrives at Mir. } Lights out following moves, as bridge moves to position #3	A. Areas 2,5 ↓ Sp. 13 B. Areas 11, 12, 13 ↓ } As P. x's Sp. 8' C. P in cell – S.R cell ↑
I₂ P.17 L.374	19	"Shake it off. Come."	They x toward center and Caliban	S.R. cell ↓ X ↑ Areas 1 2 3 4 5 6 7 14 15 * Day sky, pale blue * First use of sky
I₂ P.19 L.457	20	"So, slave, hence." Music	With music, bridge moves downstage and stage brightens	Areas 1 2 3 4 5 6 7 8 9 10 11 12 13 14 15 warm wash sky, SR cell SR study { And, if already up, get brighter

(1)

I₁
BOS'N'S WHISTLE
ENDLESS ROPE (FROM FLIES) PULLED BY TRI/STEF.
PROSPERO'S STAFF (BREAKAWAY — DISCUSS)
PROSPERO'S BOOK (BREAKAWAY — DISCUSS)

I₂ LARGE RUBY RING FOR PROS. DOUBLE
2 SPEARS FOR SOLDIERS (OUT OF STOCK — ONLY SEEN
BRIEFLY)
BLANKETS AROUND DOLL — FOR SLEEPING 3 YR OLD
MIRANDA
SHORT SWORD W/ SHEATH FOR FERDINAND
(BORROW FROM S.V.)
BENCH DR (PART OF SET)
LECTERN (UR 8' ON SET)
FOR BOOK

II₁ FOLDING CAMP STOOL — GONZALO
BRASS FOLDING TELESCOPE — ADRIAN

SWORDS — RAPIER W SHEATH (MAKE) — PROS.
↑   "   "   "   "   — ALONZO
(WE HAVE)
CROSS HILT (MAKE SHEATH) — GONZALO
S.V. CUP HILT (HAS SHEATH) — SEB.
OTHER SV CUP HILT W/ SHEATH — ANT.
SV CUTLASS (HAS SHEATH) — ADRIAN

II₂ LOW CART DRAWN BY ROPE, WITH FOUR LOGS —
DRAWN BY CALIBAN
LOGS 3' X 18"
OR
SO

BOTTLE — "MADE FROM BARK OF TREE" STEFANO

III₁   DIFFERENT LOG DRAGGER —
           A ROPE NET, W/ Y MORE LOGS — FERDINAND

III₂   WINE KEG — TO SIT ON

III₃

← 10' →

↑
8'
↓

2 POLES W/
10' STRETCHER
(1 × 3)
WITH RIBBONS
(DIFFERENT SHADES
OF GREEN)
THROUGH WHICH MEN
STRUGGLE.

4 "ISLANDERS" — FIGURES ON POLES →

THIN POLE, HOOP,
COLORED RIBBONS

IV₁

FLOOR CLOTH (SAND COLOR) FOR JUNO TO WALK
         ON   3' × 15'
   6 BUNCHES OF PAMPAS GRASS
   2 FLOWERED GARLANDS FOR CROWNS (CGST.)
   2 WEDDING CAPES (COST)

③

IV, CONT.

    GARMENTS (RAGS) IN BUNDLE

    LINE WITH CLIP TO FASTEN ON SET, WITH
        POLE (FOR "FANCY CLOTHES")

V OUTSIZE CHESS BOARD, TALL (18") CHESS PIECES

APPENDIX D

LIST OF PLAYS MENTIONED
IN THE TEXT

Note: For plays existing in many available editions, no citation will be given.

Bagnold, Enid. *The Chalk Garden*. New York: Samuel French, 1984.

Barry, Philip. *The Philadelphia Story*, in *Best Plays of the Modern American Theatre*, Second Series, 1939–1946, edited by John Gassner. New York: Crown Publishers, Inc., 1947.

Beckett, Samuel. *Waiting for Godot*. New York: Grove Press, 1954.

Boucicault, Dion. *London Assurance*, in *English Plays of the Nineteenth Century*, edited by Michael R. Booth. Oxford, England: The Clarendon Press, 1976.

——. *The Octoroon*, in *Representative American Plays*, edited by Arthur Hobson Quinn. 7th edition, revised. New York: Appleton-Century-Crofts, Inc., 1957.

——. *The Poor of New York*, in *French's Standard Drama*. New York: Samuel French, 1966.

Brecht, Bertolt. *Mother Courage*, English version by Eric Bentley, in *The Modern Theatre*, Vol. 2, edited by Eric Bentley. Garden City, NY: Doubleday Anchor Books, 1955.

——. *Threepenny Opera*, in *Bertolt Brecht*, *Plays*, Vol. 1, translated by Desmond I. Vesey and Eric Bentley. London: Methuen & Co., Ltd., 1960.

Caldwell, Erskine. *Tobacco Road*. Adapted for the stage by Jack Kirkland. In *Twenty Best Plays of the American Theatre*, 1930–1939, edited by John Gassner. New York: Crown Publishers, Inc., 1940.

Chekhov, Anton. *The Sea Gull*.

Coward, Noel. *Blithe Spirit*. New York: Samuel French, 1941.

Dighton, John. *The Happiest Days of Your Life*. London: Samuel French, Limited, 1951.

Driver, Donald. *Your Own Thing*. Music and lyrics by Hal Hester and Danny Apolinar. In *Great Rock Musicals*, edited by Stanley Richards. New York: Stein and Day, Publishers, 1980.

Eliot, T. S. *The Cocktail Party*, in *The Complete Poems and Plays, 1909–1950*. New York: Harcourt, Brace and Company, 1952.

——. *The Confidential Clerk*, in *The Complete Plays of T. S. Eliot*. New York: Harcourt, Brace and World, 1967.

Euripedes. *Medea*, translated by E. P. Coleridge, in *The Complete Greek Drama*, Vol. 1, edited by Whitney J. Oates and Eugene O'Neill, Jr. New York: Random House, 1938.

Feydeau, Georges. *A Flea in Her Ear*. Translated by John Mortimer. London and New York: Samuel French, 1968.

——. *The Girl From Maxim's*. Translated by Anne and Stuart Vaughan. Unpublished. (Note: Gene Feist's version of this play, published by Samuel French, contains a third act *not* by Feydeau.)

Gay, John. *The Beggar's Opera*, in *Twelve Famous Plays of the Restoration and Eighteenth Century*. New York: The Modern Library (Random House), 1933.

Giraudoux, Jean. *Tiger at the Gates*. New York: Samuel French, 1955.

Gorki, Maxim. *The Lower Depths*, translated by Edwin Hopkins, in *Chief Contemporary Dramatists*, Second Series, edited by Thomas H. Dickinson. Cambridge, Mass.: The Riverside Press, 1921.

Hare, David. *The Secret Rapture*. New York: Grove-Weidenfeld, 1989.

Harling, Robert. *Steel Magnolias*. New York: Dramatists Play Service, Inc., 1988.

Hauptmann, Gerhardt. *The Weavers*, in *Masters of Modern Drama*, edited by Haskell M. Block and Robert G. Shedd. New York: Random House, 1962.

Henley, Beth. *Crimes of the Heart*. New York: The Viking Press (Penguin Books), 1982.

Hochwalder, Fritz. *The Strong are Lonely*, translated by Eva Le Gallienne, in *The Public Prosecutor and Other Plays*. New York: F. Unger Publishing Co., 1980.

Hwang, David Henry. *M. Butterfly*. New York: New American Library, 1988.

Ibsen, Henrik. *An Enemy of the People*, translated by David Scanlan. New York: Bantam (The Bantam Library of World Drama), 1968.

——. *Ghosts*. Unpublished version by Stuart Vaughan, 1981.

——. *Hedda Gabler*. Unpublished version by Stuart Vaughan, 1978.

Kesselring, Joseph. *Arsenic and Old Lace*. New York: Dramatists Play Service, Inc., 1942.

Lindsay, Howard, and Crouse, Russel. *Life With Father*, in *Sixteen Famous American Plays*, edited by Bennett A. Cerf and Van H. Cartmell. New York: The Modern Library (Random House), 1941.

Miller, Arthur. *Death of a Salesman*. New York: Dramatists Play Service, Inc., 1952.

Molière, Jean-Baptiste Poquelin de. *The Misanthrope*, translated by Richard Wilbur. New York: Harcourt, Brace and World, 1965.

Murray, John. *Room Service*. New York: Dramatists Play Service, Inc., 1937.

O'Casey, Sean. I *Knock at the Door*, adapted for the theatre by Paul Shyre. Unpublished. 1956.

O'Neill, Eugene. *Ah, Wilderness!* New York: Samuel French, 1933.

——. *Long Day's Journey Into Night*. New Haven and London: Yale University Press, 1962.

Orton, Joe. *Loot*, in *Complete Plays*. New York: Grove Press, 1977.

Pinter, Harold. *The Birthday Party*, in *Complete Works*. London: St. Martin's Press, 1978.

Plautus. *The Braggart Soldier*, translated by Erich Segal, in *Plautus: Three Comedies*. New York: Harper and Row (Harper Torchbooks), 1963.

Racine. *Phaedra*, translated by Robert Lowell, in *The Classic Theatre*, Vol. IV, edited by Eric Bentley. Garden City, NY: Anchor Books, Doubleday and Company, Inc., 1961.

Rice, Elmer. *The Adding Machine*. New York: Samuel French, 1929.

Shakespeare, William
    All's Well That Ends Well
    A Midsummer Night's Dream
    Hamlet
    Henry IV, Part One
    Henry IV, Part Two
    Henry VI, Part One
    Julius Caesar
    King John
    King Lear
    Macbeth
    Much Ado About Nothing
    Othello
    Richard II
    Richard III
    Romeo and Juliet
    The Taming of the Shrew
    The Tempest
    Timon of Athens
    Twelfth Night

Shaw, Bernard. *Arms and the Man*.

——. *Man and Superman*.

——. *Saint Joan*.

——. *Pygmalion*.

Sherwood, Robert. *Abe Lincoln in Illinois*, in *Best Plays of the Modern American Theatre*, Second Series, 1939–1946, edited by John Gassner. New York: Crown Publishers, Inc., 1947.

Sophocles. *Oedipus the King*.

Spewack, Bella and Sam. *Boy Meets Girl*, in *20 Best American Plays of the Modern American Theatre*, 1930–1939, edited by John Gassner. New York: Crown Publishers, Inc., 1940.

Sterner, Jerry. *Other People's Money*. New York: Applause Theatre Book Publishers, 1990.

Synge, John Millington. *The Playboy of the Western World*, in *Masters of the Modern Drama*, edited by Haskell M. Block and Robert G. Shedd. New York: Random House, 1962.

Thomas, Brandon. *Charley's Aunt*, 2nd edition, revised. New York and London: Samuel French, 1962.

Thurber, James. *Out on a Limb*, Thurber stories and sketches, adapted for the stage by Haila Stoddard. Unpublished. 1978.

Uhry, Alfred. *Driving Miss Daisy*. New York: Theatre Communications Group, 1988.

von Kleist, Heinrich. *Amphitryon*. New York: F. Ungar Publishing Co., 1962.

Wilde, Oscar. *The Importance of Being Earnest*.

Wilder, Thornton. *Our Town*, in *Three Plays by Thornton Wilder*. New York: Bantam Library of World Drama (Bantam Books), 1966.

Williams, Emlyn. *The Corn is Green*, in *Sixteen Famous British Plays*, compiled by Bennett A. Cerf and Van H. Cartmell. New York: The Modern Library (Random House), 1942.

Williams, Tennessee. *A Streetcar Named Desire*. New York: Signet Books (The New American Library), 1947.

——. *The Glass Menagerie*, in *Masters of Modern Drama*, edited by Haskell M. Block and Robert G. Shedd. New York: Random House, 1962.

INDEX